The Textual Life of Savants

Studies in Anthropology and History

Studies in Anthropology and History is a series that will develop new theoretical perspectives, and combine comparative and ethnographic studies with historical research.

Edited by Nicholas Thomas, The Australian National University, Canberra.

VOLUME 1	Structure and Process in a Melanesian Society: Ponam's progress in the Twentieth Century ACHSAH H. CARRIER AND JAMES G. CARRIER
VOLUME 2	Androgynous Objects: String bags and gender in Central New Guinea MAUREEN ANNE MACKENZIE
VOLUME 3	Time and the Work of Anthropology: Critical essays 1971–1991 JOHANNES FABIAN
VOLUME 4	Colonial Space: Spatiality in the discourse of German South West Africa 1884–1915 JOHN NOYES
VOLUME 5	Catastrophe and Creation: The transformation of an African culture KAJSA EKHOLM FRIEDMAN
VOLUME 6	Before Social Anthropology: Essays on the history of British Anthropology JAMES URRY
VOLUME 7	The *Ghotul* in Muria Society SIMERAN MAN SINGH GELL
VOLUME 8	Global Culture, Island Identity: Continuity and change in the Afro-Caribbean community of Nevis KAREN FOG OLWIG
VOLUME 9	The Return of the Ainu: Cultural mobilization and the practice of ethnicity in Japan KATARINA V. SJÖBERG
VOLUME 10	Tradition and Christianity: The colonial transformation of a Solomon Islands society BEN BURT
VOLUME 11	Recovering the Orient: Artists, scholars, appropriations ANDREW GERSTLE AND ANTHONY MILNER
VOLUME 12	Women of the Place: *Kastom*, colonialism and gender in Vanuatu MARGARET JOLLY
VOLUME 13	A History of Curiosity: The Theory of Travel 1550–1800 JUSTIN STAGL
VOLUME 14	Exploring Confrontation. Sri Lanka: Politics, culture and history MICHAEL ROBERTS
VOLUME 15	Consumption and Identity JONATHAN FRIEDMAN
VOLUME 16	Resplendant Sites, Discordant Voices: Sri Lanka and international tourism MALCOLM CRICK
VOLUME 17	The Rationality of Rural Life: Economic and cultural change in Tuscany JEFF PRATT
VOLUME 18	The Textual Life of Savants: Ethnography, Iceland, and the Linguistic Turn GÍSLI PÁLSSON

This book is part of a series. The publisher will accept continuation orders which may be cancelled at any time and which provide for automatic billing and shipping of each title in the series upon publication. Please write for details.

Gísli Pálsson

The Textual Life of Savants

Ethnography, Iceland, and the Linguistic Turn

LONDON AND NEW YORK

First published 1995
by Harwood Academic Publishers.
Reprinted 2004
by Routledge,
11 New Fetter Lane, London EC4P 4EE

Transferred to Digital Printing 2004

COPYRIGHT © 1995 BY Harwood Academic Publishers GmbH

All rights reserved.

No part of this book may be reproduced or utilized in any form or by any means, electronic or mechanical, including photocopying and recording, or by any information storage or retrieval system, without permission in writing from the publisher.

BRITISH LIBRARY CATALOGUING IN PUBLICATION DATA

Gísli Pálsson
The Textual Life of Savants: Ethnography,
Iceland and the Linguistic Turn. –
(Studies in Anthropology & History,
ISSN 1055-2464; Vol. 18)
I. Title   II. Series
949. 12

ISBN 3-7186-5721-X (hardcover)
ISBN 3-7186-5722-8 (softcover)

DESIGNED BY   Maureen Anne MacKenzie
Em Squared, Main Street, Michelgo, NSW 2620, Australia

FRONT COVER   "Mountain" (artwork by Sigurður Guðmundsson, 1980–1982), reproduced by kind permission of the artist.

Contents

	List of Figures	vii
	Preface	ix
ONE	Introduction	1

PART ONE From Life to Text
| TWO | The Conventional Metaphor of Cultural Translation | 27 |
| THREE | The Factual, the Fictive and the Fabulous: Novel and Ethnography | 47 |

PART TWO Times, Lives and Medieval Texts
| FOUR | Sagas, History, and Social Life | 75 |
| FIVE | The Power of Words and the Context of Witchcraft | 99 |

PART THREE Lives, Texts and Modern Realities
SIX	Fetishized Language, Symbolic Capital, and Social Identity	123
SEVEN	Beyond Environmental Orientalism	145
EIGHT	Conclusions: Towards a Theory of Living Discourse	169
	References	181
	Index	201

Figures

FIGURE 1.1.	The "homecoming" of the Icelandic manuscripts in April 1971 (A Danish naval vessel brings some of the most important manuscripts back to Iceland. Courtesy of the National Museum of Iceland. Photo: Ari Kárason)	15
1.2.	"Mountain" (artwork by Sigurður Guðmundsson, 1980–1982)	22
4.1.	The world-view of early Icelanders (Adapted from early maps, see *Íslendinga sögur og þættir*, 1987, II:xxviii)	78
4.2.	The travels of medieval Norsemen	79
4.3.	Medieval sociality: from "The Section on Dependency" (From the *Jónsbók* law code of the *Skarðsbók* manuscript; fourteenth century. Courtesy Stofnun Árna Magnússonar á Íslandi. Photo: Jóhanna Ólafsdóttir)	93
5.1.	How to do things with swords: from *Flateyjarbók* (From a thirteenth-century manuscript. Courtesy Stofnun Árna Magnússonar á Íslandi. Photo: Jóhanna Ólafsdóttir)	104
6.1.	The image of the "Mountain Woman" (Ca. 1870. Artist: Helgi Magnússon. Based on a description by Eiríkur Magnússon and a sketch by J.B. Zwecker. Courtesy of the National Gallery of Iceland)	134

Preface

This book focuses on the role and significance of texts and textualism for anthropology and ethnography and, more specifically, the understanding of particular aspects of Icelandic society and history. The discussion is centred on a range of issues; moving between general social theory and ethnographic details, the immediate present and the distant past, language and production, fieldwork and the act of writing, texts (sagas, novels, and ethnographies) and "real" life. In each case, however, it draws attention to what may be called a "pragmatist" approach, a concern with action and agency as they constitute, and are constituted by, social life. Such an approach, I hold, is an important and timely remedy to current textualism, the trendy theoretical tradition often described as the linguistic turn.

Different parts of the book have been written with different contexts and purposes in mind over a period of five years or so, during which I have modified my views on several pertinent issues. Although most of the earliest material has been extensively revised to suit the present context, the reader may detect some inconsistency in both concepts and argument. I fully agree that conceptual coherence is an academic virtue, but our language necessarily retains some traces and relics from the past, our past and that of others. Some literary scholars refer to the polyphony of language and plurality of voices with the notion of "intertextuality" (see Tannen 1989: 12), faithful as they are to the facts of texts. I find it more relevant and revealing, as readers of this book are bound to notice, to use the Malinowskian metaphor of the "long conversation". Each of us is necessarily engaged in a continuous dialogue with colleagues, critics, and "informants" – and, of course, ourselves.

Dialogue does allow for reading, writing, and the interrogation of texts. My interest in early Icelandic history and the saga literature began during my early days as a postgraduate student in Manchester, England, when I came across an article by Victor Turner on Njáls saga, one of the so-called family sagas. Earlier, as a student in my native Iceland, I tended to think of the sagas, an obligatory reading at almost every stage of learning, as rather boring stuff, at any rate not for anthropologists. Turner managed to change my mind. The sagas, I thought, would be an exciting site for "fieldwork". It took me some fifteen years, however, to actually do something along those lines. While the reading of texts is an important form of dialogue, especially in the case of academics, dialogue, above all, is a mutual collaboration of socially constituted subjects rooted in history and social life, not just an exchange between autonomous, alienated beings. This book, in fact, is the product of discussions I have had with a number of people representing several rather different discursive communities. Not only has the work presented here been informed by discussions with fellow academics, but there have been general theoretical developments in the discipline, in the form of influential anthropological texts, and also persistent dialogues with Icelanders from different walks of life who have continued to provide useful and interesting topics and perspectives – fishermen, fish-workers, anthropologists, linguists, saga-scholars, and, last but not least, university students. Teaching at a small anthropology department at a small university, I have been forced (or, better, "allowed") to work on a range of themes and subjects and over the years I have taught a variety of courses, including "Ethnolinguistics", "Fishing Adaptations", "The Anthropology of the Sagas", "Ecology", and "Social Theory". For me, dialogues in the classroom have frequently been a source of inspiration and learning.

For an anthropologist, the experience of fieldwork, usuallly outside the academy, is a crucial phase of learning. The chapter on language is partly the result of discussions with fellow Icelanders, focusing on language policy and the politics of language. Similarly, the chapter on fishing, partly a revision of ideas expressed in some of my earlier writings, is very much a product of an extended discussion with Icelandic fishermen. My original fieldwork, on the south-west coast in 1979 and 1981, was part of the work for my doctoral dissertation at Manchester University. Later, in 1993 and 1994, I revisited the communities I had stayed in with new questions in mind. I have learned, as many people have before me, that fieldwork is not only important for the collection of "data" but also for the development of ideas. Fortunately, learning sometimes involves having a good time. I am reminded of an amusing moment of personal discovery during my earlier fieldwork. Once a fish producer in the community where I worked, who was expecting to export dried fish (stockfish) destined for Nigeria, showed me an article in the latest issue of *The Economist* about the instability of the Nigerian coalition government caused by tribal conflicts and interests. Worried by rumours about the negative prospects for stockfish marketing, he asked me to summarize the contents of the article in Icelandic – adding, in characteristic humour with a decidedly sophisticated expression on his face, "we only read French here!". This event brought home to me the immediate relevance of news from the larger world, of economic relations between "my place" and some of the tribal societies that had been documented in detail by anthropologists.

I want to, thank all the people "in the field" who have shared with me their company and their views on language, texts, and fishing: the numerous Icelanders I have listened to, had discussions with, interviewed, and debated with over the years; a complete list of names would be much too long. A number of colleagues have been of extensive help in one way or another in the preparation of this book and the formation of the research on which it is based. Without their comments, encouragement, suggestions, and criticisms *The Textual Life of*

Savants would never have been produced. While, again, a full list would be too long, some of the persons involved simply have to be mentioned. Paul Durrenberger (University of Iowa) and an anonymous reviewer read the manuscript and commented extensively on presentation and argument. Harwood Academic Publishers provided both detailed comments and extremely valuable advice. I have benefitted, in one way or another, from stimulating discussions and exchanges with several other people, including Richard Bauman (Indiana University), Anne Brydon (University of Western Ontario), Ástráður Eysteinsson (University of Iceland), Guðný Guðbjörnsdóttir (University of Iceland), Stephen Gudeman (University of Minnesota), Agnar Helgason (University of Iceland), Jón Haukur Ingimundarson (University of Arizona, Tucson), Tim Ingold (Manchester University), Hjörleifur Rafn Jónsson (Cornell University), and Halldór Stefánsson (Osaka Gakuin University). I wish to express my gratitude to all these people, all of whom may disagree with me on several points, insisting, as the saying goes, that the responsibility for the errors and limitations there may be must rest with me. Finally, I acknowledge my debt to several funds, institutions and agencies which have supported, directly or indirectly, the work on which this book is based – particularly the Icelandic Science Foundation, the University of Iceland, the British Council, the Wenner-Gren Foundation for Anthropological Research, and the Icelandic–United States Educational Commission.

Some of the material in the book has appeared elsewhere in a different form. A short version of Chapter Two was presented to a panel on "Understanding anthropologists' understanding" at the meeting of the American Anthropological Association in Chicago in November 1991. Much of that chapter appeared in the introduction to *Beyond Boundaries: Understanding, Translation and Anthropological Discourse* (Berg Publishers, 1993). Chapter Three is an extensive revision and elaboration of a lecture originally written in Icelandic for a conference (in June 1992) in honor of Halldór Laxness on his ninetieth birthday, and later published as "Hið íslamska bókmenntafélag: mannfræði undir Jökli" in *Skírnir* (1993(1), Reykjavík). The fourth chapter is partly based on my introduction to *From Sagas to Society: Comparative Approaches to Early Iceland* (Hisarlik Press, 1992). Some of the material in the fifth chapter, dedicated to Paul Baxter, formerly Senior Lecturer in Social Anthropology at Manchester University, appeared in David Brokensha (ed.) *A River of Blessings* (Maxwell School of Citizenship and Public Affairs, Syracuse University, 1994). Parts of Chapter Six appeared in an article ("Language and society: the enthnolinguistics of Icelanders") in *The Anthropology of Iceland* (University of Iowa Press, 1989). Chapter Seven which includes some material from my book *Coastal Economies, Cultural Accounts: Human Ecology and Icelandic Discourse* (Manchester University Press, 1991), is partly based on papers presented to the ASA conference on Anthropological Perspectives on Environmentalism at the University of Durham, 30 March to 3 April 1992, and a session on "Nature and society: A contested interface" at the conference of the European Association of Social Anthropologists (EASA) in Oslo, 24–27 June 1994.

CHAPTER ONE

Introduction

> An anthropologist... cannot banish his few patient readers for a couple of years to a South Sea atoll, and make them live the life for themselves; he has, alas, to write books about his savages and lecture about them!
> Bronislaw Malinowski, *The Sexual Life of Savages*

Until recently, and during most of the history of their subject, anthropologists tended to take ethnographic texts (the field reports of their colleagues) at face value and to treat them as more or less authentic documents about social life. Scholars might disagree on many points, of course, and interpretations might vary from case to case depending on the kind of social theory they advocated, but their common goal, with the exception of only a few and marginal dissidents, was to compare and generalize. The present intellectual climate is a very different one. Increasingly anthropological discussions are concerned with somewhat narcissistic accounts of the adventures of ethnographers and what happens to them in the field. The *making* of texts rather than their contents.

Oddly enough, this development has been reinforced by Said's book *Orientalism* (1978). I say "oddly enough" because after all Said *was* concerned with the contents of texts more than anything else. Western descriptions of the Arab world, he argued, had little to do with the reality of the Orient; such descriptions generally provided more information about those who wrote them and their relations to the Orient than the world they claimed to describe. Said's original thesis has been subject to much discussion and is not without its critics, thus Figueira suggests that the politics of the critique of Orientalism "arbitrarily links a text with certain cultural practices, it 'colonizes' a text from the past by means of present-age discourse... I question the virile compulsion to view the West's reception of the East solely in terms of possession, power, and control" (1991:5). Nevertheless, since the publication of Said's book, the word "Orientalism" is frequently used to denote any kind of "othering," including that of ethnographic texts. In this broad sense, Orientalism is a powerful literary establishment, a textual institution that domesticates, exaggerates, and misrepresents "the Other" in terms of ethnocentric and nostalgic concerns. Indeed much anthropological discourse does just that. Thomas points out that while an elaboration of indigenous views of time and history may be regarded as a "reasonable reaction" to eurocentric views of the "natives," "anthropology is a discourse of alterity... which necessarily distances the people studied from ourselves" (N. Thomas 1991:3). Such distancing is implicit in the notion of the strange and remote, central to the anthropological project in the past.[1] Anthropology, almost by definition, involves a journey—mentally, at least—into relatively strange and distant lands, an attempt to understand the unique, exotic, and bizarre. To some extent the critique of Orientalism may be extended to our renderings of western society. Anthropologists' relations to the West are no less problematic than their relations to the Orient. "Occidentalism" (Carrier 1992), essentialist interpretations of the West by westerners, similarly simplifies and exaggerates.

Not only are anthropological comparison and generalization increasingly being replaced by poetry, self indulgence, and introspection, for many anthropologists ethnographic research is primarily a battle with paper and texts. Malinowski opens one of his books with a sweeping statement about the facts of life among South Sea Islanders. Sex, he says, "dominates in fact almost every aspect of culture" (1929:xxiii). For many anthropologists savants today, it seems, the facts of texts occupy a comparable status. Textual images are used to illuminate almost every aspect of social life, and not just the making of ethnographies. Culture, as the saying goes, *is* text. Some of the chapters in this book take a critical look at the general theoretical tendency to textualize human life, the textual life of anthropological savants, while others discuss the relative usefulness of actual texts for the ethnographic and historical reconstruction of particular realities, especially Icelandic ones. I argue that although the focusing on the rhetorical and textual aspects of social discourse has generated lively discussions and led to some important insights and developments, it is imperative to reverse the current priority of text over life.

Some literary scholars may regard literature as "the most interesting thing in the world, maybe more interesting than the world" (Derrida 1992:47), but such a position is both narrowly chronocentric and strikingly ethnocentric. The committed textualist may argue that "oral literature" is independent of time and place, something that humans have produced everywhere and at all times, and that the term of the "text" (from "to weave") is etymologically quite compatible with speech, the "stiching" of oral discourse. As Ong points out however, "oral literature" is a contradiction in terms and, moreover, "when literates nowadays use the term 'text' to refer to oral performance, they are thinking of it by analogy with writing" (1982:13). This chapter introduces the relevant theoretical and ethnographic issues discussed in the following chapters, emphasizing the tension between the written and the oral, between textual representation and participation in social life. Also, it briefly describes the Icelandic context of cultural invention, the nature of Icelandic textualism, and the contents of the following chapters.

THE LINGUISTIC TURN

With European explorations in the Middle Ages and the colonial expansion that followed, western people were confronted with puzzling information about distant lands, information collected by travellers and missionaries. Although it is probably an exaggeration to say that at the beginning of the Age of Discovery exotic traditions were inherently shocking to the West, since, as Boon points out (1982:34), "distance from Europe was not yet a relevant factor in ideas of monstrosity," early explorers provided Europeans with abundant food for thought about "primitives" (what was true and what wasn't?). More importantly, with the Renaissance the whole attitude to knowledge and learning was transformed. With the voyages of Italian merchants, the birth of a new aristocracy based on wealth and "bourgeois" values, and the triumph of humanism, westerners convinced themselves that they were able to separate themselves from the rest of the Creation with the help of science and rational thinking, scrutinizing and domesticating it with their powerful but somewhat limited senses, particularly vision (Lindberg and Steneck 1972). The church lost the dominant position it had achieved centuries ago and everything became measured in human terms. The humanists assumed that "man" was able to dissociate himself from the "natural" world, to observe cultural others and the animal kingdom from a distance.

It is true that the usefulness of the category of the Renaissance is debated among historians. Thus, Le Goff suggests it is high time "that we let the air out of the inflated concept of the Renaissance" (1988:10), arguing that the past will withstand any attempt to force a periodization upon it. The term "Middle Ages," he points out, was only invented in 1469 to underline the inferiority of the "Dark Age," the period prior to the Renaissance. Nevertheless, as Le Goff himself emphasizes, certain ways of dividing up the continuity of history are "more illuminating than others" (ibid.). The Renaissance episteme or paradigm was arguably no less significant for the emergence of modernism and the development of western science than Columbus's arrival in the strange land that turned out to be the "New World."

The epistemological views represented by the Renaissance are nicely illustrated in the laws of *Perspectiva* ("seeing through") and the innovative three-dimensional space established by Italian painters during the fourteenth and fifteenth centuries, including Giotto, Paolo Ucello, and Pierro della Francesca. Early Renaissance painters painfully struggled with the perspectival view of space in the "window" of the "picture plane," the "correct" representation of depth and infinity, and the tension between engagement and detachment, trained as they were in the static and holistic world of Aristotelian philosophy and the medieval church. By the end of the Renaissance, in contrast, the art of painting increasingly focused on cognitive and spatial research, the representation of human activities and their place in nature and history; the canvas was no longer primarily decorative space for the glorification of finite orders and godly designs.

Renaissance painters were rewarded for their efforts with spectacular artistic success which enabled them to locate humans in three-dimensional space, setting them free from the rest as if they were to recede into infinity or, alternatively, leave the "visual pyramid" of the canvas and "step outside." As Panofsky (1991 [1927]) points out in his classic essay *Perspective as Symbolic Form*, the apparently trivial visualism of the Renaissance signified a fundamental shift in western worldview. Now, he argues, the ground plane of the painting permits us to read both the sizes and the distances of the bodies arranged on it. Thus, a tile pattern might be used as "an index for spatial values":

> We can actually express both bodies and intervals—and thus the scope of every movement as well—numerically, as a number of floor squares.... It is not too much to claim that a pattern of tiles used in this sense represents the first example of a coordinate system: for it illustrates the modern 'systematic space' in an artistically concrete sphere, well before it had been postulated by abstract mathematical thought. (Panofsky 1991:57–58)

Projective geometry, Panofsky goes on, "like so many subdisciplines of modern 'science,' is in the final analysis a product of the artist's workshop." In fact, for Leonardo da Vinci art and geometry were interdependent; painting, like the other sciences, he assumed, was based on mathematics and careful observation.

In a relatively brief period nature had become a quantifiable, three-dimensional universe appropriated by humans, superior and rational beings in charge of the world. This "anthropocracy," to use Panofsky's term, represented a radical detheologized departure from the enclosed universe of the Aristotelians constituted by the earth and its seven surrounding spheres. The Renaissance, the Enlightenment, and the positivist science developed by Descartes, Francis Bacon, and many others, which were to mould every kind of western scholarship, instituted a series of decisive dualisms, including those of humanity and animality, nature and society, description and reality. The positivists typically assumed, often implicitly, a radical break between empirical observations and general non-empirical statements, emphasizing the primacy of the former. Since descriptions of the empirical world acquired a separate existence, independent of what was described, they could be scrutinized on their own and compared to the real. Questions of truth, falsity, and verification, as a result, became tantalizing and primary concerns. The metaphor of visual perception, a powerful Renaissance tool, was applied to any kind of empirical demonstration. In anthropology, the tradition of privileging the visual channel is exemplified by the icons of "forms" and "structural" relations, both of which emphasize appearances (Herzfeld 1987:202). This visualist bias even applies to historiography and the understanding of the distant past: "the Latinate 'evidence,' meaning that which is manifest or in plain sight, metaphorically indicates that historical evidence brings the vanished past back into sight" (Partner 1986:105).

In the modernist, positivist project, science became a passionate, aggressive search for truth and knowledge, an epistemological orgy.[2] Given the persistent othering of the object of modernist scholarship, the Baconian imagery of sexual assault was a recurrent one. The literature on modern science is, indeed, replete with passages that describe human-environmental interactions by means of an aggressive, sexual idiom.[3] Nature appears as

> a seductive but troublesome female, to be unrelentingly pursued, sought out, fought against, chased into her innermost sanctuaries, prevented from escaping, persistently courted, wooed, harried, vexed, tormented, unveiled, unrobed, and 'put to the question?' (i.e. interrogated under torture), forced to confess 'all that lay in her most intimate recess', her 'beautiful bosom' must be laid bare, she must be held down and finally 'penetrated', pierced and 'vanquished' (words which constantly recur). (Midgley 1992: 77)

When the party wore on, the hangover set in; the crisis in representation, the "postmodern condition." The project of the Enlightenment was simply childish and vulgar scientism, a "metaphysical illusion," "the illusion of having found an Archimedean standpoint situated beyond historical and cultural contingency" (Benhabib 1992:4). In anthropology, and indeed most of the social sciences, description was increasingly seen to be situated in what it described and humans were regarded as part of nature. Panofsky, who generally emphasized the *successes* of the Renaissance project and its contribution to "science," seems to have anticipated some of these developments, suggesting that one may reproach perspective, the "mathematization" of visual space, for "evaporating 'true being' into a mere manifestation of seen things" (1991:71). An important aspect of the challenge to modernism is the *Zeitgeist* of "postempiricism" sometimes identified by the phrase "linguistic turn": the persistent theoretical tendency to textualize human life, the noisy "sirens of textuality" (Partner 1986:110).

Although the theoretical metaphor of language and texts is not a recent invention and, as Bloch reminds us (1991), anthropologists have generally tended to think of culture as "language like," the exact metaphorical implications very much depend on the theory one adopts. Consider, for instance, the enormous differences between Saussure's notion of *langue* as an autonomous semiotic system and Chomsky's concept of language as a "mental organ" (1980:39), on the one hand, and, on the other hand, Wittgenstein's notion of the "language game" (see Harris 1988), and Bakhtin's concept (1986) of "translinguistics." Obviously, the inference of the metaphoric association of culture with language hinges on what one means by "language like." Generally, the linguistic turn in the social sciences, the textualization of life, has more in common with Saussurean and Chomskian reifications than the socialization of language and writing represented in the works of Wittgenstein and Bakhtin.

It is probably a truism to say that written documents, including novels, ethnographies and histories, are powerful sources for anthropological and historical research. Increasingly, anthropologists are willing to use creative writings as authentic ethnographic sources. Equally, it is obviously important to challenge the textual authority of the ethnographer and to question the "objectivity" of field reports. The loss of faith in anthropological knowledge, however, was not primarily the result of psotmodern theorizing and literary deconstruction; ethnographers, as Fabian points out (1991), realized that positivism was unable to deliver the kind of knowledge and scholarship they were after. The publication of Malinowski's diaries, written in the Trobriand Islands at the time of the First World War, made his own method, the celebrated method of "participant observation," highly suspect. Anthropologists generally came to the conclusion that ethnographies and other texts are necessarily artifacts of and situated in particular discourses and historical contexts. Malinowski's diaries showed that writing in the third person was a far more complicated undertaking than usually assumed; ethnographic "observers" are not just passive receptors of experience, devoid of feelings and opinions. Our actions, moods, and relationships necessarily inform what we write. Ethnographers, therefore, are inevitably faced with what Labovian sociolinguistics have referred to as the "observer's paradox"; they arrive on the scene to record things as they are, but their mere presence unavoidably shapes the course of events and, therefore, their representation. The awareness of the paradox suggests a "crisis" in representation. Clearly, we have reason to doubt that it is meaningful to speak of "factual" accounts, uncontaminated by the "externalities" of the person of the reporter—by relationships, fiction, and rhetoric.[4]

Textualism and autobiography, however, are not adequate responses to the crisis in representation. For one thing, they often signify surrender to the popular dictum that in ethnography anything goes. If cultural "texts" invite several and equally plausible or implausible "readings," as textualists seem to assume, the issue of faithfulness and authenticity is beside the point. Interpretive liberalism, relentless self-indulgence, and excessive textual concerns have their own pitfalls; anthropologists become literary critics and ethnography a form of art. It is not simply the case that anthropologists critical of the fashionable inward gaze are driven by their interpretive and theoretical insecurity to suppress any serious discussion of self, text, and autobiography, although the defensive and repressive treatment of sex among Freud's contemporaries may provide a tempting analogy. It is precisely by studying others that we learn about ourselves; comparative studies provide us with the critical means with which we can assess the unconscious assumptions of our own social formation. Indeed, there are good grounds for arguing, as Mascia-Lees, Sharp, and Cohen do (1993), that theorists of the linguistic turn "stave off" their own anxiety, when losing the privilege to authorize and define, by questioning the whole basis of ethnographic truth.

A further problem with textualism, at least its strong "culturalist" version, is that it merely represents a return to the prison house of reified language in yet another form. Thus Clifford argues (1988:38) that anthropological interpretation necessarily requires "textualization" of experience, "the process through which unwritten behavior, speech, beliefs, oral tradition, and ritual come to be marked as a corpus, a potentially meaningful ensemble separated out from an immediate discursive or performative situation." In this approach, social life is reduced to a thing, a cultural "corpus" separated from action and experience. To reduce our informants to thing-like creatures imprisoned by culture is not only arrogant, it goes right against the current emphasis, on authorizing indigenous "voices," on taking notice of what we hear in the field rather than brushing it aside, canonizing it, or appropriating it on our own terms.

Literary scholarship and textualist anthropology typically minimize the differences between literature and social discourse. Thus Todorov (1990:26) emphasizes that "there is not an abyss between literature and what is not literature, that the literary genres originate, quite simply, in human discourse." Although, obviously, literature flows from social discourse, the textualization of social life which juxtaposes speech and writing necessarily amounts to a distortion, ignoring the important differences there are between natural discourse and written texts. Literary texts may be revealing and perceptive, but they are not equivalent to natural dialogues. The differences between the context of everyday speech and that of the written word are nicely captured by Habermas:

> In everyday communicative practice speech acts retain a force that they lose in literary texts. In the former setting they function in contexts of action in which participants cope with situations and—let's say it—have to solve problems. In the latter setting they are tailored to a reception that removes the burden of acting from the reader; the situations that he encounters, the problems that he faces, are not immediately his own... Literary speech acts are... illocutionarily *disempowered*. (Habermas 1992:223)

Both the textualists and positivists have tended to define the aim of anthropological practice as the mediation of experiences derived from the ethnographic encounter with "another" world, going "beyond" cultural boundaries. At present, however, one can sense a growing disillusionment with the notions of boundaries and discontinuities (see Ulin 1991, Ingold 1993a). Social theorists have raised serious doubts about the linguistic turn and the ways in which social science is currently being represented, taught and practiced, arguing that the preoccupation with text and rhetoric fails to do justice to the scholarly attempt to make sense of social life and that the big questions on the theoretical agenda need to be rephrased or rethought. Friedman, for instance, criticises the "spectacularization" of anthropology, the "overwhelming fascination with the text, ... the appropriation of the real" (1987:168). Indeed, we may be forced to go beyond the *metaphor* of the boundary in anthropological analysis, challenging the assumptions of discontinuity and otherness with which anthropologists usually begin when defining the approach and subject-matter of their discipline. The tension between these two senses of "going beyond," that is, crossing boundaries, on the one hand, and, on the other, challenging the metaphor of boundaries, is the driving force of many contemporary theoretical debates. I suggest that anthropology and the social sciences generally are well advised to abandon the model of the textualist and its reifications, focusing on practises and discourses: addressing social life and the social aspects of texts rather than the textual aspects of life.

FIELDWORK AND "FINDING ONE'S SEA LEGS"

Anthropological practice, after all, is necessarily based on what Habermas refers to as "everyday communicative practice," on intensive contact with living persons and ethnographic fieldwork. As Malinowski argued (1929:xxvi), in a somewhat patronizing tone, keeping fieldnotes and writing ethnographies is a rather unfortunate necessity. What matters most, for recent critics of the textualist approach no less than the architects of modern fieldwork methods, including the founding father Malinowski, is to participate in local life and to learn about the lives of others. Fieldwork, Gudeman and Rivera point out (1990:4), is

> a perpetual discussion . . . Texts are frozen, they are conversation-stoppers that deny the continuous remaking of social life. . . The anthropologist produces a text, . . ., but only as one part of several larger conversations; and the anthropologist must certainly have a 'good ear' as well as a facile pen.

It is high time for a reappraisal of ethnographic fieldwork, of anthropology's classic concern with the ability to listen to other people's accounts and the willingness to partake in social discourse. To listen to others, however, is by no means a straight-forward activity. For one thing, it is important to go beyond positivist notions of the anthropologist as a recipient, recorder, or inscriber of texts, unrelated and unaccountable to the people he or she writes about. As Bakhtin remarked (1986:69), "the listener who understands passively, who is depicted as the speaker's partner in the schematic diagrams of general linguistics, does not correspond to the real participant in speech communication." Both culture criticism and radical objectivism (whether it be that of a foreigner or a native anthropologist) run the risk of reductionism, of transforming the use-value of everyday life into the exchange value of marketable anthropological commodities, the quaint, the exotic, and the foreign for sale on the international markets of academia.

Parts of this book are based on my fieldwork in my native Iceland. Not only did I work in my own country, I grew up in a fishing community in a family with deep roots in the fishing industry that I was studying. It is hardly appropriate, therefore, to speak of an "arrival" story as anthropologists often do when discussing their fieldwork. This fact inevitably affected my research: the kinds of questions I addressed, my relations with local people, and the answers they gave me. Since I spoke the "same" language as the people I talked to, I was unlikely to ask some of the more stupid questions that a foreigner or an outsider might pose. And, no doubt, my prior knowledge of the language and context of fishermen and fishworkers enabled me to grasp the nuances of the expressions I recorded and to act more appropriately than would otherwise have been possible. On the other hand, had I been an outsider my identity might have been somewhat less problematic. Perhaps, I would have been more likely to ask some of the interesting questions that fieldworkers are said to ask at the beginning of their work when they, supposedly, take nothing as given. And I might have been granted the licence to ask some of the more naïve questions I kept to myself until I felt it was safe to pose them to others.

At any rate, at the beginning of my fieldwork I felt hampered by the fact that much of the information I thought I needed seemed to be kept in closed quarters. While local people found the general topic of my research—changes in conceptions of fishing—a legitimate one, some of the questions I asked, especially those concerning fishing success, competition and fishing techniques, were seen to be either idiotic or too personal. While this is a reaction many fieldworkers may experience early in their work, the likelihood of its occurrence may be somewhat stronger in the case of a native fieldworker. Why would an academic from the capital city, I was asked, make an effort to understand this particular fishing community? Why would an anthropologist talk to fellow Icelanders, for months and mostly about relatively obvious matters? For quite some time I felt as if I was not making much progress, isolated as I was on the margin of the community. I knew that some important issues were not elaborated upon in my presence and I found it very embarrassing to see some of them discussed in greater detail in newspaper accounts. The process of establishing the necessary trust and rapport, and of gaining access to the local community, seemed painfully slow.

At one point, however, during the winter season in 1981 the wheels began to turn. A highly respected local skipper invited me to join him on one of his fishing trips. "If you *really* want to know what the fishing industry is all about," he said, "you must go fishing." He may have seen his offer as a test or challenge, knowing that academics and other landlubbers who rarely go to sea (*landkrabbar*, literally "land-crabs") are prone to seasickness in Icelandic waters. I accepted his challenge, and shortly after we left harbor we were in rough seas, indeed, one of the worst storms of the winter season. For several hours, while the skipper and his crew patiently waited for the weather to improve to be able to draw the nets they had placed in the sea the day before, I was busy emptying the contents of my stomach. I did not have the stomach, in a literal sense, to do anything except adjust my body to the movements of the boat, attending to the sea. No doubt my seasickness confirmed the skipper's belief that academics were hopeless at sea. Then, miraculously, it seemed, the weather suddenly improved and, fortunately, the feeling of seasickness vanished. I found the movements of the boat pleasant and relaxing and for the rest of the trip I addressed the skipper and his crew with a variety of questions, about boats, gear, skippers and fishing tactics. Quite suddenly, my nausea had been replaced with a sensation of alertness and well-being, an "oceanic" feeling. Later on, when ashore, I found out that the attitude towards my research had changed. My questions seemed to acquire a new force and they were no longer easily avoided or ignored. I had the feeling of having suddenly become accepted as a legitimate participant in local life. Apparently, then, the fishing trip was a rite of passage. I never bothered to ask for an explanation of what happened, but several people addressed me by reminding me of the fishing trip: "so, you've been feeding the fish!"

For Icelandic fishermen the experience of nausea above all represents a temporary, transitional and possibly beneficial phase. For them, the metaphor of nausea combines emotional and cognitive aspects. To be "seasick" (*sjóveikur*) is to be unfamiliar with the rocking movements of the world. As nausea is replaced by well-being, a quantum leap in learning is supposed to take place. Getting used to or adapting to something is referred to as recovering from seasickness, "getting one's sea legs" (*sjóast*). And those who return after an experience on rough seas are said to have *found* their sea legs (*vera sjóaðir*). Given the geographical location of Iceland in the middle of the North Atlantic and the historical importance of maritime transport, Icelanders often use—now, in the age of aeroplanes, as well as in the past—the nautical metaphor of "having sailed" (being *sigldur* or *sigld*) when refering to a person who has been abroad, a metaphor which may suggest some kind of othering. Thus, a person "has sailed" if he or she has first-hand experience of foreign customs. For me, however, the fishing trip was not an encounter with an exotic land; rather it served as a useful metaphor for a critical stage in learning, an important part of my enskilment as a fieldworker. Learning, is a matter of bodily involvement, of engagement and immersion in the practical world.[5]

I had gone on the fishing trip not only to accept the challenge of the skipper but also to learn about fishing: about models of success, skippers' decisions, interactions among crew men and the community at sea. While I was almost paralyzed by nausea at the beginning of the fishing trip, later on, when I had at least temporarily adapted to the irregularities of the seascape, I was able, as a fellow passenger, to attend to the social world aboard, the tasks of the crew, and the practical matters in which they were involved. Fieldwork experiences often involve psychosomatic processes, veritable "gut reactions." Seasickness, in fact, has much in common with the symptoms identified, by both fieldworkers and medical experts, as "culture shock." The likelihood of such illnesses varies from one person to another and from context to context; some people never get sick and some are sick all the time, but most manage to recover at some stage, often without any obvious explanation. It would be wrong to dismiss the experiences of seasickness and culture shock as pathological ones; both involve bodily manifestations of a particular stage in learning.

Fieldworkers usually begin their "trip" on the margin of the community, deeply uncomfortable by their status as alienated outsiders. As they become involved in the activities of others, they move towards the center and begin to feel "at home." Often such a feeling develops gradually. In my case it did not. The reason probably had to do with the peculiar nature of the context of my fieldwork, the trip and the fishing crew. The crew is a "total institution" in Goffman's sense; a relatively complete and exclusive social world, rather like those of prisons and hospitals, where newcomers are immediately presented with a test of their belonging. Passing (or failing) the test, however, is not the issue; what is important is being submitted to it, claiming publicly, so to speak, one's earnest request to participate and belong. To take part, therefore, is likely to involve sudden development of communion. For me, the fishing trip was both an important step in the process of social learning and a meaningful lesson on the nature of fieldwork. I came to realize, as many had before me, that to engage in fieldwork is not just to "observe" and record but to participate in local life. From now on, I increasingly left my tape recorder behind and abandoned arranged, formal interviews, listening instead to the spontaneous flow of local discourse and engaging in free conversations with others. I should, perhaps, have done so right from the beginning; the radical empiricism which suggests that the knower and the known live in separate worlds and treats experience as "something passively received rather than actively made, something that impresses itself upon our blank minds or overcomes us like sleep" (Jackson 1989:5) is not, and was not, the model of the day. But lessons of this kind only tend to sink in as a result of personal experience; indeed, they are not "passively received."

Many anthropologists have discussed similar "breakthroughs"—signals of positive change—in their relationships with the people they visit. Although I find it useful to refer to my fieldwork as a journey, a fishing trip, for me fieldwork does not involve a privileged, solitary trip across boundaries to places unknown to others—to "another" world. Rather, the metaphor of the journey draws attention to the similarities in emotional as well as social experience of doing fieldwork and fishing in rough seas; in the progression, in one case, from the margin of the discursive community towards the centre, and, in the other, from nausea and seasickness to alertness and well-being.

THE ETHNOGRAPHIC CONTEXT: THE INVENTION OF ICELANDERS

The early Icelandic settlers, emigrants from Norway and the British Isles, established a stratified society which combined settled pastoralism, agriculture and fishing, and a society based on divisions between slaves, landless freemen, and freeborn landholders. An assembly (*Alþing*) was established in 930, but there was no state or centralized authority. This social formation, referred to, in the present context, as the Icelandic Commonwealth, lasted for roughly three centuries. The sagas, many of which, it is generally believed, were composed in the turmoil of thirteenth-century Iceland when Icelanders had submitted to the King of Norway, reflect social life during the Commonwealth Period and the decades following its "collapse." The period from the end of the Commonwealth to the beginning of the nineteenth century was in many ways a "silent" one (Hastrup 1990a), characterized by colonial oppression, isolation, and economic stagnation. The Icelandic independence movement sought to break out of the silence by emphasizing the contrast with the achievements of the heroic past, the Viking heritage and the sagas. Much like the Greek independence movement phrased its concern with stagnation, the fall from cultural grace, in terms of the rhetoric of European aboriginality (Herzfeld 1987:25), Icelanders presented themselves as the aboriginals of "Norse" civilization.

In the beginning, the emigrants to Iceland regarded themselves as "Norse" or "Nordic" (*norrænir*), but later they contrasted themselves as "Icelanders" with their Nordic neighbors on linguistic grounds, as is evident from an indigenous linguistic treatise, the *First Grammatical Treatise* (Benediktsson 1972), written in the twelfth century. Icelandic belongs to the Nordic languages, a subgroup of the Germanic languages which belong to the Indo-European "family" of languages. The closest relatives, from a comparative viewpoint, are Norwegian and Faroese. Icelandic is usually said to have emerged as a separate language as early as the tenth century, but the differences between Icelandic and Norwegian were probably not very great until the fourteenth century. Since then, Norwegian has undergone many changes while Icelandic has remained relatively uniform and resistant to change. No doubt, there are many reasons for the relative unity of Icelandic. During the period of settlement different Scandinavian dialects were mixed into a unified language, communications within the country were relatively easy, and there were regular travels of laborers and vagrants from one place to another. Also, a strong literary tradition encouraged further unification. Moreover, Denmark's language policy in Iceland during its period of colonial rule seems to have been weak or nonexistent. Arguably, the colonialists *expected* Icelanders to play the part of the ancestors of Norse civilization.

Foreign texts have often influenced, albeit indirectly, the historical and cultural consciousness of Icelanders; the accounts of foreign travelers have motivated indigenous constructions of what it meant to be Icelandic. Sometimes, Icelanders were pleased to see foreign accounts of their island and their history, but more frequently they were shocked to see what foreigners made of them. Some felt a strong urge to publish a "true" account of Icelanders and correct the "mistakes." Arngrímur Jónsson says in the preface to his *Crymogæa* (Iceland), written in Latin in 1609, that his aim is to defend his fatherland against ignorance and deceit, to prove to the larger world that even though Iceland is "neither Italy nor Greece," it belongs to the society of Christians and not that of "pagan barbarians." At the turn of the nineteenth century, Thoroddsen wrote four volumes on Iceland and foreign conceptions of the inhabitants for similar purposes but with Icelandic readers in mind. More recently, Sigurður Nordal, inspired by discussions with Englishmen and Americans, wrote an influential book on "Icelandic Culture," "a new Crymogæ, a defense on the behalf of the Icelanders" (1942:39). A similar work, but even more romantic and nationalistic, is Guðmundur Finnbogason's book "The Icelanders." The works of Nordal and Finnbogason provide good examples of what Icelanders wanted to be in the eyes of the larger world and what made them different from their own point of view. Both are written in the context of the nationalist movement, constantly cashing cheques on deeds committed seven hundred years ago, to paraphrase Nordal's cynical remark.

The collapse of the Icelandic Commonwealth in 1262, signified the beginning of a long period of Scandinavian domination. After just over a century of Norwegian rule, Iceland passed with the mother country to the Danish crown. The nature of Danish colonialism—from 1380 to 1944, when Iceland gained full independence—varied from one period to another, but generally, for more than half a millennium of Danish dominance, Iceland retained a special status in the colonial empire preserving much of its cultural and legal autonomy. The Icelandic independence movement, largely inspired by Icelandic students and scholars in the cultural metropolis of Copenhagen, supported its claim for independence with reference to the somewhat exaggerated "dark age" of foreign oppression, emphasizing Iceland's literary-historical heritage, prior to the period of foreign domination, embodied in the Icelandic language and the sagas. Unfortunately, they argued, during the period of Danish colonialism a significant part of that heritage, important books and manuscripts about the Commonwealth, had been accumulated in Copenhagen. Some were sold to Danish scholars and collectors while others were requisitioned by the colonial authorities. Thus in 1662 the Danish king ordered that he be sent two copies of every book written in Icelandic or printed in Iceland. Still others were appropriated by Icelandic scholars in Copenhagen, in particular Árni Magnússon (d. 1730), who were anxious to save the "national treasures" from the "miserable conditions" of sixteenth and seventeenth-century Iceland. The movement of Icelandic nationalists that flourished in the nineteenth and twentieth century insisted upon the return from

Copenhagen of every manuscript that had originated in Iceland and for Icelanders this was one of the most symbolic demands of the politics of decolonization. Iceland gained home rule in 1918 and soon after (in 1925) the Icelandic Parliament formally requested the return of all "national antiquities" stored in Danish museums.

For several decades, Danish and Icelandic authorities were to debate and negotiate the "ownership" of Icelandic manuscripts stored in Copenhagen (more than two thousand manuscripts, at times with much emotion, heat, and fervour. The sagas, many Danes argued, represented the "Old-Norse" (*oldnordisk*) tradition of the distant past, a time when "Danish language" (*dönsk tunga*) was the common cultural denominator of the Nordic world, and therefore, they reckoned, the manuscripts were properly deposited in Denmark, and for good. For many other Scandinavians (Swedes and Norwegians), the Icelandic texts were Norse creations which only happened to be recorded and temporarily guarded in Iceland by Norse emigrants. German nationalists, by the way, entertained a similar idea (although they did not, it seems, claim to possess the scripts), emphasizing the pan-Germanic roots of the sagas and the Viking spirit and integrating them in their national heritage. For Icelanders, however, the sagas not only qualified as the major accomplishment of the Nordic and Germanic traditions; they were nothing less than world literature: yet they belonged to Icelanders and nobody else. "No Germanic people, in fact no nation in Northern Europe," Nordal wrote in 1931, "has a medieval literature which in originality and brilliance can be compared with the literature of the Icelanders from the first five centuries after the settlement period" (cited in Byock 1992:43). In the words of Einar Ólafur Sveinsson, another authoritative indigenous scholar, the saga literature "is still a vital force, it is the root that draws the juices from the soil of ancient times, passing them on to the lively and maturing branches of modern culture" (Sveinsson 1959:103). Clearly, the manuscripts, the sagas, and the distant past were caught up in discursive battles, ideological struggles, and relations of power. Much like other colonial and post-colonial subjects Icelanders needed a past, a "golden" age of monumental achievements. By appealing to the "facts" of linguistic antiquity, historical continuity, and external threats (foreign slang), the Icelandic intelligentsia and the nationalist movement were able to ensure the support of Scandinavian (and European) intellectuals. The manuscripts were to be returned in stages, the last ones in 1996.

In April 1971, some of the most important exiled manuscripts were handed over to the Icelandic authorities at a formal occasion in Reykjavík (see Figure 1.1). Thousands of people turned up in a festive mood to participate in and experience the event that marked the "homecoming" of the manuscripts. In addition to the formalities of speeches, flags, handshakes, and brass bands, there was much spontaneity and informal carnivalesque. According to newspaper accounts, crowds of students chanted a John Lennon song popularized all over Europe and North America

FIGURE 1.1   *The "homecoming"...*

in demonstrations against the war in Vietnam, "All we are saying is give peace a chance." Suddenly they would switch to an Icelandic version singing "All we are saying is return the manuscripts" (*Allt sem við viljum er handritin heim*), playfully mixing the youthful international movement of the late 1960s and the more serious mood of Icelandic nationalism. After more than three centuries' absence from Icelandic soil, as the speechmakers put it, the manuscripts were back home.

The sagas and more recent texts, chronicles and folk tales, have provided an important avenue for the fetishization of Icelandic culture and the national heritage. Jónsson (1989) and Hastrup (1991) have drawn attention to the ethnological invention of Icelandic traditions and their role for the nationalists' construction of cultural identity. The Icelandic intelligentsia established a number of "old traditions," for example *þorrablót*, an annual food ritual modelled on a selective and exaggerated reading of written accounts. While the word *þorrablót* occurs in some of the sagas—the etymology of the term suggests a feast of sacrifice (*blót*) during the "month" of mid-vinter (*þorri*) in the old Icelandic calendar—we have little evidence on the nature of the ritual. By the end of the nineteenth century, however, the *þorrablót* represented an attempt to imitate a Viking ritual, emphasizing particular rules for drinking, speaking, and singing. Icelandic newspaper from 1881 provide accounts of the "resurrection" of the ritual: "In ancient times during mid-winter it was customary to gather for a feast and now several men, members of the archaeological society, have introduced that tradition" (see Jónsson 1989:449). Motivated by the rhetoric of a "national" past, a group of men got together, decorated with "ancient" symbols and relics, to have a drink, making speeches and honoring the gods of heathen times.

During the 1950s and 1960s, the feast of *þorrablót* was reinvented once again, this time by restaurant owners in Reykjavík. The formality of the event stressed the consumption of "purely Icelandic" or "typical" Icelandic food, based on an improvised reconstruction of the food ritual of Commonwealth Iceland. As time went on, the restaurant owners in Reykjavík set the standard for the whole country. As Hastrup points out, "by 'eating the past' the Icelanders continue to celebrate themselves—in the past tense" (1991:236). Now, the menu usually includes burned sheep heads (including the brain and the eyes), blood sausages, "rotten" shark, dried fish, and marinated ram's testicles. Much of this is considered exotic, but the more exotic the more Icelandic. Those who manage to consume testicles, brains and eyes have a stronger claim to being "truly" Icelandic than those who don't. The emphasis on collective, *national* identity should not blind us to the fact that cuisine varies from one group to another. Ethnological accounts of Icelandic traditions, Jónsson argues, typically ignore differentiation and the social context of cultural inventions, focusing instead on continuity, origins, and etymology. "Icelanders wander about this economic and political void—equal, ethnic, and in festive mood" (Jónsson 1989:452).

During the twentieth century, the sagas have been one of the most important foundations, if not the most important, on which Icelanders have built their public image. By the end of the campaign for political independence and during the years that immediately followed full independence, many of the sagas were published in new standard editions in order to define more clearly the traditions of Icelanders. At the same time, modern Icelandic was standardized. In the rapidly expanding school system of the 1950s and 1960s, standardized Icelandic was strictly enforced, in theory, at least, to ensure equality and cultural homogeneity. Language discourse continued to focus on purity, but this time the problem was an internal one: the polluting effects of the "language of the street." Since independence, Icelandic society and identity have undergone major transformations. Most importantly, the Second World War and the Cold War redefined Icelandic society and its place in the world. The economy was modernized in a couple of decades or so, shifting the focus from agriculture to expansive and highly mechanized fishing, a class system emerged with new forms of inequality, and politically and culturally Iceland moved closer to America than ever before although it retained fairly close relations with its "Nordic neighbours." More recently, with the end of the Cold War and the increasing political and economic integration of Europe, Iceland has, again, moved closer to the east. In this new context, the textual imagination of Icelanders will, no doubt, have to face a series of threats and challenges. In particular, notions of Icelandicness, language, tradition, and cultural boundaries are subject to change. With the dominating position in recent years of the English language in the global village of the mass media and electronic communications, the idea of the external threat has been reinvented. Now, however, the bad guys are neither easily discernible nor near at hand, and they are no longer Danes. Somewhat paradoxically, given the current forces of European integration and globalization, Icelanders and Danes (and, for that matter, members of the other Nordic nations) continue to see themselves as having much in common, and perhaps more than ever before, as the inhabitants of a cultural island, so to speak, situated in the margins of Europe and the larger world.

ETHNOGRAPHY IN THE MARGINS: INDIGENOUS TEXTUALISM

As the preceding discussion indicates, the social discourse of Icelanders has its own form of textualism. It would be wrong, however, to assume that the current bookish outlook of Icelanders, their preoccupation with pure Icelandic, ancient texts, and the literary heritage, represent an unbroken tradition extending to the distant past, the Commonwealth Period. For one thing, the nature and practice of literacy varied from one time to another; over the centuries Icelandic textualism has taken several forms, moving from runic inscription and the copying of manuscripts to printing and, finally, mass production of different kinds of texts—or, from "scribal culture" to "print culture" and "print capitalism."[6] This is not to submit to the ethnocentric techno-determinism that has characterized western discourse on texts, particularly "printing," only to draw attention to the historical transformation of literacy and the textual imagination.[7]

Literacy seems to have been introduced to Norse society with the runic alphabet in the second or third century A.D.; some of the stone inscriptions that have been found in eastern Norway date from that period. We do not know much about the role and context of early runic inscriptions, but it is likely that they assigned authority to exchange and claims of inheritance and property. The Norse settlers in Iceland brought with them their runic practice and later on, with the introduction of the Roman alphabet and the acceptance of Christianity in the year 1000, a powerful literary tradition emerged, enabling the recording and codification of the past, language, and the laws, and, of course, the production of sagas. We know that some Icelandic vellum manuscript date back to the winter of 1117 or 1118. Some were probably written as early as 1096 when important tax law were enacted, and some even earlier. The manuscript called "The First Grammatical Treatise," written by an anonymous Icelander sometime between 1125 and 1175, testifies to the perceived need for composing an alphabet "for us Icelanders" in order that it might become "easier to write and read ... both laws and genealogies ..."[8]

It is difficult to confidently identify the cultural context in which the sagas were written, read, and copied (most of the existing manuscripts were edited and revised in medieval monasteries) and we may never be able to specify the actual literary practices of medieval Iceland and the nature of literacy. This is one of the key problems in the "new" ethnographic perspective of literacy studies.[9] It seems, however, that by the end of the Commonwealth Period literacy was largely restricted to particular classes of men, to chieftains and the wealthiest farmers. Much evidence also indicates that the sagas were written for public performances, not for individual or private consumption. Often the sagas were read aloud at domestic gatherings when there was little else to do than to enjoy a good story in the company of others: thus the frequent references to *sagnaskemmtan*, storytelling. Occasionally, the saga writer deliberately addresses the person performing at such gatherings, keeping in mind the reader as well as the audience. Reading the sagas was a highly valued art, much like verbal performance generally was a means of earning honor in real life.

Whatever the nature and context of literacy in early Iceland, the sagas provide important evidence on an indigenous discourse on language, a rich discourse comparable in detail and complexity to those described for some contemporary realities in recent ethnographies, for example the elaborate "talking about talk" (Goldman 1983:200) among the Huli of New Guinea. For early Icelanders, both the spoken and written word, gossip and oratory as well as books and runic inscriptions, were imbued with immense powers, analogous to the physical force of an army. One way to assault someone was to attack personal honor through insulting verses or stories. Such attacks could have very severe consequences, escalating into feuds and warfare. Storytelling was also a means of *bestowing* honor on others, particularly for bravery in battle and generosity in gift-exchange. Aware of the potential impact of stories for their reputation, the actors would often stage a performance hoping it would later be celebrated in stories. This is what Bauman refers to as the "performance of honor": "the display of honored qualities in action itself represented a performance form carried out with a view toward eliciting recognition and advertisement through verbal performance" (1986:146). Above all, however, it was witchcraft that demonstrated the "biting force" of the word, to borrow saga jargon, the force that ensured physical effects. In the scribal culture of early medieval Iceland, a written word or symbol could be used by anyone, and for good as well as evil ends. Malinowski remarks (1922:428) that while the Trobrianders used certain words when exercising magic, he was not "under the delusion that the composers or inventors of magic had a theory about the efficiency of words." Medieval Icelanders, in contrast, judging from saga accounts, seem to have had an elaborate folk theory of speech acts.

Paper was introduced to Iceland in the fifteenth century and the first Icelandic press was established in 1530. With the Protestant Reformation in the sixteenth century and the Danish colonial regime, there was a general shift from copying and fairly restricted circulation of vellum manuscripts to massive multiplication on paper, from script culture to print culture, although the early practice of writing on calfskin continued until well into the seventeenth century. However, while the production of books became cheaper than before, it was strictly controlled. For a long time, the only publishing house in the country was governed by the church. Now, the motivation for textual production had less to do with local politics—with social honor, heroic battles, and personal deeds—than state control, law, religious indoctrination, and, above all, domestic discipline. Around 1750 a series of official ordinances and regulations were applied to almost every aspect of domestic life. In particular, they focused on the rearing of children and domestic discipline (*húsagi*), attempting to improve moral standards and to prevent too much independence of *ungdómur* (literally, "young people")—a category which, significantly, embraced both children and domestic laborers.[10] Literacy was an important means for improving moral standards, but it was largely restricted to males (heads of households) and religious texts. In the wake of the Reformation, textual production became the monopoly of the officials of the church and the state and any kind of personal "magic" in the form of writing was deemed to be an evil act. Despite considerable differences in the form and frequency of witchcraft accusations from one time to another, one thing seems to have remained constant throughout the medieval period: the firm folk belief in the magical power of words.

General literacy in Iceland, as many other places in Europe, came with the Enlightenment, several decades later, however, than on the continent. Literacy and schools encouraged innovation and the efficient production and transmission of knowledge. With the development of print capitalism and the nationalist upheaval in the early twentieth century, Icelandic textualism was reinforced. For one thing, the publication of dictionaries and works of grammar reified a "proper," standardized version of modern Icelandic. Equally important, Icelanders' textual heritage of the sagas was rediscovered and popularized. The sagas supplied the national roots, and evidence of a glorious past and monumental literary achievements. Icelanders, in sum, submitted to the tyranny of the text. This new form of textualism, whose inception was both domestic (the national elite) and foreign (Danish intellectuals, notably the linguist Rask), has largely informed the traditional "Icelandic school" of saga studies, an approach that has undoubtedly prevented the development of ethnographically informed medieval historiography in the study of the sagas.

No doubt the deep historical roots of the textual heritage and its significant role for the independence movement and the construction of Icelandic identity helped to establish a strong emphasis on books and texts in independent Iceland.

Icelanders like to see themselves as a highly literate nation. They tend to believe that they publish and read more books than other people do: "Indeed, the alleged addiction of Icelanders to reading books and the proportionately large number of bookstores are among the few items of information about Iceland that have reached the outside world" (Tomasson 1980:116). Much evidence, on the other hand, indicates a discrepancy between Icelandic representation and practice in this respect. While the possession of some of the standard saga editions is one of the hallmarks of an educated household and leather-bound volumes are bought by the meter, saga reading seems much less important than the number of volumes in Icelandic homes would indicate. Much like during earlier times, the sagas are consumed publically, not individually; frequently they are staged and performed on formal occasions—this time, however, largely for maintaining and reinventing the national image of the Icelanders.

In the textual life of Icelanders, language, culture and history are not only understood in terms of a glorious literary past, with reference to the continuous written records of Icelanders of their society and history from the time of settlement in the late ninth century; many Icelanders, in particular the intelligentsia, like to apply a highly bookish approach to both contemporary realities and the past, an approach that has much in common with the "scriptism" of modern Greece, another society on the "margins" of Europe. Herzfeld observes that

> in Greece, local claims to European identity clashed with European claims of Greek otherness. The commonly held nineteenth-century view of Greece as ... a mere survival of the Classic age ... clashed with the Greeks' own aspirations for recognition as a modern European nation. One possible resolution ... lay in presenting Greece as fixed in time before modern history, the definitive locus of European *aboriginality*. (Herzfeld 1987:54)

If we substitute "European," in Herzfeld's text, with Nordic (or Scandinavian) and "Greece" with Icelandic, we have a fairly accurate description of the Icelandic cultural context. In both Greece and Iceland, the ambivalent combination of modernity and aboriginality motivated a persistent concern among the indigenous elite with the "language question" and the "textual heritage": a preoccupation with cultural purity and external threats and an exaggeration of linguistic unity and cultural homogeneity.[11]

The bookish approach of Icelanders to their society, identity, and history is particularly evident in contemporary discourse on language policy. Language tends to be treated as a sovereign "thing," a collective institution independent of and above those who speak it who are reduced to mere instruments of language. Language becomes a phantom object: a commodity fetish, to paraphrase Marx (1976:165). To some extent, such an approach is an offspring of western discourse on language, culture and texts, including Saussurean linguistics. Of no less importance, however, as we have seen, are the particular historical developments in Iceland; the saga literature, the colonial background, the Protestant Reformation, the independence movement, and Icelandic nationalism. Together these forces have shaped the cultural invention of contemporary Icelanders.

It is probably fair to say that, in focusing on literary achievements and the written word, Icelandic culture pays relatively little attention to visual sensibilities. Thus, many of the visual arts, including painting, sculpture, photography, and film making, were fairly late arrivals on the Icelandic scene. Despite the important role of visual images in the modern era, the transmission of the Icelandic cultural heritage in the school system and the mass media overwhelmingly emphasizes textual traditions and their continuity to the present day. Icelanders, it is sometimes pointed out, are visually "illiterate." Traditionalists complain, however, that teenagers are being corrupted by television and videos and that, consequently, knowledge of "culture" and the past, of Icelandic language, identity, and literary heritage, is rapidly disappearing. Although such claims, of course, are not unique to the context under discussion (the "back-to-basics" slogan is heard in many places nowadays), they rarely take the extreme forms of the Icelandic ones.

The image of the "Mountain" (see Figure 1.2) by Sigurður Guðmundsson, an Icelandic artist, nicely illustrates some aspects of Icelandic textualism. Not only can Icelanders scarcely exist without commodities, books, in particular; the textual heritage, much like other essentials of modern life such as food and clothes, puts its stamp on them: their *"habitus"* in Bourdieu's (1990) sense of the term, their bodily dispositions. The textual determinism of the Icelandic context is, in fact, in many respects reminiscent of the "textual habitus" described in Messick's book about a particular Muslim society, *The Calligraphic State*, "a set of acquired dispositions concerning writing and the spoken word.." (1993:251). As we shall see later, however, Guðmundsson's image of the "Mountain" also suggests another very different "reading," more akin to postmodern environmental discourse than any kind of vulgar determinism, whether textual or ecological.

OUTLINE OF THE BOOK

The first part of this book focuses on anthropological textualism and the general theoretical issues involved: ethnography, representation, and social understanding. Chapter two examines the usefulness of applying the metaphors of boundaries, cultural translation, language and texts, important metaphors in most schools of anthropological thought, to social life. Such metaphors, I maintain, need to be replaced by a new ethnographic concept emphasizing democratic communion. If the modern scholarly imagination is burdened with the facts of texts, much like

Victorian writers and South Sea Islanders seem to have been troubled by the facts of life, it is not as farfetched, perhaps, as it may sound to proceed with a lengthy discussion of a particular novel. This is not to argue that fabricated texts are equivalent to field experience and ethnographic evidence, although novels may be highly informative in this respect. I try to show in the third chapter that much of what the Icelandic writer Halldór Laxness has to say about travel accounts in his novel *Christianity at Glacier* is highly relevant for the current anthropological debate on the authenticity of field reports and ethnographic authority, the question of whether, and to what extent, one should believe the person who has a grip on the pen. Laxness's novel, I suggest, is not simply a parody of anthropological narcissism, it offers a sophisticated critique of othering, positivist scholarship, and "Orientalist" ethnography, in Said's sense of the term. Anthropology, or any discipline for that matter, must respect the norms of "good conversation," what German social scientists refer to as *Sprachethik*. I shall illustrate these issues by a critical discussion of the writings of some of the anthropologists who have recently worked in Iceland, focusing on the ethnographic writings of Kirsten Hastrup and the way in which she has responded to indigenous critique of her works.

Most of the ethnographic and historical content in the second and third part of the book relates to Iceland, past and present. The second part, on times, lives and medieval texts, largely focuses on the sagas and the Commonwealth period. The central issues discussed are the ethnographic authenticity and comparative usefulness of

FIGURE 1.2   *"Mountain"* (by Sigurður Guðmundsson)

the sagas and, generally, what to make of them. Icelandic scholarship has tended to approach the sagas from one of two textual extremes; one approach treats the sagas as pure fiction, the works of literary geniuses, while another, saga fundamentalism, regards them as absolute historical truth. For decades medievalists and literary scholars have studied the sagas as pieces of text, but recently anthropologists and social historians have begun to address them from a new angle, with comparative and ethnographic questions in mind. I shall draw upon these insights to argue that the sagas are powerful ethnographic documents about the saga age. The fourth chapter is devoted to a general discussion of the sagas, the context in which they were produced, and the development of a social approach in saga studies, while the fifth applies such an approach to a particular aspect of the medieval world: the magical power of words and texts and the changing context and practice of witchcraft accusations. For medieval Icelanders, texts were imbued with a force of their own, much like magic things, including gifts and weapons. Textual powers, whether they were embodied in runic inscriptions, codified law, or books of witchcraft, might have profound, even fatal, consequences for those subjected to them as well as those who possessed them.

The third part of the book concentrates on particular aspects of social life in contemporary Iceland and its interpretation. Some discourses on modern realities, in particular those relating to language, culture, and identity, I suggest, are impaired by the hegemony of texts and textualism. Chapter six focuses on the role of language policy for the formation of social identity and the allocation of symbolic capital in the modern class system and the emerging Icelandic nation state after the Second World War, while chapter seven discusses fishing and economic production, focusing on the issues of property and differential access to natural resources. The discourses on language and production contain a plurality of voices, but each of them has been dominated by a particular voice emphasizing specific notions of sociality and individual differences. The dominant voice, though, has come from different directions: the discourse on language has largely been developed from above, by academics and the intelligentsia, whereas the one on production has been developed from below, by fishermen and laborers. Recently, however, discursive power has moved in the opposite direction: discussions on language are more relaxed and democratic than before, while discussions on production, especially fisheries management and catch quotas, have become more elitist.

The final chapter summarizes the general arguments advanced in the book as well as specific conclusions with respect to Icelandic ethnography and history. I distinguish between three different modes of ethnographic production each of which represents particular relations and moralities: the colonialist, textualist, and, finally, the one of living discourse. The living discourse, I conclude, with its emphasis on democratic communion and the continuity of the social world, represents a truly post-Orientalist ethnographic order.

NOTES

[1] There is an extensive literature on the subject; see, for instance, Todorov 1988, Torgovnick 1990, and Bongie 1991.

[2] The ambitions and assumptions of the modernist project are nicely illustrated in Rabinow's ethnography of French intellectuals *French Modern* (1989).

[3] Francis Bacon spoke of "entering and penetrating... holes and corners" (cited in Bordo 1987: 108).

[4] It is tempting to think of narratives of nature and the environment as more "factual" than those dealing with social life, but interestingly there are identical debates in the field of environmental history. Cronon (1992), for instance, examines two very different accounts of the droughts on the Great Plains in the 1930s, the "Dust Bowl," in the light of the "postmodernist assault on narrative" (Cronon 1992: 1349). "The two authors," he argues (p. 1347), "dealt with virtually the same subject, had researched many of the same documents, and agreed on most of the facts, and yet their conclusions could hardly have been more different."

[5] Elsewhere I have applied the theoretical perspectives of practice and embodied knowledge to learning and enskilment (see Pálsson 1994a).

[6] For a discussion of the notions of "script culture" and "print culture," see Anderson 1983 and Parry 1985.

[7] Warner has argued (1990) that the technological determinism associated with printing assumes the value-terms of modernity and ignores the reciprocal interaction between a medium and its politics.

[8] See Benediktsson 1972:35.

[9] On the "new" ethnographic perspective, see, for instance, Street 1993. Much has been written on the production and use of literature in early Iceland and it is impossible, in the present context, to discuss the relevant issues except very briefly. For useful and informative accounts, see, for instance, Guttormsson 1989, Lönnroth 1991, and Ólason 1989.

[10] See Guttormsson 1983:13.

[11] There are important differences as well between the contexts of Greek and Icelandic discourse on independence and national identity. Thus, while both Greeks and Icelanders may be said to have occupied the margins of a larger civilization, the otherness they faced—on the other side of the fence, so to speak—derived from rather different sources; the Greeks were troubled by the Orient, the engulfing threat of Turkish language and culture, whereas Icelanders contested their image as "brute primitives" or "medieval survivals," an image frequently emphasized in foreign accounts.

PART ONE

From Life to Text

Chapter Two

The conventional metaphor of cultural translation

> ... the learning of a foreign culture is like the learning of a foreign tongue: at first mere assimilation and crude translation, at the end a complete detachment from the original medium and a mastery of the new one.
>
> Exactly as I have to write in English, and translate native terms into English, so also I have, in order to make them real and comprehensible, to translate Melanesian conditions into our own.
>
> Bronislaw Malinowski, *The Sexual Life of Savages*

Social scientists, I argued above, have increasingly gone along with the traditional claim of the literary scholar that the text is "the thing." In one sense, however, the textual emphasis is not a new phenomenon in anthropology. For quite some time, anthropology has been regarded as an "art of translation" (Crick 1976:164), a textual exercise facilitating understanding across boundaries of time and culture. Given such a metaphor, the role of the anthropologist is to go behind the baffling chaos of cultural artifacts, to discover order in the foreign, and to transfer implicit meaning from one discourse to another. Anthropologists are presented as semiotic tour guides, escorting alien "readers" in rough semiotic space. The defining of anthropologists as professional, cultural translators has appeared in anthropological discourse in various contexts and under different guises, depending on theoretical and historical concerns. This chapter charts the theoretical landscape of cultural translation. It begins with a discussion of the idea of the divided world, in particular the three worlds scheme, its place in western discourse, and its implications for anthropology. It then moves on to the implications of the notion of translation, the parallels between linguistics and anthropology, and the relative usefulness of the metaphor of translation in relation to anthropological practice. Finally, it deals with the idea of a culturally divided world and "cultural dyslexia" (defined as a failure to "read" other cultures and come to terms with difference) and alternative visions of both social life and its understanding.

For American anthropologists, the metaphor of cultural translation has been a particularly compelling one. Not only has the concept of "culture" been of central importance to them, linguistic models and metaphors have generally been regarded as highly relevant and useful for analysis of cultural phenomena. The cultural determinism inspired by Boas and the linguistic determinism of Sapir and Whorf, therefore, have much in common. Sapir and Whorf, as Feleppa notes (1988:56), regarded the "linguist's translation problem (and the ethnographer's problem generally) as one of 'calibrating' radically different conceptual schemes of reference." Similar ideas are evident in French structuralist anthropology. Lévi-Strauss (1963) applies the method of distinctive features, borrowed from the linguistics of Jakobson, to analysis of ethnographic details, including kinship systems. For him, radically different cultural systems are transformations of one another.

More surprisingly perhaps, given the difference in theoretical developments, in particular the primary concern with the social rather than the cultural, British anthropologists have also found the notion of cultural translation appealing. Significantly, a collection of essays published in honour of Evans-Pritchard was entitled *The Translation of Culture* (Beidelman 1971). It opens with a quote from Evans-Pritchard's *Theories of Primitive Religion*, which suggests that the "semantic difficulties in translation" are the "major problem" with which anthropologists are confronted. Asad suggests (1986) that while the idea of cultural translation may not have been unanimously accepted by all the founders of the British school of social anthropology, it was nevertheless an important one. Asad's claim, however, that Malinowski never thought of his work in terms of the translation of cultures is not altogether correct. In his early essay on "The problem of meaning in primitive languages," Malinowski refers time and again to issues of translation. Malinowski points out, with reference to his Trobriand ethnography, that native conceptions are often foreign to European vocabulary and that direct translation is therefore impossible: "Such words can only be translated into English, not by giving their imaginary equivalent... but by explaining the meaning of each of them through an exact Ethnographic account of the sociology, culture and tradition of that native community" (1923:456). "The ethnographer," Malinowski goes on, "has to convey... [the] deep yet subtle difference of language and of the mental attitude which lies behind it, and is expressed through it" (ibid.:457). Although Malinowski's essay is largely concerned with the problems of translating primitive *languages*, at times the author clearly draws some general lessons for ethnographic practice (Malinowski 1929:xxv). Malinowski, then, was not immune to the linguistic metaphor of translation, even though he advanced a theory of language both very different from those of Boasian anthropologists and structural linguists and highly relevant for a discursive theory of ethnographic fieldwork: the pragmatist notion of language as being a mode of action rather than a normative instrument of expression.

No doubt there are several reasons for the popularity of the idea of translation in anthropology. Given the close and prolonged relationship with linguistics, the imagery of grammar and the text was always implicit. Inspired by the success of structural linguistics, Kroeber asked, "what is the cultural equivalent of the phoneme?" (1952:124). Cultures (or languages) might be different, anthropologists reasoned, but they were tangible facts; in other words, systematic or "grammatical" phenomena, which lent themselves to objective description and analysis. The role of the ethnographer was to discover the rules that governed the system and to translate them into anthropological "language." One of the reasons that anthropologists often talk about their project in terms of cultural translation is that they think of culture as something with the properties of language. The rise of positivism was another, related development that stimulated the use of the metaphor of translation. Keeping in mind the promises of machine translation and autonomous linguistics, ethnographers felt confident that discovering general "laws" behind cultural diversity, transforming "emics" into "etics," was a relatively simple and straightforward task. To do "ethnoscience," for instance, it was not necessary to bother with social theory at all, only to pay attention to minute details.

The problem of translation has been a central concern for diverse schools of anthropological thought: "anthropology's most important theoretical problem" (Larsen 1987:1), "at the heart of the anthropological enterprise" (Tambiah 1990:3). Indeed, if there is a root metaphor which unites different anthropological paradigms, it is the metaphor of cultural translation. Keesing has rightly warned against the tendency to read into the apparently conventional metaphors of other peoples saliences that may not be there, the danger of "mistranslation," pointing out that we cannot assume that other people's metaphors "have qualitatively different depths of meaning for them than our ways of talking have for us" (1985:208). How "deep" is our conventional metaphor of cultural translation? Is it something that anthropologists have to live by?

ONE WORLD, TWO, OR MANY?

The idea of translation necessarily suggests some degree of cultural difference and othering. Since the Middle Ages, western people have been fascinated with the idea of the Other and travels to distant lands. Western discourse has assumed a binary distinction between the primitive and modern. The anthropological usefulness of such a distinction, however, has often been questioned, almost right from the start. And since the 1960s, it has been hotly debated. With decolonization, functional anthropology (the "child of colonialism" as some people had it) was subject to intense criticism because of its preoccupation with isolated, timeless tribal societies; Worsley, in an article suggestively entitled "The end of anthropology?," questioned whether anthropology, given its dualist vocabulary, had any future at all (see Asad 1973:9). Anthropology, some of the critics argued, was a discipline fatefully shaped by the forces of the past. Decolonization meant there was no longer an anthropological object to be perused by detached and distant observers; there was no longer a fundamental division between the West and the rest. In short, anthropology had become obsolete. More recently, Kuper (1988) has advanced an equally critical argument: not only is the category of the primitive a historical construct, an idea reflecting the times and fashions of those who use it, the idea of primitive society is a fabrication which should be removed forever from the agenda of anthropology.

The arguments of anthropology's critics in the 1960s, which envisaged the end of the discipline with the dissolution of the Other, were often discussed in rather simplistic and conspiratorial terms, but they nevertheless spoke of real concerns. Was not anthropology bound to wither away with the disappearance of the "primitive" and the power relations that formerly sustained it? However, the events of the following years were to prove the critics wrong. While the pattern and timing varied somewhat from one country to another, generally anthropology became a highly fashionable academic subject and its practitioners entered an expanding market. On the other hand, the new relationship between Europe and its former colonies significantly altered the practice of anthropology, introducing new emphases of change and inter-social relationships, of development, and anthropology within western societies. One aspect of this development is that western anthropologists find it increasingly difficult to work in former colonies. As Keesing points out, this will not help to dismantle the idea that the logic and cosmologies of non-western people are very different from our own: "Unfortunately the shrinking opportunities for prolonged, sustained fieldwork, combined with some of the fashions of contemporary symbolist anthropology, may have precisely the opposite effect" (1985:212).

To explain adequately how anthropology flourished despite the apparent dissolution of its subject matter would, no doubt, require detailed and complex analyses of the professionalization of the social sciences, new systems of funding, and academic expansion in the anthropological metropoles; analyses which would take us far beyond the scope of the present book. One important factor, however, was the fact that "the primitive," far from being discarded from the conceptual baggage of anthropology, was subsumed under a less simplistic and seemingly more neutral scheme: the division of all societies of the globe into three worlds. The Cold War, and its ideological offspring modernization theory, added a new binary distinction to social scientific discourse whereby the "developed," modern world, the world of technological sophistication, was subdivided into capitalist ("free") and socialist parts: the First World and the Second, respectively. The residual category of the underdeveloped world—euphemistically renamed the "Third World"—within a somewhat modified division of social scientific labor remained the speciality of anthropologists, since it was a world governed by tradition, religion and irrationality (see Pletsch 1981). Not surprisingly, in former, particularly African, colonies, anthropologists became *personae non gratae*. Those who taught anthropology at African universities were sometimes forced to call their subject "sociology." British anthropologists, however, who tended to think of their subject as "comparative sociology," easily identified with such a label. The First World, in contrast to the Third, was the subject of sociologists and economists, since it was a world of utilitarianism and rational thinking, unaffected by religious and ideological constraints.

To some extent the notion of the Third World is merely a new, technical term for an older underlying concept of the Other. The idea that societies are separated by permanent boundaries, and yet rather elusive ones (for the exact lines of division have always been a matter of debate), is still very much with us, even if under a new guise. While we tend to take the three worlds scheme for granted, in fact it raises many questions. Pletsch suggests that, like other "primitive systems of classification," the three worlds scheme has its own *raison d'être*. He emphasizes the significance of the Cold War context, arguing that, from the point of view of "we" who inhabit the First World, the Second is more modern and less exotic than the Third, yet its very modernity, combined with its threatening ideology, makes it particularly dangerous: "the socialist world is . . . the dangerous and inscrutable enemy that motivated the very invention of the three worlds concept . . . And *vis-à-vis* the first world, it is the "other" in the most profound sense" (Pletsch 1981:576). The three worlds scheme has assumed considerable authority in social scientific discourse, in part due to the Cold War.

In the early years of the Cold War, western academics rediscovered the Greek concept of the "ecumene" (*Oikoumene*). For the Greeks, the ecumene encompassed the known and inhabited world beyond which lay the foreign world of darkness and barbarism. Twentieth-century geographers and anthropologists tend to use the concept of ecumene as a synonym for "culture." Kristof, for example, defines ecumene as "communities of thought and culture" (1959:282), and sees the boundaries between ecumene as relative: "it may be sometimes meaningful to speak of the ecumene of the human race as a whole, but it may, at other times, be equally meaningful to differentiate between the ecumene of the Pygmies, of the Eskimos, of the Chinese civilization, of the Islamic faith, etc." (ibid.:277f). And for Kroeber, ecumene consists of a "specific, preponderant, interwoven mass of culture" (1945:19). Sometimes, however, the concept of the ecumene was restricted to the ideological boundary between the "free" world and the "socialist." Kristof points out that his use of the ecumene concept is similar to what Cold War political science refers to as "cultural blocs," the East and the West. These blocs are "worlds apart": in other words, different ecumene separated by ideological boundaries.

The Second World, despite its otherness, it seems, was too modern for western anthropologists.[1] Academic anthropology is still largely concerned with the *Third World*, although the anthropological study of the West enjoys increasing popularity. Outside universities, development work is the major market for anthropological expertise. The concept of "interface," recently introduced by students of Third World rural development, echoes the idea of discontinuity implicit in the three-worlds scheme, the plural notion of the ecumene, and their predecessor the concept of "primitives." In Long's usage, the concept of interface depicts "areas of structural discontinuity inherent in social life generally but especially salient in 'intervention' situations" (1989:221). Interfaces, he suggests, characterize situations "wherein the interactions between actors become oriented around the problem of devising ways of 'bridging,' accommodating to, or struggling against each others' different social and cognitive worlds" (ibid.:232). But while the concept of "interface" assumes that humans live in separate worlds, it also may represent an attempt to understand cultural continuity, the flow and exchange *across* boundaries; the building of "bridges."

Some time ago, Barth pointed out (1969:11) that anthropological reasoning tends to assume wrongly that boundaries are unproblematical. Anthropologists, he suggested, tend to think of boundaries between social groups as permanent, "natural" demarcations and to project some concept of ethnicity onto the realities they describe. Leach developed a similar argument, pointing out that while in some places in the Kachin Hills Area social groups are clearly segregated in other places they are "jumbled up" (Leach 1954:60). Some Kachins are highly conservative about language, while others "seem almost as willing to change their language as a man might change a suit of clothes" (ibid.:49). Indeed, the salience of concepts of ethnicity and boundaries may derive more from agrarian discourse, from state ideologies and nationalist rhetorics, than the realities of non-state societies: that is, from "us" rather than "them." Some anthropologists advance the radical suggestion that we adopt the strategy of *assuming continuity* and then ask questions about the conditions of its suppression, about rupture and estrangement: trying to understand why the bridges "break down," to continue the metaphor, rather than why they are constructed.

Those who challenge the prevalent assumption of discontinuity may be informed by very different considerations. Some anthropologists emphasize the inevitable experiential continuity of the human world irrespective of time and place. For them, there is nothing particularly "modern" (or "postmodern," if you will) about the phenomenon or state of continuity. Such an argument echoes Heidegger's remarks about the bridge, an argument which, as literary scholar Barbara Johnson points out, might well have been written to explicate the issue of translation:

> It does not just connect banks that are already there. The banks emerge as banks only as the bridge crosses the stream. The bridge designedly causes them to lie across from each other. One side is set off against the other by the bridge. Nor do the banks stretch along the stream as indifferent border strips of dry land. With the banks, the bridge brings to the stream the one and the other expanse of the landscape lying behind them. It brings stream and bank and land into each other's neighborhood. (Heidegger, cited in Johnson 1985:149)

Others emphasize recent changes, arguing that modern means of communication, including transport systems, space technology, and computers, have turned the life-world of humans into a rapidly contracting cultural universe.[2] Significantly, international lawyers now speak of some areas—areas which belong to all humans (including the high seas)—as "global commons." Indeed, modern "information society" seems saturated with cross-cultural details. Popular culture is no longer preoccupied with assimilating the otherness of the contemporary human world, for this is a world where apparently nothing remains to be discovered. At least the exotic increasingly appears as just as understandable, or *mis*understandable, domain as that of our familiar home. In the absence of a convincing "real" other, modern storytellers and mythmakers resort more and more to the strategy of "importing" strangers. The ideological project of "exoticism" manages to recover alternative space, an "elsewhere" from outer space or former times.

Cultural elements are not only exchanged in the modern world at a faster rate than ever before; increasingly, political issues which formerly might have been regarded as purely "local" in nature, at best multinational, assume global, international significance. The Cold War came to an end, rather suddenly and unexpectedly. The superpowers have signed a series of agreements on disarmament, and the authoritarian regimes of the Eastern bloc have disintegrated one after another, so rapidly that it seems necessary to assume some kind of ideological domino effect. The Berlin Wall has been demolished and turned into souvenirs, and the "Iron Curtain" is rapidly disappearing into folklore and history. If one assumes that the development of the three worlds scheme and the present social scientific division of labour were the results—partly, at least—of the Cold War, then anthropology is likely to change in the post-Cold War era. The rethinking of the western, Orientalist notion of the Other (which began some time before the end of the Cold War) is bound to accelerate. Anthropologists and historians often emphasize that essentialist notions of the Other must be discarded.[3]

Related to the notion of discontinuous worlds and the Other is the popular anthropological idea of ethnographic production as cultural translation. To what extent is it a useful one, we may ask; what kinds of problems are associated with it and what explains its authority in anthropological discourse? We may well begin by considering the nature of translation proper, of the reproduction of a text (a "source") in a different language (a "target").

RELATIONS OF ETHNOGRAPHIC PRODUCTION

Translation has a long history in the West. It is said to have begun with the translation of the Hebrew Old Testament into Greek. The histories of translation studies, literary criticism, and Biblical scholarship are closely intertwined (see Frye

1982). While approaches to translation have not always been the same, translation is never innocent but necessarily infused with attitude. Decisions about whether or not to translate, what texts to select, and what kind of receptor language to use are not as straightforward as one might think. In some cases, the Koran for example, a holy text has been carefully guarded against translation by the faithful. Another point is provided by eighteenth-century German nationalists, who argued that to preserve the German national character it was important to prevent contamination from other, alien languages. In *Fragmente*, the philosopher Herder suggested that a language would greatly benefit from guarding "itself from all translations" (cited in Steiner 1976:78). In this case, the idea is not to protect a holy text from being translated, as with the Koran, but rather to avoid the corrupting influence of translations on the *medium* of translation, irrespective of what is being translated. In both cases, however, a boundary is being erected between insiders and outsiders by means of language.

In the opposite instance, where translation is encouraged or at least practiced, the attitude also varies from context to context. An important factor is the relation of power between source and receptor, as Lefevere and Bassnett emphasize (1990:11):

> although idealistically translation may be perceived as a perfect marriage between two different (con)texts, bringing together two entities for better or worse in mutual harmony, in practice translation takes place on a vertical axis rather than a horizontal one. In other words, either the translator regards the task at hand as rising to the level of the source text and its author or . . . the translator regards the target culture as greater and effectively colonizes the source text.

A translated text often indicates the relative submissiveness or superiority of the translator and the authority of the receptor culture *vis-à-vis* the source; much like a litmus paper changes colour according to degree of acidity. For anthropologists, such an observation strikes a familiar note.

Gender is one source of differences in approaches to translation. Some leading students of translation talk about the relationships between translator and author not only in terms of a predator-prey relationship (in Steiner's words, the translator "invades, extracts, and brings home" (1976:298)), they also tend to employ a violent sexual language. Translation is an "act of appropriative penetration" (ibid.). The content of the source-text is represented as a passive, female prey to be appropriated by a male translator. This is, as Neild has put it, the language of the one-way street, of the "brutal rape" (1989:239). Chamberlain (1988) discovers related notions of a patriarchal code behind the metaphors of "chastity" and "faithfulness" which translators often use when talking about their works. Literary scholars and professional translators, concerned with the "right" image of their source, frequently discuss the faithfulness or "equivalence" of the target (see, for example, Hatim and Mason 1990), legitimating their authority and originality. Such concerns indicate that national "fidelity" (ethnicity, laws, and the maintenance of order) is at stake, the enforced imagined community of the nation state. An example of this is the Italian proverb *"traduttore, traditore"*; "translator, traitor" (see Gutt 1991:170).

The patriarchal, marital code of the literary scholar, it seems, manages to survive even the most radical, deconstructive onslaughts. Thus, Derrida speaks of the "translation contract," defined as "hymen or marriage contract with the promise to produce a child whose seed will give rise to history and growth" (1985:191). Johnson takes the analogy between translation and matrimony into somewhat smoother and more neutral territory—arguing that the translator may be regarded "not as a duteous spouse but as a faithful bigamist, with loyalties split between a native language and a foreign tongue" (Johnson 1985:143). Yet she suggests that, perhaps, the project of translation is best described as incest: "through the foreign language we renew our love-hate intimacy with our mother tongue. We tear at her syntactic joints and semantic flesh and resent her for not providing all the words we need . . . if we are impotent, it is because Mother is inadequate" (ibid.). Such are the perverse pleasures of wrestling with texts.

The influential thesis of Steiner's *After Babel* may also be challenged for its eurocentric bias. Herzfeld points out that Steiner's cultural relativism is restricted to endo-European culture: while for Steiner "familiar diversity makes translation within the European historical community both difficult and potentially deep, 'translation at great distance turns out to be the trivial case' (Steiner 1975:393)" (Herzfeld 1987:89). For Steiner, Herzfeld goes on, "translation from exotic languages is at best an 'invention' and a simplification, whereas European literatures compel our attention to the complex minutiae of difference." This suggests, in anthropological terms, that authentic cultural translation is only possible close to home: beyond our neighbors there is only rhetoric, caricature and distortion.

Following the insight of Lefevere and Bassnett (1990), and assuming that cultural "translation" takes place on *both* the vertical and horizontal axis, one may speak of different relations of ethnographic production. How ethnographers, as visitors or guests, meet their hosts (and how they are met by them), how they manage their lives among them, and how they report what they experience, varies from case to case. It is useful to distinguish between two ideal types, in the Weberian sense, admittedly at some risk of oversimplification. In some cases, ethnographers "colonize" the reality they are studying in terms of a universalist discourse, asserting the superiority of their own society in relation to that of the "natives." This is the "classic" Orientalist ethnography produced during the heyday of western colonialism: cultural translation reminiscent of the "brutal rape" referred to above. In Malinowski's words (1922:8), "the Ethnographer has not only to spread his nets in the right place, and wait for what will fall into them. He must be an active huntsman, and drive his quarry into them and follow it up to its most inaccessible lairs."

In some other cases, ethnographers "submit" themselves to their hosts by relativizing their world, idealizing and romanticizing them. Such an approach is epitomized by the works of many of the "textualists" and "postmodernists" which were developed in response to the fervent critique of the links between anthropology and imperialism, particularly during the Vietnam War. Anthropology had to be "reinvented." However, as we shall see later, in some respects textualism is just as much a one-way street as the colonialist discourse of the past.

It is imperative, I think, to develop an alternative approach for ethnography, a post-Orientalist approach that emphasizes the role of conversation. Several anthropologists have suggested such a model and, again, there are obvious parallels in literary discourse. Neild (1989) and Chamberlain (1988) suggest a feminized approach to translation which underlines the reciprocal or hermeneutic nature of the enterprise (see also Robinson 1991:49). Thus, Neild emphasizes, if the process of translation is to be described as a love affair, an adequate theory of translation must recognize the role of empathy and seduction; the author "reaches out" to the translator, altering his or her consciousness just as the translator alters the text (1989:239). Similar perspectives have been developed with respect to the notion of the "separative" self in some other disciplines. Thus England argues that the neoclassical idea of the separative self and subjective utility, an idea which logically excludes the possibility of interpersonal utility comparisons, of "translating one's own and another person's metric for utility," must be replaced by the notions of empathy and connected selves:

> Assuming that interpersonal utility comparisons are impossible amounts to assuming a separative self, and to denying the possibility of an empathic, emotionally connected self. But if we assume instead that individuals *can* make interpersonal utility comparisons, then surely we would conclude that as scholars we, too, are capable of making such comparisons. (England 1993:42)

Somewhat unexpectedly, the language of seduction may well be accommodated within the metaphor of the predator and prey mentioned above. The translators' language of seduction, in fact, is strikingly reminiscent of the language employed by some groups of hunter-gatherer-fishermen. Hunting activities are frequently regarded as love affairs where hunters and their prey seduce each other: hunters must enter into relationships with game animals in order to have any success and *vice versa*.[4] Prey animals may refuse to be killed, and to make the animal consent to its death the hunter must possess a particular magical power. Only if properly applied will the animal offer itself to the hunter. To kill an animal is to engage in a dialogue with an inhabitant of the same world; animals are social persons and humans are part of nature. In the hunter's view, there is no fundamental distinction between nature and society. Just as the hunter may "fall for" a potential prey, then, the translator may be "seduced" by a text. And, perhaps, just as an animal may refuse to be killed, a text may refuse to be translated.

CULTURAL DYSLEXIA

If we take the textual metaphor seriously, presenting culture as text, anthropology becomes a study of reading. "Doing ethnography," Geertz remarks (1973:10), "is like trying to read (in the sense of 'constructing a reading of') a manuscript—foreign, faded, full of ellipses, incoherencies, suspicious emendations, and tendentious commentaries, but written not in conventional graphs of sound but in transient examples of shaped behavior." For psychologists, the successful reading of a written text, is a highly complex mental operation. It is a research topic in its own right. The failure to read, or the state of "dyslexia," broadly defined as reading maldevelopment in normal people not resulting from a defect of the senses, is an issue that also has bothered psychologists. Positivist anthropology, as already mentioned, has emphasized the successes of cultural reading, as has the model of autonomous linguistics; whatever their "surface" differences, languages (or cultures) are similar in structure and, therefore, translatable. The opposite idea, however, of "cultural dyslexia" has always enjoyed some popularity, focusing on the *inability* to read the alien, cultural worlds of other people, drawing attention to the difficulties and failures of translation more than to the successes. At a time when some of the walls of the real world, which effectively separated people in the past, are crumbling, notably the Iron Curtain, some modern social theorists lead one to believe that cultural barriers are insurmountable and that people live in fundamentally different worlds. They remain sceptical of the translator's enterprise, emphasizing, like Quine (1960), the inevitable difficulties of radical translation.

While debates about the quality of translation have, perhaps, been more methodological than theoretical, some anthropologists have drawn attention to the theoretical and ideological differences that separated various schools of thought. Much has been written, for example, on the mutual "antagonism" of North American anthropologists and British social anthropologists (see Watson 1984). Ortner's claim that "we do not . . . hear stirring arguments any more" and that anthropologists "no longer call each other names" (1984:126–7) certainly seems an overstatement. Can we really expect two anthropologists who represent separate academic communities, as different as, say, an Anglo-Saxon community and a Russian one (two communities separated for decades due to the Cold War), to be able to communicate intelligently about their projects? "To fly from London to Moscow, from anthropological discussions at one end to similar discussions at the other," Gellner points out, "is to shift from one climate and atmosphere to another"

(1988b:3). But if national anthropologies are mutually unintelligible or, at least, difficult to translate, we may ask, is there much left of anthropolgy's interpretive and comparative enterprise? This, however, is to stretch the differences between academic communities beyond the reasonable. Despite his claim about differences in "atmosphere," Gellner in fact claims to transcend the cognitive boundary between the Soviet anthropologist and the British, pointing out the contrasts of "instinctive thought-style" of the Soviet anthropologist and the Anglo-Saxon one. Thus, the Anglo-Saxon "idea of an 'ethnographic present' ... with its tacit bias towards a stability assumption, is barely thinkable in Russia" (Gellner 1988b:2-3).

If people (including anthropologists) are "translating" all the time and apparently with success, must there not be more or less successful translations, more or less authentic reproductions of the source "text" in the receptor language? And, if this is the case, what criteria should be applied for deciding what constitutes an authentic, successful translation? Similar questions and issues have been raised in many other fields of scholarship, including philosophy, literary theory and translation studies. Keesing has criticized his fellow anthropologists for their excessively exotic readings of cultural texts, for producing interpretations that are "simply wrong, constructed out of misunderstandings and mistranslations" (1989a:459). This kind of ethnography which is the anthropological equivalent of what literary scholars call "translationese," translation that sounds like a translation, is not a novel phenomenon. In the last century, Henry Maine attacked social theorists for their biased ethnographic approach. They "uniformly ceased to observe and began guessing," he said, when dealing with the customs of "archaic" society, while they "carefully observed the institutions of their own age and civilization" (1861:70).

Some modern cultural critics, however, cease to observe at all, whether at home or abroad. In maximising the strangeness and alienation of their own world, the cultural critics invent Other in the familiar (Spiro 1990:57). Orientalist scholarship is practised at home on the assumption that humans generally, even close neighbours apparently speaking the same language, are far removed from each other in cultural terms. For many cultural critics, the contrast between "observing" and "guessing," emphasized by Maine, is not an important one, for if cultural texts invite several, equally plausible readings the issue of faithfulness and authenticity is beside the point.

It may be argued, on the other hand, that despite their apparent liberalism, allowing for many readings of cultural texts, interpretive anthropologists in fact practice an authoritarian approach, eliminating alternative interpretations of their ethnographic material. Oddly enough, those who advocate interpretive anthropology, even those who claim to subscribe to a "reflexive" approach, emphasizing the interaction between informant and ethnographer, sometimes take a rather defensive stance when challenged by others. Perhaps, such a defensiveness is primarily a response to the conditions of constructing ethnographies in the modern global ecumene. Nowadays, texts and translations move from one continent to another in only a matter of days or hours, even minutes. The innocence of the exotic and the faraway is forever lost as our informants, whether we like it or not, read what we write and challenge our conclusions, almost from the moment we publish them. When confronted by the natives, it may be tempting to resort to ethnographic substantivism, assuming there are as many interpretations as there are interpreters, taking refuge in the protective environment of the ivory tower.

We may find it convenient, for certain purposes, to refer loosely to anthropological practice as one of "mediating" between cultures, as an "art of translation." Anthropologists, much like literary translators, are bound to be troubled by questions of ethnographic "faithfulness" and "accuracy". Witness the well-known debates of Redfield and Lewis on Tepoztlan and Mead and Freeman on Samoa. Indeed, it seems impossible to avoid the idea that "careful translations," which render indigenous conceptual systems "as faithfully as we can" (Keesing 1985:205), are the only feasible antidote to misinterpretation and overinterpretation. It is one thing, however, to refer broadly to the anthropological enterprise—our attempt to make sense of ethnographic realities—as one of translation, and quite another to describe culture as a text. Metaphors operate much like a railway system, for as we speak metaphorically we confine our thoughts to a particular "track"; as we change our root metaphors, we "shunt" or "switch" our thoughts from one line to another. The application of the textual metaphor in anthropology, as we shall see, is a tricky one. And we need not be stuck with it.

Before we discard the metaphor of translation, however, and dissociate anthropology from "translation studies," we may well remind ourselves that there are many ways of translating. In fact, some of the works of those who study translation proper may be more "anthropological" than textualist ethnographies. Thus, Robinson has forcefully argued for the importance of moving from text to life: "Translation theorists, like their colleagues in the other so-called human sciences, like to talk about texts, intertextualities, structures of correspondence, and the like—all hypostatized abstractions. But the reality of translation and all human communication is *people*" (1991:21). It is rather ironic to hear social scientists speak of a general "linguistic turn," moving from life to text, at a time when students of translation, most of whom are linguists and literary scholars, increasingly refer to a "cultural" turn (Lefevere and Bassnett 1990:4), moving from word and text as translation units to discourse and social context.

SOCIAL UNDERSTANDING

The issue of "mediation" or "translation" logically assumes some degree of misunderstanding. If people fully understand each other, there is no need for translation. There exists a rich literature attempting to explain why the *in*ability to assume the role of others varies from one context to another. For instance, social thinkers from the Enlightenment onwards, including Montesquieu and Simmel, have debated the effects of competition, commerce and capitalism on attitudes towards "strangers" (see Haskell 1985). Some have argued that commerce is detrimental to role-taking abilities and humanitarian sensibility, erecting boundaries between people. Others, however, have emphasized its interactive and moral virtues. Competition, Simmel argued, "achieves what usually only love can do" in that it "sharpens the businessman's sensitivity to the tendencies of the public, even to the point of clairvoyance" (cited in Hirschman 1982:1652).

Anthropologists have addressed such issues in an ethnographic context, attempting to understand the reasons for and maintenance of standing misunderstanding. Durrenberger (1975), for example, provides an account of recurring "dramas of misunderstanding" in Thai-Lisu interactions in northern Thailand. The Lisu are egalitarian while the Thai are hierarchic. The two groups, therefore, have different ideas of contract and obligation which partly explains their mutual misunderstanding and mistrust. Discourse analysts have similarly examined the reasons why different groups in the "*same*" society repeatedly fail to understand each other. For Tannen (1990), male-female communication in North America is cross-cultural communication. She has argued that even though boys and girls grow up together in the most intimate relationships within the most fundamental social unit, the family, they often develop different styles of conversation. Tannen largely attributes the communicative differences between men and women to differences in social relations, much like Durrenberger does with respect to ethnic differences in northern Thailand: men have a hierarchical style, emphasizing difference and ranking, like Thai; women, like Lisu, are egalitarian, emphasizing connection and communion. As a result, men and women frequently misunderstand each other.

Clearly, one factor important for the maintenance of misunderstanding is the relative power of the groups involved, the "terms of trade." As a Sacramento Valley native once explained to a visitor: "Everything in the world talks, just as we are now, the trees, the rocks, everything. But we cannot understand them, just as the white people do not understand Indians" (cited in McEvoy 1986:31). Massive misunderstanding is an aspect of discourse, rooted in particular historical circumstances and relations of power, in the political economy of cultural dyslexia.[5] But do not Thai and Lisu, we may wonder, or, for that matter, husbands and wives in North America, somehow manage to communicate, despite the "enormous" gulf between them? The weary philosophical debate on the possibility of a private language partly focuses on whether two people, speaking languages that apparently have nothing in common, will be able to understand each other and set up a working language literally from scratch. Wittgenstein's contribution to the debate emphasized that two people involved in a common task, say a builder and an assistant, will inevitably come to an "agreement in definitions." The "language" they use is, of course, the same as that of Thai and Lisu: "The common behaviour of mankind is the system of reference by means of which we interpret an unknown language" (Wittgenstein, cited in Harris 1988:108). Western observers of encounters between European and non-European peoples were often surprised by "how easily the language of expression and gesture could overcome cultural barriers" (Bitterli 1986:28).

Cultural theory generally assumes, on the other hand, that as a model of social life, the tower of Babel is a more adequate one than the Wittgensteinian notion of the "common behaviour of mankind" for it postulates that people necessarily erect elusive, mental structures ("culture") over their heads. Carroll (1987:4) discusses the misunderstandings that occur between French and Americans as due to the different "cultural texts" through which they are likely to perceive their worlds. If one assumes that people inevitably have problems with comprehending others, such difficulties are likely to *increase* with greater interdependence. Thus Fagan (1984:14) argues: "Few people find it easy to accept those who are different from them, whether the difference be that of color, creed, or simply way of thinking. This inability of humankind to comprehend others heightens the tensions in our industrial and nuclear world." Given a textual approach to social life, the difficulties due to misunderstanding will not be reduced in the global ecumene.

The concepts of culture and boundaries which are implicit in most discussions of social understanding—have been the subject of much theoretical debate. Asad argues that anthropologists must challenge Eurocentric history by analysing how pre-capitalist societies made their own history and that the "concept of culture is crucial in such an enterprise" (1987:604). He is careful, however, to dissociate his own concept from both the traditional notion of culture as a bounded, homogeneous entity and the Marxist notion of the superstructural and ideological. For him, culture has more to do with social practice than a state of mind, as he speaks of "cultural discourses that constitute objective social conditions and thus define forms of behaviour appropriate to them" (ibid.:605). Rosaldo also seeks to redefine the concept, challenging the tacit assumption of the "cultural invisibility" of the anthropologist, the notion that "'they' have culture and 'we' do not" (1989:198), drawing attention to the borderlands between cultures rather than difference and unity.

Others adopt a more critical stance with respect to the culture concept, at least in the plural. Leach criticizes his colleagues for postulating cultural differences where none exists: "When you encounter an anthropologist who writes about cultures in the plural . . . watch out!" (Leach 1982:43). Drummond has raised similar doubts, pointing out that the process of "communicating across cultures" is more complex and difficult than is commonly assumed. For him the problem lies with the notion that "there are distinct, bounded cultures out there, little worlds waiting for their fieldworker to step off the boat and proceed to elucidate" (Drummond 1987:219), not with the concept of culture itself. He advocates the culture concept of anthropological semiotics, stressing the priority of sign production: "Groups or societies don't generate culture; culture brings forth societies" (ibid.:220). It may be argued, however, that the emphasis on the priority of culture and sign production necessarily suggests a programmatic and oppressive concept of social life as a normative world devoid of creative agency. And this is precisely the problem with the metaphor of the cultural translator and the text alluded to above. Culture tends to be regarded as an autonomous entity independent of the people who represent it, as an external force exerting its influence upon the mind and body of the individual. Not only are people alienated from each other, they must be forever alienated from their own constructs.

The notion that there are many cultures and not just one, it has sometimes been argued, necessarily invites some kind of disillusionment. As Ricoeur pointed out long ago (1965:278), "Suddenly it becomes possible that there are just *others*, that we ourselves are an 'other' among others. All meaning and every goal having disappeared, it becomes possible to wander through civilizations as if through vestiges and ruins. The whole of mankind becomes a kind of imaginary museum." From this point of view, the act of translation is an "aimless voyage" (ibid.). Ingold (1993a) draws attention to the privileged but awkward status of the anthropological voyager in such a cultural universe, emphasizing that the idea of cultural translation actually *establishes* dicontinuities rather than overcomes them in that it artificially presents the world as something already divided. The metaphor of the translated text involves a fetishism of culture, of transforming the use-value of everyday life into the exchange value of exotic commodities for sale on the international academic market. Despite its somewhat attractive language of relativism, Ingold claims that the alienating discourse of cultural discontinuities logically places the "observer" in a position of absolute superiority: the "natives" are depicted as being imprisoned by culture, while the anthropologist is presented as culture-free. The translator, to continue the linguistic metaphor, is not a polyglot but a person without language. Indeed, to present anthropologists as cultureless experts in cultural reading and regard the rest of humanity as cultured dyslexics, is indicative of ethnographic immunity, an attitude of arrogance. Ingold suggests that anthropologists need to rethink their discipline, to develop a new discourse that reclaims the continuity of the social world, and that such a discourse has no place for the concept of culture. That is quite a challenging argument, given the weight of the culture concept in anthropological thought.

Placing oneself in the role of the detached "observer," treating other cultures as mere museum pieces for academic and theoretical consumption, is not only arrogant and irresponsible but also unrealistic, given the fact that observations are inevitably situated in a particular historical and political context. The notion of the anthropologist as impartial "observer" derives from the kind of objectivism that characterizes the social theories of Saussure and Durkheim. Indeed, Saussure comments that when we hear people speaking a strange language, "we perceive the sounds but remain outside the social fact because we do not understand them" (1959[1916]:13). This follows from the distinction between the individual and social in his theory. According to Saussure, language (*langue*) is a system of inherent relationships, best understood as an autonomous entity outside the individual. Such a radical distinction between the outside and inside, the individual and social, fundamentally misconstrues the nature of human life, for it assumes an observer *removed* from society. One cannot remain outside the social fact, no matter how great the cultural "distance" or the thickness of the language "barrier." As Said emphasizes, "there is no vantage *outside* the actuality of relationships between cultures, between unequal imperial and non-imperial powers, between different Others, a vantage that might allow one the epistemological privilege of somehow judging, evaluating and interpreting free of the encumbering interests, emotions, and engagements of the ongoing relationships themselves" (1989:216–17). I am reminded of my own experience of fieldwork and fishing, of nausea and seasickness. Recovering from seasickness, I came to the conclusion that to do fieldwork is not simply to listen, observe and record but to "tune in" to others until one's attentiveness resonates with theirs.

As we move from text to life, assuming, to paraphrase Heidegger, that cultural translation "does not just connect banks that are already there," we are bound to rephrase the old question of how people communicate across cultural boundaries and ask instead: how do we learn to understand the social world to which we belong? In other words, how do people become socially competent? Interestingly, some students of literary translations have addressed similar questions, emphasizing the need for a "people-centred" theory which discusses translation "in terms not of structural equivalence but of *what translators and readers do*—how people interact in the many different activities surrounding translation" (Robinson 1991:135). If a textualist approach to social life leads to what Volosinov called "passive understanding," "the kind of understanding . . . that excludes active response in advance and on principle" (1973[1929]:73), a pragmatist social approach means engaging in practical activities. Thus, one may argue that learning means not simply absorbing or assimilating a normative structure or a stock of knowledge, but rather to be caught in an ever-flowing stream of practical acts, verbal and non-verbal. We become competent social beings by becoming attentive and responsive to our relations with others which is a matter of "enskilment," not enculturation.

There are good grounds for arguing that the child first develops social cognition as a member of a family. As Dunn suggests, "children are motivated to understand the social rules and relationships of their cultural world *because they need to get things done in their family relationships*" (1988:189). Such understanding is quite complex, even at an early age. Some children, it seems, are capable of sharing a perspective at eighteen months, and before long most children are able to understand familial relations—relations of authority, hierarchy, age and gender—and reason intelligently about their social world. But, as Ingold points out, if children can do this, "why cannot fieldworkers?" (1993a:222). The evidence on children's social cognition contrasts sharply, of course, with the culturalists' thesis, mentioned above, about grown-ups being incurable dyslexics both at home and abroad.[6]

To speak of the enskilment of the fieldworker as growing up, emphasizing the affinity of the ethnographer and the child, is illuminating, and in more than one sense. Not only does the construction of ethnographies by definition entail social learning; communication and the development of social understanding are necessarily affected by the form of life involved. Rational consensus and authentic understanding are the products of what Habermas calls the "ideal speech situation," a symmetrical discourse that allows for general participation relatively free from constraint. For him, the "ideal speech situation" represents

> the necessary but general conditions for the communicative practice of everyday life and for a procedure of discursive will-formation that would put participants *themselves* in a position to realize concrete possibilities for a better and less threatened life, on *their own* initiative and in accordance with *their own* needs and insights. (1989:69)

Idealistic as the notion of the ideal speech situation may sound, it provides a model for a new ethnographic order emphasizing life rather than text, reciprocal communicative interaction rather than domination. It is a mode of scholarship that may be described as the "living discourse." In a world of decolonization and continuity (the modern, global ecumene), such a post-Orientalist approach to ethnography is far more realistic than its predecessors, the modes of the colonialist and the textualist.

If one assumes that anthropologists are experts at cultural translation and interpretation, must one not conclude that anthropology has a significant role to play in the contemporary world? While anthropologists are usually eager to point out the importance of their insights and expertise in the academic context, they are often reluctant to use their skills in the outside world. There are many reasons for such an attitude and some of them are easily understandable. The work of some anthropologists who have attempted to apply their knowledge to the promotion of intercultural understanding (particularly in the area of business and tourism) tends to be rather shallow and simplistic, relying as it does on short field trips and superficial ethnographic knowledge. Also, giving in to naïve demands for committed action-research—the innocent plea, for instance, of the 1970s for "relevance" and political engagement—would eventually lead to theoretical stagnation. Many anthropologists would contend, however, and quite rightly, that the discipline must be more conscious about its role in the past, its current practice, and its social responsibility in the future.

As we have seen, the anthropological notions of the cultural translator and the discontinuous world, implicit in the comparative enterprise, have been both persistent and powerful. Recent developments in social theory, however, suggest that we rethink the issue of translation, of going beyond boundaries. Wolf argues that ethnographers have *always* been "in a world of sociocultural billiard balls, coursing on a global billiard table" (1982:17). Other reasons as well suggest that modern practitioners of anthropology rethink the metaphor of translation and bounded cultural units, and these have more to do with events in the so-called "real" world than any developments in the academy or anthropology alone. For one thing, over the last years the human social and ecological habitat has seen spectacular developments. Each of us is necessarily engaged in a long, *global* conversation; a conversation, incidentally, that is threatened with powers far more destructive and decisive than texts and poetry.

Modern humans, whether they like it or not, inhabit an endangered "global village" in a very genuine sense. As the process accelerates, anthropology need not become less important.[7] The characteristics of the global village, the exponential increase in cultural flow (texts, sounds, and images) and the sudden breakdown of "insurmountable" cultural and political walls (in particular the end of the Cold War), however, invite anthropologists to revise their image of the discontinuous world, breaking up the boundaries of their cherished tribes and villages. The issue of national and cultural boundaries within the global context has been extensively studied in some fields of scholarship, especially political science. While there has been some interest in "globalization" in recent years, anthropologists have generally avoided the international context, faithful as they tend to be to all kinds of microcosms.

The futuristic image of the global village need not, however, be a particularly realistic one. We should not underestimate the human capacity for reinforcing existing barriers, inventing new ones, or reinventing those of the past; after all, over the last years we have witnessed recurring "territorial" conflicts, not least in Eastern Europe, the former Soviet Union, and the Middle East. Nor should one conclude that the global village is necessarily a "better" world than its predecessor. The erosion of boundaries, some people argue, simply means more boring sameness, greater exploitation and an increasing gap between North and South in terms of standards of living. As Kuper (1988:240) points out, the modern image of the global village may be just as much a transformation of our image of our own society as the earlier image of primitive society. But while we may well keep Kuper's sober remark in mind, we can hardly escape the conclusion that, given the extensive changes that have taken place in the world system over the last years, the prevailing anthropological preoccupation with cultural discontinuities is somewhat archaic and obsolete. If the travellers and ethnographers who recorded comparative data many decades (even centuries) ago were coursing on a global ethnographic "billiard table," then the comparative anthropologist of the post-Cold War era, the age of cultural flow and continuity, is surely on slippery ground.

NOTES

[1] The relative neglect of the Second World in the anthropological literature may be partly due, however, to the fact that indigenous governments did not allow fieldwork by western social scientists. Even if fieldwork was permitted, it was likely to be troublesome. Those anthropologists, for instance, who worked in China often felt constrained by the close supervision of their official hosts.

[2] See Hannerz 1992.

[3] See, for instance, Sharabi (1990) and Prakash (1990) on the Arab world and India, respectively.

[4] The metaphor of seduction, however, is complex and tricky. Speaking of Cree representations of human-animal relations, Brightman points out (1993:194) that some indigenous accounts, including the ones of seduction, attest to mutualism and communion in human-animal relations while others indicate hierarchy and domination; such accounts, he claims, can be placed along a "continuum between reciprocity and exploitation". "The question of whether Crees believe one or the other model to possess greater validity," Brightman concludes (1993:200), "is exceptionally difficult to address."

[5] See, for instance, Schieffelin and Crittenden (1991) on first contact in some Papuan societies.

[6] Some non-developmentalist psychologists, however, similarly emphasize the evidence for people's shortcomings in dealing with the cognitive demands of their life: "the adult is viewed as a creature whose most impressive intellectual triumphs are matched by equally impressive failures" (see Flavell and Ross 1981:310).

[7] Samuel suggests that "anthropology as translation will become a less relevant activity, but anthropology as a science will have a new and increasingly important function" (1990:28).

CHAPTER THREE

The factual, the fictive and the fabulous: novel and ethnography

The difference between a novelist and a historian is this, that the former tells lies deliberately and for the fun of it; the historian tells lies in his simplicity and imagines he is telling the truth.

Halldór Laxness, *Christianity at Glacier*

Once a thing is put into writing, the composition, whatever it may be, drifts all over the place.

Plato, *Phaedrus*

This chapter focuses on exoticism in ethnographies, novels, and travel accounts, the experience of fieldwork, and the notion of "the Other." While the last section takes a critical look at some recent anthropological works on Iceland, particularly those of Kirsten Hastrup, much of the chapter is devoted to a discussion of a fictive travel account, the novel *Christianity at Glacier* by the Icelandic writer Halldór Laxness. The amount of space given to a novel may strike the reader as a little odd, given the overall stress on social life in this book and the general emphasis within anthropology on the priority of ethnographic fieldwork over text and fiction. This is not to suggest that ethnographies are first and foremost to be treated as fiction or creative writings and that the characters of the novel are just as "real" as the people anthropologists get to know in the field. Nor is it to argue that the testimony of the novel and the voices we hear during fieldwork should be attributed the same kind of significance. Laxness's work, obviously, *is* creative writing. It is a fabricated text. However, not only can it be read as ethnography, as a more or less informative and authentic account *of* Iceland; more importantly, it may be interpreted as a contemplative discourse on the tension between text and social relations and the kind of pursuit we normally associate with fieldwork: as a critique of textualism and a celebration of the pragmatics of life, of being-in-the-world in the Heideggerian sense of the term. Behind the apparent simplicity and humorous, perhaps absurd, chronicle of the novel there is an equally fascinating theoretical account highly relevant for anthropological discussions of representation, texts, and natural discourse. Laxness's novel, I shall argue, advances a sophisticated challenge to Orientalism, to scientism, positivist "observers," and culture critique. Last but not least, it provides a useful starting point for a critical discussion of some ethnographic representations of Iceland.

STRANGERS AND JOURNEYS

The category of "the Other" inevitably suggests fundamental assumptions about human nature and social life. Leach asserts, echoing a remark by Foucault, that while the species *Homo sapiens* is a unity in a zoological sense, the notion of "people not like us" is a cultural universal: "because of their cultural inhibitions all men everywhere behave *as if* they were members of many different species" (1982:58). Leach attempts to show that humanitarian efforts informed by the United Nations Declaration of Human Rights, efforts that preach tolerance, individualism and human unity, are seriously misguided in that they contradict the very essence of human nature, the persistent tendency to separate "us" from "them." Others might argue that the role of humanitarian efforts is precisely to challenge the "human nature" *constituted* by political and economic orders that operate on the assumption that people are members of many different species. One of the problems in dealing with Leach's assertion about human nature is that discussions of boundaries and the category of "the foreign" tend to be heavily ideological and rhetorical in tone. Leach admits that his aim is "to provide moral justification for . . . non-egalitarian presuppositions" (ibid.:56).

Assertions for and against statements about the alienated and fragmented nature of humanity are often grounded in the ethnography of "primitive" societies. As Gellner remarks, we tend to solicit the vote of "Stone Age" people in debates about moral issues, as if they were the "Constituent Assembly of Mankind" in continuous session (1988a:23–4). If we were to seek the advice of such an assembly, it would hardly be conclusive, and certainly not unanimous. Many accounts of hunter-gatherer societies do support Leach's claim. According to nineteenth-century travellers in north-west Alaska, for instance, Inuit kept a constant watch for foreign trespassers into local territory. "Strangers were assumed to have hostile intentions unless they could prove otherwise, and they had to do that very quickly or blood would flow" (Burch 1988:99). The Inuit term for themselves, as is often pointed out, suggests that they saw only themselves as fully human. Often, however, strangers were seen as a threat, and a very real one, primarily because they represented the advancing frontier of colonial powers (Schieffelin and Crittenden 1991). While the Batek of Malaysia have strong emotional ties to their area (*pesaka*), where they have grown up and feel "at home," they do not seem to be particularly on guard against "strangers." On the contrary, they "are not territorial in any of the usual senses of the term" (Endicott and Endicott 1986:140). The Batek do not even "think of areas as having definite boundaries" (ibid.:157).

The distinction between "them" and "us" is no doubt recognized in most, if not all, languages. Much evidence suggests that making social distinctions is part of the human endowment. Young children seem to be predisposed to evoke a rudimentary categorization of social kinds.[1] But to extend the modern notion of the Other into the distant past, the pre-history of "primitive" bands would surely amount to an over-simplification. The systematic, one-sided appropriation of otherness, the Orientalism identified by Said was not a recognized, legitimate subject on the agenda of Stone Age assemblies. Orientalism, Said emphasizes, is a mode of representation "erected in the thick of an imperial conquest" (1989:211). Quite possibly, the advent of writing and literacy marked a critical shift with respect to accounts of the outlandish. At any rate, the authority and significance of such accounts were greatly enhanced by new means of recording and preserving them, when they became parts of state ideologies. In Europe during the Middle Ages, the desire to experience both difference and the crossing of boundaries became institutionalised in the literary genre of the travel account. The medieval world-view contained the category of *Homo viator*, a person who ventures on some kind of pilgrimage into distant lands, for personal pleasure or to save his soul, who then returned with extraordinary stories of anomalous beings, erotic adventures and dangerous events.

From the medieval era onwards, westerners have remained preoccupied with a radical distinction between "them" and "us." Such a distinction was not only underlined in the genre of the fabulous travel account. Often, particularly during the nineteenth century, it surfaced in semi-ethnographic novels which freely mixed descriptions of historical realities with imaginary events, in order to give a "real" taste to the exotic. Fact and fiction went hand in hand for the purpose of exaggerating differences. Herman Melville's autobiographical novel *Typee*, which describes the encounter between civilization and New Guinea savagery, is one example. In it, a French admiral who enters the scene to take possession of the place ("Tior") is confronted by the local patriarch-sovereign who holds a battle-spear in his hands: "The next moment they stood side by side, these two extremes in the social scale—the polished, splendid Frenchman . . . exhibited upon his person all the paraphernalia of his naval rank . . . while the simple islander, with the exception of a slight cincture about his loins, appeared in all the nakedness of nature. *At what immeasurable distance, thought I, are these two beings removed from each other*" (Melville 1846:35, emphasis added).

For anthropology, a discipline that specializes in scrutinizing the Other, the category of the "primitive" has been a particularly powerful device. The idea of the primitive has always remained on board even while anthropological theorizing has undergone radical changes and many concepts and theories have been discarded. Not only has the idea of primitive society served a variety of ideological purposes, providing, for example, a mirror image of modern society, it has generated some excellent scholarly discussions.

Much creative writing, in particular the travel novel, shares the anthropological concern with journeys to distant, exotic lands. Bakhtin emphasizes that generally the travel novel involves a static conception of the world, underlining spatial boundaries. Not only is the hero of the travel novel "a point moving in space," his or her adventures enable the author "to develop and demonstrate the spatial and static social diversity of the world (country, city, culture, nationality, various social groups and the specific conditions of their lives)" (1986:10). Differences and contrasts are, therefore, amplified:

> There are almost no intrinsic ties at all, and there is no understanding of the wholeness of such sociocultural phenomena as nationalities, countries, cities, social groups, and occupations. Hence these novels typically perceive alien social groups, nations, countries, ways of life, and so forth, as 'exotic,' that is, they perceive bare distinctions, contrasts and strangeness. (ibid.:11)

Thus, the "two extremes in the social scale" identified by Melville. This brings me to Halldór Laxness's work *Christianity at Glacier*, a novel about an Icelander who embarks on a journey in his native country.

HALLDÓR LAXNESS ON TRAVEL ACCOUNTS

Laxness (1902–) is an extremely gifted and productive writer who has produced a number of important novels, plays, and short stories, in Icelandic. While many of his greatest novels were written in the epic tradition, drawing upon the literary styles of the sagas (including their "magic realism," a narrative mode often associated, outside Iceland, with recent South American novels), throughout his career he has refused to be easily categorized. Repeatedly he has surprised his readers by exploring new themes and new forms of writing, reinventing the sagas and modernizing the Icelandic novel. A committed socialist in his early career, always ready to combat injustice and exploitation, he later became disillusioned with the politics of the class struggle, turning to other more individualistic forms of humanism, notably the teachings of Lao Tse. For years, Laxness was not only the most consequential novelist in Iceland but also the most important intellectual and critic, a veritable giant on the national literary and political scene. His novels are full of perceptive and critical social commentary and, generally, Icelanders did not receive his works well until he achieved international renown, when he won the Nobel Prize in 1955. Yet he has thoroughly reshaped their national identity with his novels, providing Icelanders with a powerful image of their history and destiny. Several of the characters he created have become household names in Iceland, including the key characters of two of his most important novels *Salka Valka* and *Independent People*, focusing on the struggles of a young woman in a fishing village and a poor peasant in the countryside, respectively.

Christianity at Glacier, a novel Laxness wrote relatively late in his career, added at least two characters to an already rich reservoir of Laxnessian household names:

Jón Prímus, a priest in a rural constituency, and Embi, a young theology student sent to the countryside to collect information for a factual report for the Bishop of the state church. The novel is not just about adventures and travelling, nor is it simply a humorous, biblical allegory, as one may be tempted to believe on first reading. It is a highly complex novel with several themes and intricate structures. Most importantly, given our present preoccupation, it shares with the works of Bakhtin and Said the concern with the *accounts* of travellers, including the travel novel. It focuses on the significance of the encounter with otherness, what to make of what we see and hear, how to write a report, and how to interpret the reports of others—in short, how to do anthropology.[2]

It is by no means easy to explain why Laxness decided to deal with such "anthropological" issues, in a novel apparently about the mundane reality of rural Icelanders and their relations with the national church. At least four explanations suggest themselves. For one thing, Laxness's "natural" fascination, as a creative writer of twentieth-century Iceland, with the literary heritage of his ancestors, particularly the sagas, inevitably suggested larger "textual" concerns, for example, the truthfulness and historicity of medieval manuscripts. Also, he seems to have been well versed in some of the relevant philosophical works produced by his contemporaries abroad, in both Europe and the United States. Furthermore, because of his conversion to Catholicism early in his career he was drawn to theological discourses on the related issue of the relationship between scripture and social life. Finally, some evidence indicates that Laxness was in fact inspired by, if not drawn to, anthropology. Thus, he seems to have been attracted by the works of V. Stefánsson, whose parents were Icelandic but living in North America. His journeys among the Inuit soon became popular reading in Iceland. Laxness refers to Stefánsson's journeys as "extremely poetic" (1986[1925]:122). In one of his memoirs, Laxness describes his encounter with a Dutch anthropologist who "for decades had stayed on distant islands inhabited by savages" (Laxness 1963:194–5) and, at the time Laxness met him, was studying brothels in Barcelona. Laxness and the anthropologist stayed at the same time in a small hotel, where they regularly met over a cup of coffee. Laxness provides the following observation of the relativist observer:

> If the people in this company were impressed by the anthropologist, he was not as impressed by them. What bothered him most of all was to generally have to communicate with civilized people, which he regarded as both more boring and in every way much cheaper than savages—although, to be sure, he was too well educated either to totally discard civilized people or to generally elevate savages above the sun.

Apparently, the presence of the anthropologist encouraged Laxness to speculate on the similarities of fieldwork and storytelling: "Often, both then and later on, I wondered what would happen to a storyteller [*sagnamaður*] if he were obliged to adequately render the social life that continuously surrounds him" (ibid.:186). As one of the guests of a Spanish hotel de famille, Laxness notes, he could not escape from becoming "involved" in the lives of other guests:

> The guest ... cannot avoid paying attention to ... personal relations among individuals. It seems as if, from sitting at the same table, he is sentenced to develop an interest in eavesdropping and gossiping about these unfamiliar persons ... I urge to myself that, as an individual, I should have no interest in this company and that I should avoid them as far as possible ... And yet every man demands, by merely being around, that one pay special attention to him...
>
> In such a hotel, every man is in fact involved in the personal affairs of others and, at the same time, a social participant with particular rights and obligations with respect to their lives. (ibid:187–8)

If a disinterested guest is necessarily somehow involved in the lives of the people he or she stays with, a participant observer or a professional anthropologist can hardly have any escape route at all. Perhaps such reflections sparked off the idea of the novel *Christianity at Glacier*. It is no exaggeration to say that Laxness has been preoccupied with the nature of travel accounts. In his early career as a creative writer and essayist, he frequently went on long journeys to faraway places, sometimes for the purpose of escaping from the routine and familiar life of his fellow Icelanders. "To evade everyday squabbles at home and innumerable local obligations" (Laxness 1963:185), to be able to write in solitude, but also in order to immerse himself in the lives of others, to learn from the people he met and the noisiness of their world, as if he were an anthropologist.

The "plot" (one of them, at least) of *Christianity*, from which I shall quote extensively, commences with the meeting of the Bishop of the Protestant Church of Iceland and the theology graduate, Embi ("Emissary of the Bishop: EmBi for short"). The fact that the reader never learns Embi's real name and that he frequently refers to himself as "undersigned" and in third person not only bears witness to the scholarly demand for objectivity, to leave him without a name is to avoid classifying him, to remove him from social history and the order of names. The Bishop has summoned Embi to his office in the capital saying that there's "something that needs investigating out there in the west" (Laxness 1972[1968]:10), by the Glacier at Snow Mountain (Snæfellsjökull). The Bishop intends to send Embi on a three day trip to find out if the rumors about Pastor Jón Primus are true or not and what the congregation say about him. The priest, it is said, is not much of a Christian, he doesn't have his church repaired, he doesn't baptize the children, and he doesn't bury the dead. Embi, we are told, is good at writing. "I've had my eye on you since last year, when you wrote up the minutes of the synod for us," the Bishop says, "It was a masterpiece, the way you got all their drivel down, word for word" (7). Although

Embi seems an ideal candidate for the enquiry, it is not clear to him what to do: "what kind of 'technique' could one expect from an ignorant youth in such a predicament? What am I to say? What am I to do?" (15). The Bishop's answer is simple:

> We're asking for a report, that's all... Let them talk, not argue with them... Not be personal—be dry!... Write in the third person as much as possible. Be academic, yes but in moderation. (15–16)

For the Bishop, an "academic" report is an "objective" one in the sense that the writer's opinions are irrelevant for what he writes. Embi's frequent references to the details and techniques of tape recording emphasize the detached and factual nature of his report:

> I sat slightly behind the visitor, and the silent recorder ran smoothly between the changes of spools from my parka pocket. Unfortunately, for a long time there is a piercing bleat at 30-second intervals, it's the ewe that's looking for her lamb outside on the paving. (141)
>
> The tape ran out at this point, so I did not catch the last arguments... I changed spools as carefully as I could, trusting that these two oldsters were so advanced in years that they had a buzzing in their ears and would not notice my fidgeting. (150–151)

Embi suspects that it may not be that easy to follow the Bishop's commands, to separate objective research and personal opinion. He says to the Bishop: "Am I not even to say what I think about it, then?" But the Bishop answers steadfastly:

> No no no, my dear man. We don't care in the slightest what you think about it. We want to know what you see and hear, not how the situation strikes you. (16)

Embi is true to his mission. As it says in his report:

> He came to the conclusion that he had no right to complain. He had been sent here only to look for facts... It's about as unscientific as it would be dishonest to stop a scientific process in mid-stream on moral grounds—for instance, because one's feet are freezing. (23)
>
> I was just sent here like any other ass to make inquiries about things that don't concern me at all and which I don't care about at all. (225)

Before Embi embarks on his long bus ride and his trip to the exotic west, he raises the question of what to do if his informants attempt to deceive him:

> Embi: But what if they start filling me up with lies?
> Bishop: I'm paying for the tape... One must take care not to start lying oneself!
> Embi: But somehow I've got to verify what they say.
> Bishop: No verifying! If people tell lies, that's as may be. If they've come up with some credo or other, so much the better!... Spoken words are facts in themselves, whether true or false...

> Embi: And if I find them out in a lie?
> Bishop: Never speak ill of anyone in a report. Remember, any lie you are told, even deliberately, is often a more significant fact than a truth told in all sincerity.
> (16–17)

Once Embi arrives in the west, however, he is unsure about what exactly he is supposed to record. He is anxious to establish, beyond any doubt, what constitutes a legitimate "fact."

At the priest's house he is met by a puzzling woman named Pestle-Thóra. She greets him with loads of coffee and gigantic, juicy cakes of various sorts, and later in the story she remarks that "nothing less than seventeen sorts is thought genteel here" (113). Embi is irritated by the sweetness of the food he is offered. He is "paralyzed by the sight of these innumerable cakes arrayed around such awful coffee" (26), for he is hungry and expects to be treated with substantial food.[3] He is also baffled by a bizarre story told by his host. Pestle-Thóra first asserts that "nothing ever happens to anyone. Noone sees anything" (28), but Embi manages, having drunk a lot of coffee and swallowed several cakes, to get her talking. Pressed by Embi's enquiries, she tells him of her experience of a ram with straightened horns, a fairy ram that she once saw on her walks in the misty mountains: "For a long time I couldn't take my eyes off this beautiful animal which I knew didn't exist here in the valley nor down by the shore nor anywhere in Iceland" (30). Embi wonders if the fairy ram and Pestle-Thóra's story are to be regarded as objective, palpable facts, comparable to the other and apparently more tangible "goods" offered at her reception. Is there no limit to the kinds of food that a hungry person consumes?

Another woman, Gudrún, similarly contests the young researcher's sense of the real with her long and winding stories. Embi writes in his report:

> This has become rather complicated. It keeps adding to itself, however small the questions... The woman leads me round in circles, and no doubt there are many still to come. (221)

Embi feels compelled to set the record straight: "Is that not a little exaggerated, madam? I'm in considerable doubt whether I ought to put this on record" (220). Gudrún, however, has no mercy: "Aren't you just a tiny bit limited, my little one?" (217). As many novice ethnographers, Embi in fact seems more than "a tiny bit limited" at times. Once, when a potential informant hands him a bottle of Danish akvavit, Embi declines the offer at first, but then changes his mind, apparently to establish rapport. "The undersigned finally lets himself... be talked into accepting the bottle, and pours a few drops of tepid akvavit into his palm and rubs it into his hair" (97).

Jón Primus, the focus of Embi's enquiries, turns out to be no less difficult than Gudrún and Pestle-Thóra. Again, Embi must beg his informant not to deceive him:

"I am a young man and it's easy to fill me up with lies. But I hope the story you've been telling me has some truth in it" (85). On several occasions Jón Primus deliberately challenges Embi's notions of truth and science. For the former, the search for truth simply involves adding one fabula to another. Discussions between Embi and pastor Jón about these issues often focus more on historiography and temporal distance than field reports and faraway places. "They lied so fast in the Middle Ages," Jón Primus argues, "they hadn't even time to hiccup" (182). The same applies, however, to the modern scholar. The historian is a simple-minded novelist who "tells lies in his simplicity and imagines he is telling the truth." Embi asks pastor Jón if he has studied history and the priest responds:

> When I discovered that history is a fable, and a poor one at that, I started looking for a better fable, and found theology. (86)
>
> I do not see how the Creation can be turned into words; . . . History is always entirely different to what has happened. . . And the closer you try to approach the facts through history, the deeper you sink into fiction. (88)

Pastor Jón's philosophy, then, treats language with modest respect. If representations are nothing but fabulas, there is little point in listening to what people say.

Embi's report describes many weird and chaotic events at Glacier. "Incalculable agents are involved in this," he comments in one case (173). Clearly, much of the experience of his "fieldwork" is beyond his comprehension. "One asks and asks and always the answers become more incomprehensible than the questions. In the end one becomes an idiot" (214). The identification of the Bishop's emissary as "Embi" ("Umbi," in the original Icelandic text) is hardly a mere shorthand expression or a coincidence. It is too similar to the term "imbecile" and the equivalent expression in Icelandic slang *imbi*. Embi seems to depart for the capital city both ignorant and in a state of mind that is often described as culture shock:

> I shivered and shook for a little while longer until I sighed hopelessly into the fog: Where am I? (267)
> I was a little frightened . . . I took to my heels with my laces flapping about my ankles, and I ran as hard as I could back the way I had come. I was hoping that I would find the main road again. (268)

Embi, it seems, failed to find his sea legs and was profoundly troubled by his adventures at Glacier. Yet he learned a lot, at least about matters unrelated to "religious" practice, in the Bishop's sense of the term.

The beginning of fieldwork usually involves much strain of the kind experienced by Embi. Successful fieldwork requires membership in a new discursive community in somewhat unfamiliar surroundings, and, often as well, the learning of a new language. Normally, however, much of the strain associated with the first phase of fieldwork disappears, when the guests begin to feel at home among their hosts—"going native," in anthropological jargon. Clearly, this does not apply to Embi who only spends a few days doing research at Glacier. It may be tempting, therefore, to assume that the author is simply suggesting that Embi, who seems to return relatively ignorant about pastor Primus and his congregation, makes the mistake of leaving too early, before things begin to make sense. On closer inspection it should become clear that the "message" of the novel is far more general and important. *Christianity* can in fact be read as a surprisingly modern anthropological treatise combining elements of very different genres of "ethnographic" writings, novels, and travel reports. It calls to mind the fascination with the fantastic that appears in *Tristes Tropiques* (Lévi-Strauss 1973[1955]), the theoretical and hyper-reflective textual discourse of *Writing Culture* (Clifford and Marcus 1986), the private confessions of *A Diary in the Strict Sense of the Term* (Malinowski 1967), and some of the mocking parody and novelized treatment of *The Innocent Anthropologist* (Barley 1983) and *Far Afield* (Kaysen 1990).

ANTHROPOLOGY AT GLACIER: THE "CRISIS" IN REPRESENTATION

There are good grounds, then, for regarding *Christianity at Glacier* as an essay on knowledge and representation. The journey to the congregation at Glacier is the *rite de passage* of a novice traveller barely able to cope with the unpredictability of events in the field. Embi attempts to follow the unrealistic demands of the scholarly community and his report to the Bishop is an exaggerated and distorted account of an indigenous Other. The voice of pastor Primus is that of nagging epistemological doubts. The Bishop's project thus represents the Orientalist enterprise. It may not be a befitting comparison, but if the tumultuous reception in the Arab world of Salman Rushdie's novel *The Satanic Verses* is to be interpreted, partly at least, as a protest against the dominance of western texts and the distortions of Orientalism (see Ruthven 1990), we would not expect Embi to be a hero at Glacier.[4] Laxness's theme, in other words, is exoticism at home, or culture critique. Although it may sound a little farfetched to extend the theological discourse of the novel to that of critical anthropology, the differences between the approaches of missionaries and anthropologists have not always been that clear.[5]

One of the epistemological issues taken up in *Christianity* is that of data collection. From the point of view of the positivist scholar, the predicament of the scientist appropriating the real is not unlike that of Embi during Pestle-Thóra's reception. Much as her table bends under a heavy load of colorful, bulging cakes, reality is laden with various kinds of data, saturated with "facts." Embi, however, is offered juicy cakes while he seems to be looking for more solid food and similarly the ethnographer may not immediately get the "right" kinds of facts. Malinowski (1922:9), for instance, dwelt on the problem of "preconceived ideas" in anthropological fieldwork. On the other hand, the facts—and, by the same token, the cakes on the table—are a fixed number and, moreover, they are tangible phenomena accessible to all those invited to the feast. The role of the observer consists in consuming the goods and such an activity, it is assumed, is both straightforward and "objective." The positivist's agenda is clear: "eat and thou shall be satiated! One piece at least of every dish!" The analysis, furthermore, is independent of the gathering of data. In the academic division of labor, digestion is a separate department, independent of consumption. Thus, for some scholars ethnology and ethnography differ primarily in that the former gets the facts whereas the latter theorizes about them. In the Bishop's words: "I'm asking for facts. The rest is up to me" (16).

The guidance that many anthropologists have received before embarking on a field trip is similar to that of Embi. The Bishop's guidelines could well have been borrowed from a methodology textbook. "One should simply say and do as little as possible. Keep an eye on things" (15). The main thing is to "get all their drivel down, word for word." But once the novice ethnographer arrives in the field, problems are likely to arise. As Laxness remarks in one of his essays (1963:187), "the more volumes an author writes about a particular person, the further he is removed from this man, and the same applies when he is writing about himself, until finally he cannot see that man, not even through a binocular." Those who intend to record *everything* that happens in front of their eyes are no better off than Embi at Pestle-Thóra's reception. It is simply impossible to get everything down, whether spicy cakes or intriguing facts; one must decide what to select and what to ignore, and such a decision ultimately involves sociality and some kind of value judgement. Although eating to some extent is a spontaneous, mechanical activity without much systematic reflection on the act itself and eating will continue, "even if the very idea of 'meal' as we know it disappears" (Mintz 1985:200), solitary eating as well as collaborative feasting are necessarily social activities, not just the physical absorption of energy. Just as it is difficult to imagine eating without some form of "table manners," to continue the gastronomic metaphor, it is impossible to think of data collection without any kind of social convention, protocol or etiquette.

Embi's recurrent remarks about posing questions to informants also underlines the aggressiveness of the positivist's search for objective truth. Significantly, he refers to his interview with the vestry-clerk at Glacier as an "interrogation" (8). Asking questions, as literary scholar and novelist Milan Kundera points out, is "not merely a practical working method for the reporter modestly gathering information with notebook and pencil in hand," the reporter's insistence that the people he or she interviews tell the truth and nothing but the truth—the "Eleventh Commandment," as Kundera calls it—is a "means of exerting power":

> The journalist is not merely someone who asks questions, but the one who has a sacred right to ask, to ask anyone about anything. But don't we all have that right? And is a question not a bridge of understanding reaching out from one human being to another? Perhaps. I will therefore make my statement more precise: The power of the journalist is not based on his right to ask but on his right to *demand an answer*. (Kundera 1990:109–10)

The notion of the detached "observer," who doesn't get personally involved, is another but related issue addressed in Laxness's novel. Thus, Embi remarks: "What was the strange web of events into which I had suddenly become interwoven?" (258). In the end, it seems, he has some doubts about his neutrality and the procedures of the "scientific process":

> I start packing my epuipment, the tapes and shorthand notes, into the kitbag in the hope that I haven't entangled myself in anything for which I shall have to suffer later; and secondly, that I shall never be reckoned other than an impartial reporter of Christianity at Glacier. (115)

Clearly, *Christianity* is preoccupied with the distinction between fact and fiction. A distinction of this kind, it may be argued, must have been made by humans all along. One of the characteristics of *Homo sapiens* is precisely the capacity for "displacement," the ability to speak of things or events distant in either space or time, and, by extension, the ability to invent. Our words enable us to summon the attention of others from one place to another and, moreover, back and forth in time, and, knowing that, others need not believe that what we say necessarily conveys the truth. Human discourse is free and elaborate in the sense that it need not incessantly stick to the facts at hand. This is contrary to the apparently enslaved and restricted communication of other species, for instance the calls of chimpanzees and birds or the dance of bees. Bees, as is well known, are capable of communicating with conspecifics and ethologists (with the help of von Frisch they became famous for their ability to summon others to a food resource by simulating a figure-of-eight movement). Nevertheless, deception, fiction, and exaggerated language remain the privileged arts of humans, of *Homo rhetoricus*.

While the distinction between fact and fiction may be a pan-human phenomenon, the fuss about the detachment and authenticity of human accounts, of the kind discussed in *Christianity*, is very much a "western" phenomenon. It is unlikely, for instance, that the Bishop's ideas about the boundary between truth and fantasy are identical to those of prehistoric hunter-gatherers. With the Renaissance, built largely on Arab writings, Europeans imagined that they were able to separate themselves from the rest of the world and examine it objectively. As a result, established notions of fact and fiction were transformed. The religious establishment lost the supremacy it had achieved long ago and everything became measured in human terms. Somewhat ironically, pastor Primus, the rebel theologian in *Christianity*, may be seen as a spokesman for the church during the "Dark Age," while the Bishop represents the secular and "humanistic" views of the post-Renaissance.

The kind of critique of scientism and the responses to the crisis in representation offered in *Christianity* are diverse. One approach is that of the postmodernist, emphasizing the embedded and rhetorical nature of any kind of social discourse.[6] The rhetorical element of scholarly practice is not a brand-new discovery. Long ago, Marx (1976) questioned the validity of "bourgeois" economics, tearing it apart and drawing attention to its "ideological" aspects. Nevertheless, recent analyses of scholarly practice and the ways in which scientific discourses are historically constituted have both enriched theoretical discussions in the social sciences and heightened the literary awareness of their practitioners.[7] As I have argued elsewhere, the predicaments of the novelist and the ethnographer have something in common:

> To do ethnography is to familiarise oneself with local action, to participate in the social life of a particular place, and to report the experience, usually in writing. The way one does the reporting depends on a host of personal and contextual factors, some of which also pertain to the writing of a novel. The discourse of the anthropological monograph, therefore, much like that of the novel, is located within a specific historical context. And since the discourse between informant and ethnographer is a dialogue carried out in a specific context of power relations, not simply the stating and recording of 'objective' facts, ethnographic 'truth' is far more elusive than strict empiricists like to think. (Pálsson 1991:55)

Some of the advocates of postmodern anthropology are willing to go much further, reducing life to text. For them, ethnographic realities are essentially *manufactured*, for aesthetic or therapeutic purposes. Not only do they reject *any* distinction between the making of ethnographies and "creative" writing, they also discard the possibility that we are able to know each other and the world around us, abandoning any notion of truth and authenticity. Human life is analogous to the ruins of the tower of Babel. It is a world of mutually unintelligible languages and one hundred percent illiteracy. The Bishop's emissary knows even less when he returns than when he departed for the congregation at Glacier. The Bishop's search for truth must be a relatively pointless enterprise. Another and, in my view, more realistic response to the crisis in representation is to abandon the models of the text and the tower of Babel, emphasizing the continuity of the social world. A close reading of *Christianity*, as we shall see, invites such a response.

Laxness has often addressed the differences and the correspondences between factual description and plain fiction and between the accounts of guests and natives.

Sometimes, especially in his earlier works, he discusses these issues in heavily positivist terms, emphasizing the difference more than the similarity. In an article written in 1925 he goes straight to the point:

> Although they may be intelligent and honorable, natives (*þjóðerniseinstaklingar*) who are firmly adjusted to a particular place . . . are often poorley equipped to understand the totality to which they belong in an uncolored light, that is objectively (*hlutdrægnislaust*). The eyes of the guest may be perceptive, but many guests are known to have lied about Icelandic realities . . . I think I am in a good position to make objective observations, since I stayed in the country partly as a guest, enjoying the benefits of both the eye of the guest and the knowledge of the native . . .; at times I have felt as if I had the pulse of social life under my fingertips. (Laxness 1986:11)

As we have seen, however, in *Christianity* Laxness has thoroughly rejected the notion of "objective observation." Elsewhere, indeed, he has expressed his views on the matter in a somewhat scholarly manner. There he addresses the problem posed by the dual role of the "chronicler and fabulist" by introducing the person "Plus X," a person who persistently follows the narrator like a shadow:

> Who is Plus X? He is a nameless gate-crasher with an invalid passport, forever present like a peeping tom whenever one opens a book of fiction. This commander never places himself modestly at the bottom of the hierarchy of characters; he is not satisfied with anything less than the seat of honor near the center-stage of the narrative, even though the author may go out of his way to distinguish himself from the narrator. (Laxness 1965:73)

Perplexed by the intrusion of the personality and history of Plus X, despite the author's earnest attempts to leave him in the background, Laxness suggested it might be wise to cease writing works of fiction "for a while" in order to get a better idea of what writing is all about. Some years later, many anthropologists came to a similar conclusion, focusing on the act of writing rather than what they might write about. Confused by the company of the gate-crasher, no matter how impersonal and objective the style of their presentation, some of them decided to abandon the ethnographic enterprise turning instead to fiction and textual analyses of the writings of their colleagues. Laxness, however, seems to be no less critical of the model nowadays associated with the cultural critic and the textualist than that of the positivist. Social life cannot be appropriated on objectivist terms, nor can it be reduced to a text. What matters most of all is engaging in social life, being-in-the-world, what I am referring to as the living discourse.

More than any other character in *Christianity*, Jón Primus is Laxness's spokesperson for the celebration of social life. It is true that Jón Primus thinks that language is a messy thing devoid of informative value; "nothing," he argues, "is so pointless as words" (185). He repeatedly looks to the communications among other species, notably birds, with intense nostalgia. "It's a pity we don't whistle at one another like birds. Words are misleading..." (87). Embi the arch-positivist protests as usual: "... must we not, since we are here, whistle at one another in that strange dissonance called human speech? Or should we be silent?" (88). Jón Primus agrees, but only up to a point. To talk to other people, he suggests, is not quite as senseless an activity as it may sound. Words are a potent source of joy and delight. "It is pleasant to listen to the birds chirping. But it would be anything but pleasant if the birds were always chirping the truth" (241). For Jón Primus, as Embi remarks, humor and good company are more important than theoretical argument and factual information: "Philosophy and theology have no effect on him, much less plain commonsense. Impossible to convince this man by arguments. But humour he always listens to, even though it be ill humour. A typical Icelander perhaps" (182).

It may be tempting to regard such comments as evidence for the pastor's retreat from the world. There are strong grounds, on the other hand, for a different conclusion. Often, the criticism of Jón Primus is directed against the authorial power of the writer and the domination of texts. His obligation is to life itself, not to the Bishop, his emissary or the church. "This parish under Glacier is actually a good living," he remarks, "but it is a little difficult sometimes, especially for horses" (187). When the Bishop writes to the vestry-clerk for information on pastor Jón, the vestry-clerk comments: "Not a living creature in this place would choose to be without pastor Jón for a single day" (13). For the pastor, responsibility to the church is a negation of life. Embi discovers, despite his apparently limited learning abilities, that the local church has been nailed up and the pastor has no intention of offering sermons to the dead: "No paper could be found in the house on which to write funeral sermons, and no time for writing, and besides he had forgotten how to write—pretexts" (181). One of the persons at Glacier dies during Embi's stay, and Embi asks Jón Primus why the church has been nailed up and what could be done about it, to which the pastor cynically responds: "The glacier stands open" (65).

The priority of life over text in Jón Primus's approach to life is underlined in his rejection of almost any kind of dogma. Consider the following dialogue with a person named Dr. Syngman:

> Pastor Jón: I have only one theory... I have the theory that water is good.
> Dr. Syngman: For colds, or what?
> Pastor Jón: Unqualified. One doesn't even have to go by my theory unless one is thirsty. (151)

When questioned about the faith of pastor Primus, the vestry-clerk remarks:

> We have never been aware that pastor Jón had any particular doctrine; ... it's not that we here are against doctrines, least of all if there's no need to follow them. Doctrines are for entertainment. (42–3)

The vestry-clerk admits that Pastor Jón is "none too quick" at burying the dead, but hastens to add that the priest is "the only person hereabouts who can shoe a horse properly" (42). Pastor Jón's nickname "Primus," in fact, serves as a recognition of his *real* profession in life, namely shoeing horses and reparing things, including primus stoves, which has little to do with the church and its doctrines. Texts and dogmas are mere trivia. Pragmatism, if you will, is the priest's only dogma.

THE NEO-ORIENTALISM OF ICELANDERS: THE WORK OF KIRSTEN HASTRUP

To move from the "ethnographic" insights and observations of Laxness the novelist to anthropological works on social life in Iceland, I shall take a look at the writings of some of those who have recently studied Iceland, emphasizing the ethnographic works of the Danish scholar Kirsten Hastrup. Hastrup's works are an obvious choice. Not only has she published several theoretical papers on fieldwork partly informed by her encounter with Iceland, she has written at length on a whole range of Icelandic issues, including the world-view of the saga age, witchcraft, gender relations, food rituals, and national identity, contributing extensively to the rapidly growing anthropology of Iceland, arguably more than anyone else. Hastrup is to be credited for bringing anthropology to the study of medieval Icelandic and Scandinavian sources, drawing attention to their ethnographic potential, often with imaginative analyses, informed by comparative studies and powerful theoretical paradigms.

While Hastrup's works demonstrate detailed knowledge of Icelandic history, texts, and language, there are serious problems, as we will see, with some of her interpretations, especially those pertaining to modern Iceland. Some of these problems raise larger questions of general relevance far beyond the ethnography of Iceland, and it is important to identify them and address them frankly and openly. Even more importantly, her attitude to ethnographic authority, especially her approach to what Appadurai (1988:17) has called "the problem of voice," needs to be challenged. This approach, I argue, represents a "neo-Orientalist" position. My aim is not to review in detail the works of Hastrup, nor to provide an overview of the Icelandic ethnography which has been done elsewhere, only to draw attention to competing claims to ethnographic authority—focusing on disagreement more than concensus, in particular the tension between native and non-native accounts, the sources and significance of disagreement, and the ways in which anthropology deals with it.[8]

Much of Hastrup's work on Iceland centers around the dualistic notions of inside and outside, and the corresponding distinction between the domesticated and the wild. In her view, these are fundamental and "persistent" categories (1987:96) evident in both medieval documents and modern discourse. Hastrup argues (1990b) that the categorization of the inside and outside has profound implications for gender roles and identities in modern Iceland. Only men, she suggests, engage in productive activities in the realm of the outside, in the pursuit of wild animals (*veiðar*), be it fishing or hunting. "Women are . . . excluded from the men's wild" (1990b:276). She substantiates her claim with reference to her fieldwork experience, relying on the anecdotal remarks of an old man on the farm where she stayed who apparently was "completely taken back" (1987:97) when the female fieldworker attempted to transgress the engendered boundary between the inside and outside, joining the males on their expeditions into the wilderness of the mountains (herding domesticated sheep temporarily located in the wild).

Einarsson suggests, on the other hand, on the basis of his intuitive knowledge as an Icelander, that the old man's remark should not be taken at face value and that the issue involved concerned skill and experience rather than gender: the identity of the newcomer, the Danish fieldworker, rather than women's roles. Hastrup, he argues, has "definitely run astray in the pursuit of over-interpreting . . . utterances and events to suit her theoretical bias" (1990:73) and structuralist framework of binary oppositions. Hastrup's claims about the importance of dualistic categories in the medieval world-view have similarly been challenged by some social historians, legal scholars, and anthropologists, who argue that she places too much emphasis on legal texts and older secondary works. Miller, a legal scholar, concludes that she often ignores the "ethnographic" evidence of the sagas and that "there is something rather forced about [her] . . . models" (1986c:185).

Hastrup also uses anecdotes or idiosyncratic "events" with reference to her argument about fishing expeditions in the aquatic wild, insisting that women at sea represent a violation of cognitive boundaries and cultural traditions. When she attempted to go fishing she soon discovered that "not all skippers would allow women on board, because they were a bad omen and would destroy the all-important 'luck'" (1990b:19). Again, Hastrup seems to overinterpret what she hears and sees in the field. In this case, much ethnographic and historical evidence runs counter to her claims. It is true that, during the period of peasant production, Icelanders defined membership in the category of the "inside" in terms of both the territory of the farmstead and the social relations of the domestic economy. Hastrup rightly points out that in peasant society female muteness did not exist, in the sense that women no less than men participated in the discourse of the "inside," the realm of culture as opposed to nature. But while women were insiders in the peasant economy, in Hastrup's sense, they were definitely not excluded from fishing in the realm of the "outside." Even though women's roles and responsibilities within the household, particularly in relation to pregnancy, breast-feeding and caring for young children, often ensured that they stayed home while the men went fishing, there were no clear-cut categorical barriers preventing them from joining fishing crews on their expeditions into the wild. Indeed, both men and women participated in fishing.

Some Icelandic women, including Þuríður "the Foreman" (*formaður*) who began her fishing career in the 1790s, were well known for their expeditions at sea. Eighteenth and nineteenth-century accounts make it quite clear that fishing was a natural thing to do for a woman and that women's participation was "customary." These were not just curious exceptions that had to be noted for the record because they violated some norm. With the growth of capitalist fishing and urban centres, however, women *did* become muted. As I have suggested, with the weakening of the subsistence economy, the inside lost its spatial connotation and the spatial inside and the social one no longer coincided. "Women remained insiders in the sense that they still belonged to the domestic unit, but according to the new cultural model they became social outsiders, devoid of power and economic productivity. Social membership, belonging to the inside, became independent of space and redefined in social terms alone, in terms of the emerging relations of the market economy" (Pálsson 1991:165)

Hastrup's ethnography parallels that of Embi's in *Christianity* on several points. For one thing, both of them elaborate on their fabulous encounter with the "unreal." Whereas Embi runs into a fairy ram in the cloudy mountains, Hastrup meets a fairy human:

> a nebulous human figure appeared in the mist. I knew instantly that it was a man of the 'hidden people' (*huldufólk*) who visited me... Ever since the Middle Ages *huldumenn* have been known to seduce Icelandic womenfolk.... (1990b:285)

The fact that two apparently independent accounts, novel and ethnography, converge on this score need not to be taken as a confirmation of authenticity. More likely it signals the presence of the person Laxness called Plus X. Relying on brief fieldwork, isolated anecdotes, and written texts, silencing their "faculties of disbelief" (Stefánsson 1992:280), Embi and Hastrup give priority to stories of the past and idiosyncratic, personal experience rather than actual social practice in the reality of Icelanders. While Embi, however, returns from the field convinced that the local voice is too perplexing for him to understand, on the basis of only a brief acquaintance, Hastrup does not seem to harbor such doubts.

Leaving aside specific points of contention, it is essential to address the more general issue of ethnographic authority and disagreement. The debate between Einarsson, a native anthropologist, and Hastrup is quite revealing in this context. In his critical review of some of Hastrup's works, Einarsson wonders if "something-... [has not] gone wrong" when the "natives" do not recognize even the simplest ethnographic facts in the narrative of the ethnographer, a "story in which they are the main characters?" (1990:76). Hastrup's response, however, largely ignores his arguments and observations She maintains that it would be a poor anthropology that "contented itself with the native points of view," that "there is an implicated truth behind the explicit statements to which no 'native' has immediate access," and that the "rigorously scientific evaluation" of the outsider is superior to the "facile—allegedly 'empirical'—refutation" (1990c:81) of the native anthropologist. These are quite bold claims. If we take them seriously, there is no point in listening to the experience of the native anthropologist. "The activities of both sexes," Hastrup insists elsewhere, "continuously re-create the boundary between inside and outside. *I certainly experienced this myself in the course of my fieldwork*" (1990b:302; emphasis added). Whom shall we believe, the "Plus X" of Hastrup's account, to borrow Laxness's term, or that of Einarsson and on what grounds could we possibly make our choice? The native account, it may be argued, is necessarily situated in the ethnographic context in question and it is quite possible that some of Einarsson's ethnographic observations (and, of course, my own) do not hold. Surely, however, observers' accounts, too, are situated in their own context. What difference in context would justify Hastrup's claim to ethnographic privilege?

This raises the larger question as to what distinguishes between knowledge gained during fieldwork, whether by a native or a non-native anthropologist, and ethnographic production *outside* the field? Bloch argues (1992:129) that anthropologists need to be no less worried than the native that the ethnographies they produce may have lost "what it was really like." He emphasises that anthropologists should be aware that by writing up indigenous knowledge they are "rendering into a text something that is not a text" (1992:129). A similar point has sometimes been made by historians with respect to the past: "History as usually written," Durant and Durant observe, emphasizing the appeal of the irregular, "is quite different from *history as ussually lived*: the historian records the exceptional because it is interesting—because it is exceptional" (cited in Starr 1989:345-6, emphasis added). Is it possible, then, to textualise the knowledge acquired in the field without distorting its character? Is Hastrup, perhaps, necessarily distorting both the native's experience and her own for the purpose of communicating with the academic community, in order to produce "sound" ethnography and "good" scholarship?

In recent articles, Hastrup (1992, 1993) attempts to advance a general theoretical argument which would allow her to ignore *any* argument developed by a native anthropologist:

> At the autobiographical level ethnographers and informants are equals; but at the level of the anthropological discourse their relationship is hierarchical. It is *our* choice to encompass their stories in a narrative of a different order. We select the quotations and edit the statements. *We* must not blur this major responsibility of ours by rhetorics of 'many voices' and 'multiple authorship' in

> ethnographic writing...
> Because any scientific discourse must make claims to speak over and above the acts observed or heard..., there is an inherent hierarchy in the relationship between the interlocutors. To deny that is also to remain insensitive to the violence inherent in fieldwork. (Hastrup 1992:122, emphases in the original)

The rhetoric of violence and the one-way street is reminiscent of the patriarchal translators discussed in the previous chapter who enforce their brutal language and theoretical devices upon their texts. As soon as the ethnographer begins to write culture, Hastrup suggests, he or she "interpenetrates" (Hastrup 1990b:309) a radical Other as a "translator of culture" (ibid.:307). Icelanders are her possession, the victims of her text. "The people are 'mine' not as individuals, of course, but as inhabitants of the world my writing creates" (Hastrup 1992:126). For a woman who contributed to the feminization of anthropology some years ago, equipped by the notions of silencing and muteness, the "violent" theoretical landing must be rather embarrassing.

There may well be grounds for some form of objectivism that breaks with the immediate experience of the actors. On the other hand, the radical theoretical distinction between the context-bound native and the objective observer draws upon a highly suspect modernist epistemology. As McCloskey notes, modernism "renames as scientific methodology the scientist's... metaphysics, morals and personal convictions... One suspects, as have many who have thought about the matter in recent years, that scientific knowledge is not so very different from other knowledge" (1985:16). At times Hastrup seems to subscribe to a positivist idea of anthropology, the possibility of "a neutral scholarly position" (1987:99). When confronted by a native anthropologist, however, she tends to take refuge in an equally dubious approach, an approach which, for her, represents the dissolution of the history of modernism and the transition to postmodern anthropology (1992:128), insisting that anything goes as far as ethnographic analyses are concerned and that indigenous views are irrelevant, except perhaps as "data." Irritated by the critique of the native anthropologist, she sometimes wears both of her hats at the same time, taking the positions of both the modernist and the postmodernist. Thus, she argues that while anthropologists "should be prepared to face the criticisms made by subjects of study... with good grace, there still is *no simple truth* to be told.... 'The native point of view' is part of the ethnography, but the goal of scholarship is not just to record the world *as seen from a particular point of view*" (Hastrup 1993:176, emphasis added). Natives live in a final world and, by definition, they have a viewpoint, but Hastrup hasn't. And, by implication, devoid of a viewpoint the foreign anthropologist speaks some kind of truth, but the native doesn't: "The native voice may speak native words, but... it does not speak cultural truths" (ibid.:177).

Hastrup's theoretical defence, however, emphasizing the hollowness of natives' accounts, can hardly be the central issue in the present context. Keeping in mind that her "privileged" access to the realities of fishing and farming in modern Iceland is based on what must count, by any standard, as extremely short fieldwork (on our occasion, at least, only "a couple of months" (Hastrup 1987:97)), her claims about the ethnographic authority of the "outsider" seem somewhat out of place. Despite the brevity of her fieldwork, she feels confident to ignore the arguments and criticisms of the native anthropologist. Hastrup's claim to privileged representation, emphasizing that "in speaking with two tongues—native and anthropological—[Einarsson] tends to blur the issues involved" (1990c:82), is unlikely to satisfy the scholarly community.

For one thing, the discrepancy between Hastrup's interpretations and those of some indigenous anthropologists, with respect to the salience and significance of the dichotomy between the inside and outside in Icelandic society, is not simply a matter of native and foreign points of view. Hastrup's thesis about the temporal continuity of dualistic concepts and their anthropological interpretations is not fully shared by other ethnographers of Iceland. Durrenberger, a foreign anthropologist, echoes the critique of the native, arguing that Hastrup's conclusions "failed to match or even characterize accurately what [he] ... saw and heard in Iceland" and that they were "overdetermined by the anthropologist's conceptual structures and underdetermined by evidence" (1991:91). Significantly, in her otherwise interesting analysis of the Icelandic food ritual called *þorrablót*, Hastrup herself encourages such an interpretation: "Nature and culture alternate as agents in this process. Obviously, then, the Icelandic meal is eligible for structural analysis, by exposing simultaneously the entire culinary triangle. We may conclude that the modern Icelandic *þorrablót* is an almost 'overdetermined' expression of the panhuman concern with the paradigmatic distinction between nature and culture" (Hastrup 1991:235).

Moreover, Hastrup's own words on how to draw a boundary between cultures and where to locate homes and borderlands, a central problem not only for her argument but also for any kind of culture theory like her own, are far from clear. At times she refers to her work in Iceland as an anthropology at home, "among friends," that is, "among a people who, one way or another, belong to the *same* cultural area." At other times she describes the cultures of Icelanders and Danes as "parallel" ones, "developed from a shared ... background" (1987:94). And yet, leaving aside the difference between the identical and the parallel, for her Iceland is essentially "remote" and "exotic" (1990b): "Even in the case of cultures as closely connected as the Icelandic and the Danish the experiences of the inhabitants of these spaces are worlds apart" (1990b:15). By implication, any culture, even a neighboring one or one's own, is an exotic world. For Hastrup, Iceland is not simply remote and exotic in a relative sense. Iceland "proves to be implicitly exotic from the anthropological perspective. It is not only that it is 'strange' or 'unfamiliar' to the Danish ethnographer participating in Icelandic life, there is the much more profound truth that Iceland covers a separate reality. All cultures constitute worlds of their own, worlds that in turn define their own realities" (1990b:14). Hastrup's words neatly support the frequent claim that anthropologists have a tendency to create a false sense of difference, to the extent that "signs of similarity become embarrassments" (Carrier 1992:203). Ardener's argument that "social anthropologists 'at home' may be very far away indeed" (1987:50) is up to the point.

As we have seen, for Hastrup the concept of culture is a central one. She is well aware of the charges levelled against such an analytical construct by practice theorists, the recurrent claim that it theoretically alienates and imprisons the actor. She responds to such arguments by suggesting that "mentality" (a virtual synonym for "culture") is "a prison to which the captives hold the keys" (1990a:4). Such an answer will not do. Assuming that the prisoners retain the keys to their cell will hardly resolve the issue of structure and agency, for captives, by definition, are not free. Judging from Hastrup's response to Einarsson the indigenous anthropologist, on the other hand, Icelandic culture is a prison to which Hastrup holds all the keys. Unconstrained to observe the rules of "good conversation," the *Sprachethik*, Hastrup simply dismisses Einarsson's critique on her work as "a relatively unpretentious essay by a young colleague" (1990c:81). Significantly, perhaps, while Einarsson's critique was generously followed by a comment from Hastrup, her later article in *Social Anthropology* (1993), indirectly a critique of Einarsson, did not return that hospitality; the "observer's" account was not accompanied by a response from the native.[9] The attitude of privilege is also reflected in Hastrup's failure to acknowledge the contributions of other ethnographers who have worked on Iceland, especially (but not exclusively) those of Icelanders. In a review of one of her works, Stefánsson draws attention to the "polemic" aspects of her text, criticizing her for "authoritatively chastising unnamed competitors for trespassing [her] territory" (Stefánsson 1992:279).[11] Native anthropologists, by definition, are removed from the community of ethnographic modellers.

Hastrup's ethnographic works, I have argued, based on only a few weeks in two rural communities, by necessity provide a restricted account of everyday life. More importantly, her attitude to ethnographic authority is difficult to accept, as several reviewers of her works (both Icelandic and non-Icelandic) have pointed out.[10] The Lévi-Straussian rhetoric of detachment, evident in Hastrup's work, has been the subject of much critical discussion. As Todorov points out (1993), while Lévi-Strauss and many of his followers tend to emphasize the advantage of distance (the view from that strange place called "afar"), in actual practice most anthropologists identify with the people they study, cultivating closeness rather than distance. Attempting to solve the apparent paradox, Todorov suggests that detachment *with respect to oneself*, irrespective of whether one is working "at home" or "abroad," is the important issue.

In such a view, "being an outsider is only an advantage if one is at the same time a perfect insider" (Todorov 1993:84). Hastrup's ethnography has not benefitted from that advantage. Her approach, we have to conclude, is *neo-Orientalism par excellance*: while the natives are no longer colonial subjects, they are nevertheless treated as if they were.

The anthropology of Iceland is already a sizable and pluralistic meeting ground of both inside views and outside voices, indigenous and foreign scholars. If anything, the voices of the guests outnumber those of the natives. Like the better-known debates of Redfield and Lewis on Tepoztlan and Mead and Freeman on Samoa, the controversies on Icelandic ethnography discussed above raise fundamental questions regarding the making of ethnographies and their authenticity. In anthropology generally, ethnographic authority is increasingly being challenged on several fronts. Ethnographers sometimes find their writings twisted and appropriated by colleagues who happen to work on similar social groups or identical issues. More importantly, given our present concern, ethnographies are frequently challenged by people subject to anthropological analyses who find writings about them both "unreal" and parodic. It is "not so much a sense of outrage that would betray wounded egos," Americo Paredes emphasizes, "as a feeling of puzzlement, that *this* is given as a picture of the communities they have grown up in. Many of them are more likely to laugh at it all than feel indignant" (Paredes, cited in Rosaldo 1987:92). Ethnographers can no longer ignore criticisms of the writings and the analyses they produce, nor can they pass over the critique of their colleagues. As a result, they frequently find themselves arguing and debating both with their "informants" and their fellow ethnographers, often revising their position in the process, and not only during fieldwork proper but also later on, even years after they have "left" the field. It is vitally important, I think, to pay attention to the ways in which anthropologists deal with disagreement. Ideally, ethnographic disagreement should be settled with reference to some form of communicative ethics, a moral standard that allows for free and unrestricted dialogue. To her credit, Hastrup *did* respond to indigenous critique. Her response, however, was not argumentative, evading the issue of the debate.

Hastrup's rejection of native accounts, of course, has a long tradition behind. It is the modernist projection with its radical separation of the "native" and the "scholar." Malinowski, as Leach points out (1970:134–5), ridiculed the validity of native accounts, even though they might turn out to be close to or identical to his own. "He specifically mocked at the account of Trobriand social structure that one might expect to obtain from a professional Trobriand informant, . . . though when he himself attempted to write a concise description of 'The Constitution of Trobriand Society' . . . the result resembles most strikingly that given by his imaginary despised 'informant'." Nowadays, the neglect of the native voice usually takes more covert forms, but it is nevertheless there. Anthropologists' informants are often silenced "once the writing for an academic audience starts" (Wright 1992:642).[12] Hong, a native of Taiwan, presents an interesting critique of the essentialism of Taiwanese ethnography, the failure of some of the ethnographers to engage in a dialogue with the natives about their observations, the obliterating of the names of informants, and the responses of the academic community to indigenous critique. Trying to make sense of what was written about Taiwan, Hong wrote several letters for further information on some of the straight-forward ethnographic facts mentioned in one specific article. There was no response from either the anthropologist invloved or the editor of the journal that published the article. Even more uncomfortably, there was no response to Hong's enquiries from the ethics committee of the American Anthropological Association. Hong's attempt to publish some of the objections in academic journals elicited interesting comments from anonymous reviewers: Hong, they said, was "blinded by native categories," a victim of "reverse Orientalism." "Natives interested in what is written about their culture," Hong concludes, "are apparently a frightening spectre to anthropologists! When a beam of light is cast on them, they freeze like deer" (1994:7).

Ethnography has important elements of rhetoric and fiction. To return to the novel *Christianity at Glacier*, Laxness suggests on one level that it may be difficult to tell exactly when a fieldworker (ethnographer or historian) "gets things right." Sartre's novel *Nausea* (1959) belongs to a similar genre; much like *Christianity* it takes the form of a diary (it even includes an "Editors' note," pointing out that "these notebooks were found . . ."), speculating at the same time on the fallacy of othering and the limits of objectivity:

> This is what I have to avoid, I must not put in strangers where there is none.
> I think that is the big danger in keeping a diary: you exaggerate everything.
> You continually force the truth because you're always looking for something.
> (Sartre 1959:7)

Unlike *Christianity*, however, *Nausea* emphasizes the inevitability of alienation, the implausibility of finding one's sea legs. To abandon the possibility of understanding and truthfulness, however, is to evade dialogue. And to evade dialogue, as Laxness insists, is to abandon life. Any attempt to understand Laxness's own literary achievement, including how he acquired his "anthropological" insights, would, no doubt, run into some of the epistemological problems faced by Embi during his field reasearch at Glacier. It should be clear, nevertheless, that Laxness's travels in his native Iceland early in his career, his extended visits to different parts of the country and his prolonged discussions with people from different walks of life made him hypersensitive to Icelandic realities, as if he, to use his own words, "had the pulse of social life under his fingertips."

Jón Primus, one of the key characters in *Christianity*, offers a commanding critique of the alienation that results from the preoccupation with dead words and texts, the "naked corpse of the word" (Bakhtin 1981:292). For anthropologists, the key issue of authority and representation is not so much whether or not their writings consent with the discourses of the actors but rather the way in which they *continue* the ethnographic conversation. The discourses of different groups of modellers are not separate islands of history unaccountable to one another. Perceptive analytical insights often derive from the ability to empathize with the people we study, although such attachments, under the standard norms of science, are often rendered invisible as soon as the ethnographer returns from the field. To democratize anthropological discourse does not necessarily mean to agree with everybody or to take everything one hears at face value, but rather to recognize the continuity of the discursive community and the inevitability of difference and disagreement, embracing and participating in both the flow and unity of social life. After all, the act of writing up is inevitably situated in a boundless community of practice, a community that admits no radical distinction between modellers and informants. Ethnography is best regarded not as monologic reproduction of the Other but as a "long conversation," a noisy Bakhtinian "dialogue."

NOTES

[1] See, for instance, Hirschfeld 1988 and Carrier 1992:207.

[2] Such a reading of the novel is underlined in the film *Christianity at Glacier* by Laxness's daughter, Guðný Halldórsdóttir, based on the novel.

[3] Such a sugary welcome, however, is not uncommon in Iceland; Mintz observes, we may note, in his treatise on the anthropology of sugar, *Sweetness and Power* (1985:197), that "Iceland was the biggest per-capita consumer [of sugar] as of 1972—about 150 grams per person per day."

[4] This argument, perhaps, only makes sense as long as one assumes that Icelanders, to paraphrase Umberto Eco, do not "share in the fictional agreement, the suspension of belief" (Eco, cited in Ruthven 1990:160).

[5] Interestingly, when the publication of the journal *Practical Anthropology* ceased (in 1972), a new journal *Missiology: An International Review* was established, continuing the editorial policy of the former (Mandelbaum 1989:49). Hanson (1979) has much to say about the parallels between the predicaments of the missionary and the anthropologist. For valuable anthropological and historical studies of missionary work and ideology, see Hvalkof and Aaby 1981, Mudimbe 1988, Comaroff and Comaroff 1992. Mudimbe (1988:65) is less critical of missionaries than most anthropologists, emphasizing the significance of amateurism in the works of the latter: "Contrary to most anthropologists' ten months or, at best, two or three years of field research, many missionaries spent almost their whole lives among Africans."

[6] The label of the "postmodern," it is often pointed out, is a fairly elusive one and hard to define, as the extensive literature on the subject demonstrates. It is difficult, therefore, to

generalise about those who use it to refer to their own practice; see, for instance, Harvey (1989), and *Postmodernism* (special issue of *Theory, Culture and Society* 1988, 5 (2–3)).

[7] See, for instance, Stocking 1983, Ellen 1984, Clifford and Marcus 1986, Geertz 1988, Jackson 1989, and Sanjek 1990 on anthropology, McCloskey 1985 and Brown 1993 on economics, Gaskins 1992 on legal scholarship, and Atkinson 1990 on sociology.

[8] For an overview of the ethnography of Iceland, see Durrenberger and Pálsson 1989, Pálsson and Durrenberger 1995.

[9] Not only does the title of Hastrup's article "The native voice—and the anthropological vision" allude to Einarsson's article, the text explicitly refers to it, as the work of an "Icelandic critic," "an anthropologist (studying his own culture, like most Icelandic anthropologists)" (Hastrup 1993:175). "I would retort," Hastrup adds in relation to Einarsson's critique, "that everyone has the right to comment; while—of course—the backgrounds for commenting may differ. The native background is one; anthropology is another."

[10] "Ironically," Stefánsson goes on, "in her effort to distinguish herself from her colleagues in Iceland, it appears as though she had tripped and fallen through the looking glass."

[11] See, for instance, Stefánsson 1992 and Brydon 1993.

[12] Wright's main worry is that fellow anthropologists debating on her own ethnography, on the basis of what *they* assume she meant by her writings, "position" her as an informant.

PART TWO

Times, Lives and Medieval Texts

CHAPTER FOUR

Sagas, history, and social life

> Clearly the present is endowed with a capacity to understand the past in ways that it cannot understand itself: history takes place behind man's back as well as in front of his face. But a text is also a function of specific human intentions . . . and it is a large part of our task to understand how these intentions went into its making. Much of what we come to know about texts was also available to their makers, albeit in a variety of unfamiliar cognitive forms, and to empower our critical abilities by devaluing theirs is to initiate an exchange that will ultimately rebound upon ourselves.
> Lee Patterson, *Negotiating the Past*

Despite its rhetoric and limitations, the ethnographic novel provides a useful route to social life, being "the form, *par excellence* of an imagined but 'realistic' community" (Smith 1986:169). If ethnography turns out to have an element of fiction, the chronicle, the novel, and the fabula have some ethnographic content. Thus, Laxness's novels, including *Christianity*, offer an important insight into Icelandic society. His descriptions of the lives of Icelanders are often surprisingly reminiscent of anthropological field reports and they usually appear authentic and convincing. Sometimes the novel is a last resort. Baxter remarks, with respect to many areas of modern life, that "it is difficult, often impossible, to observe at all, let alone as a participant observer . . . so it seems sensible to use the published observation of those who have participated" (1991:123). Written texts may allow anthropologists, he argues, to "follow Evans-Pritchard's way of putting 'flesh and blood' into our analyses." This applies, of course, especially to students of the past. We simply haven't got much else to work on.

What to make of the records of the past is no easy matter, however. To what extent, we may ask, are we able to understand medieval realities in terms of concepts derived from modern societies? Generally, the "historical anthropology" advocated by Gurevich and the French "*Annales* school" warns against the imposition of modern criteria on the minds of people of earlier centuries, even though it also emphasizes historical continuity. Gurevich cautions that "we are not dealing with the ethnography of an exotic, 'primitive' culture" and that medieval culture "does not seem so foreign to us" as we are "bound to it by many threads" (1988:176), emphasizing at the same time that it is different and that we should "resign ourselves to the fact that medieval culture is other" (1988:216).

This chapter explores the comparative context of the Icelandic sagas and the ways in which they can be used to extract information about social life and its transformation. Such an exploration, as we shall see, demands a wider discussion of the ethnographic and historical validity of the sagas and the degree of "otherness" represented by the saga-world. The sagas have been extensively studied as pieces of text, as literary and historical documents, by generations of saga scholars. Despite its progress and insights in some respects, this scholarly tradition has remained relatively silent on many pertinent and important issues, particularly social and comparative approaches. For two decades or so, however, several anthropologists, archaeologists, literary scholars, and social historians have been identifying and exploring the value of an alternative approach, an approach which reverses the priority of text over life. From their point of view, the sagas are potentially valuable as ethnographic documents. Despite their limitations as historical evidence, the sagas are a rich reservoir of social information, a potential source for the comparative understanding of Commonwealth society and history. As Bauman argues, "if we can turn literary models to the study of society, we should find it equally productive to apply sociological perspectives to literary texts" (1986:134).

While we may refer to the sagas, for the sake of simplicity, as a single class of documents, for many purposes it is both necessary and legitimate to speak of different "genres" of sagas. We should be aware, however, of the definitional difficulties involved. In fact, the notion of literary genre has been subject to much debate. As Todorov points out (1990:16), to define genre as a "class of texts" is mere tautology. Some genres of sagas, in particular the category of the "Sturlunga saga," are embedded in our "field-notes" while others are not. Unlike that of the "family sagas" the category of the "Sturlunga saga" is not imposed by later writers and scholars.[1]

A social and comparative approach to early Iceland and the sagas emerged already at the beginning of the twentieth century in the work of the anthropologist Bertha S. Phillpotts (1913). Several other scholars were aware of the ethnographic potential of the sagas, although they did not elaborate on it. Thorstein Veblen argued, for instance, that *Laxdæla saga*

> ... remains ... an ethnological document of a high order; perhaps standing in this respect at the head of the list ... More intimately and more naïvely than any other, this saga reflects the homely conditions of workday life in its time, together with the range of commonplace sentiments and convictions which animated this workday life. So that it is fairly to be taken as a competent though perhaps accentuated record of late-Pagan and early Christian manners, customs, convictions and ideals among the Germanic peoples at large. (Veblen 1925:vi)

Also, Marcel Mauss opens his classic essay on exchange and reciprocity (1954[1923–4]:xiv) with a citation from an Icelandic document (*Hávamál*) on gifts and friendship. Years later, in the late 1960s and the 1970s, a social and comparative approach simultaneously gained momentum in different settings and academic communities—in the works of historians, anthropologists, and literary scholars.[2]

Generally, however, comparative works have remained relatively insular in different discursive communities, frequently on the margins. Meanwhile, "saga scholarship" proper, notably the "Icelandic school" has typically ignored, and at times been quite hostile to, these developments.

The emerging social focus in recent saga studies is not only a cumulative result of the works of the scholars involved and the expanding scientific communities they belong to. Nor is it simply a healthy remedy to the somewhat ethnocentric bias of traditional saga-scholarship. Equally important, recent theoretical developments in anthropology, historiography, and literary studies have very much pushed interdisciplinary enterprises to the fore, inviting scholars in several fields to readdress similar questions involving the relationship between fact and fiction, representation and reality, life and saga.

THE SAGA WORLD

The sagas are not just about Iceland. Early Icelanders often contrasted their social world with those of distant Others across the sea (see Figure 4.1), engaging in their own bizarre form of othering and cross-cultural comparison. Indeed, some sagas suggest a form of folk Orientalism, largely based on foreign accounts imported through the gateway of Byzantium: an Orientalism informed by classical Latin heritage and the hegemony of the Greek empire. Thus *Alexanders saga* (1925:163) describes the inhabitants of the "land of India" as "men and women covered with hair and with different colours, nine feet tall, without clothes, and living from . . . fish, . . . among them were people called cenocephali, they have dog's head and they bark." Another saga, *Hauksbók* (1892–96:165–67), provides a particular chapter on the "nature of different peoples"; one group of people "is not affected by the poison of the snake," some have "such a large lower lip that they can throw it over their head while they sleep," and others have "no tongue but indicate everything with signs."

Oriental stories of this kind reached early Iceland through a long network of Nordic travellers, Viking raiders, and merchants, by way of Russia or the Mediterranian (see Figure 4.2). Some Nordic travellers went as far as Jerusalem, others continued to "Sarkland" (Arabia and Africa in medieval Scandinavian terminology). Thus the royal Viking of Sweden, Yngvar the Traveller (Víðförull), went on a long journey down the Volga River to the Caspian Sea, reaching Sarkland in the year 1041. His story is the subject of a famous text, *Yngvars saga Víðförla*, which describes encounters with dragons and monsters of various kinds. While partly based on travels and observations, such accounts were heavily reliant on the texts of classical geographers and encyclopedic works. Eventually, they found their way into Icelandic texts, particularly the genre of the fantastic "lying sagas" or *lygisögur*.

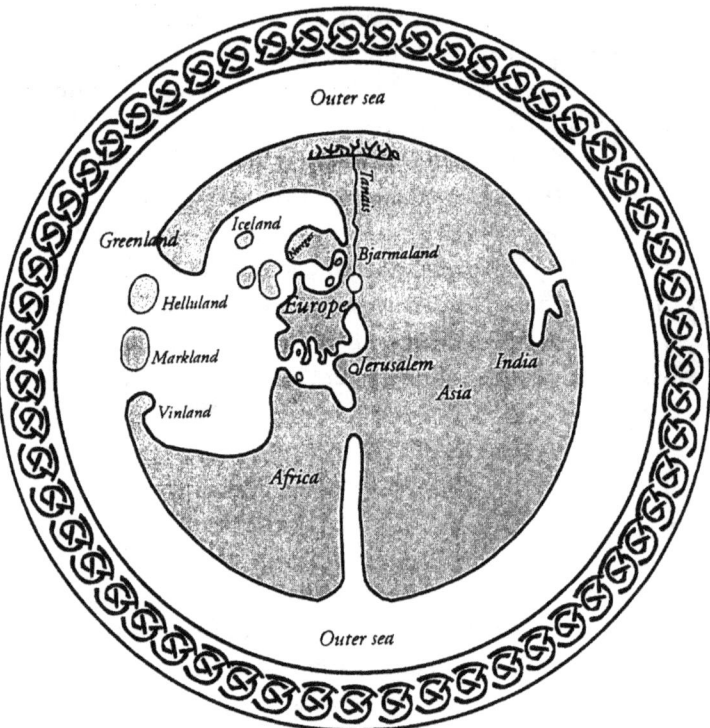

FIGURE 4.1   *The world-view of early Icelanders*

In many ways, therefore, medieval Icelandic texts were rooted in western discourse. Despite all the accounts of the travels of the Vikings and the numerous textual traces of other lands and histories evident in Icelandic manuscripts, the ordinary Icelander must have lived in a relatively isolated social world, given Iceland's location in the North Atlantic. Medieval Icelandic references to other societies are therefore largely mythical and second hand, borrowed from other European texts. None of this, of course, is unique to the world-view of early Icelanders, for similar ideas captured the imagination of other Europeans (Hodgen 1971). Some sagas, including *Eiríks saga*, also refer to alien groups close at home, notably indigenous peoples on the western shores of the North Atlantic. We know that Norse settlers from Iceland and Norway stayed for extended periods in neighboring Greenland and North America. Viking settlements have been discovered in several places in both Greenland and L'Anse aux Meadows in northern Newfoundland and a good deal of archaeological scholarship has attempted to explain why these settlements did not survive (see McGovern 1990). Although in Icelandic the concept of *skrælingi* was quite a loaded one, with the dual meaning of "barbarian" and "native of Greenland,"

SAGAS, HISTORY, AND SOCIAL LIFE 79

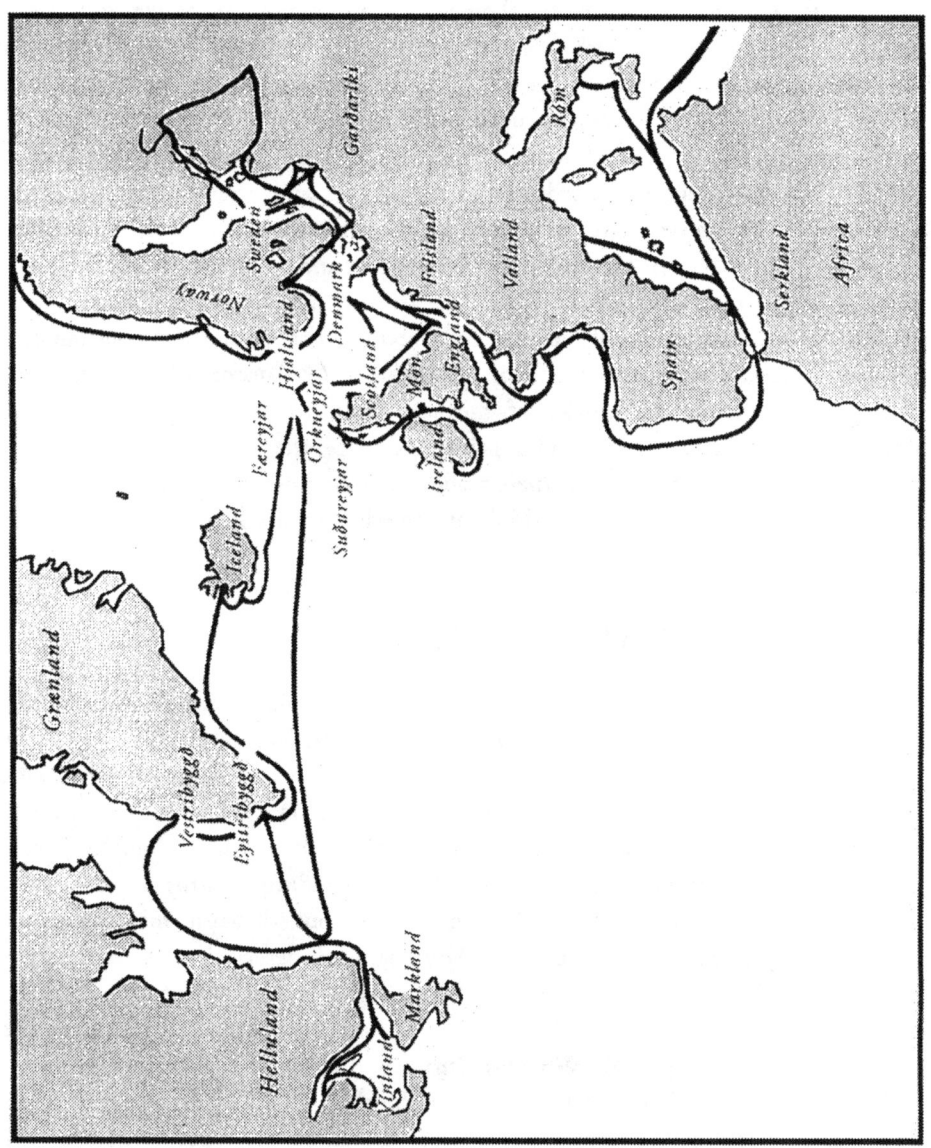

FIGURE 4.2 The travels of medieval Norsemen

the first-hand accounts by early Icelanders of their western neighbors are far less fantastic than those about the Orient.

Not only are the sagas partly concerned with distant lands, equally those that purport to focus on Icelandic realities sometimes add "alien" material to their indigenous accounts. Thus, exotic themes as well as a range of classical literary devices, plots, styles, and metaphors are occasionally borrowed from abroad. This does not, however, necessarily detract from the ethnographic value of the sagas. While the authors may have depended extensively on foreign texts and rhetoric, sometimes producing "mere" translations of European texts, their works must somehow mirror their own needs and circumstances and, therefore, the reality of early Iceland. The same is true, of course, for foreign translations of the sagas. Thus, Japanese reproductions of saga accounts, in both text and comics, clearly impose alien cultural elements onto the Viking world to make it more comprehensible to Japanese readers. Stefánsson shows that Japanese comic book artists do not feel constrained by the need to preserve the integrity of the original texts (Stefánsson 1993). In fact, they freely modify the characteristics of the saga-idols, to ensure their "successful" translation. Despite its distance in both time and space, the saga-world seems to have a particular appeal for modern Japanese readers, as a kind of "science fiction," for they readily identify with what they think are the heroic deeds and morality of the "Vikings."

EXPLORING THE "FIELDNOTES"

Turner long ago drew attention to the ethnographic usefulness of the sagas. The sagas, he said, "read like exceptionally well-filled ethnographic records and diaries" (1971:371), "full of the very materials that anthropologists rejoice in when vouchsafed to them by informants in the field" (ibid.:351). In Turner's language, the sagas were "nothing but connected sequences of social dramas" (ibid.:353). More recently, several historians and anthropologists, including Hastrup (1985), Miller (1990), and Durrenberger (1992), have pointed out through more systematic analyses, that many saga narratives parallel ethnographic descriptions from other parts of the world. As Miller puts it, the world of the sagas "has the virtue of looking very much like some worlds that we can prove to have existed and in fact have been carefully studied" (1990:76). Whereas Turner switched from literature to anthropology partly to be able to work in a society "not too dissimilar to ancient Iceland" (1971:351), Hastrup and Durrenberger were drawn to the sagas because of their training in anthropology. In Durrenberger's case, fieldwork was decisive as well. "Because I had lived in a society in which witches, sorcerers, ghosts, feuds, hauntings, factions, and vengeance were daily realities, the sagas seemed true and believable to me" (Durrenberger 1992:4).

Admittedly, the sagas are relatively silent on many aspects of social life. Often, for instance, they are mute with respect to various means of exploitation, chieftains' capacity to appropriate the products of ordinary farmers and the sexual exploitation of women. Careful comparative reading of the sagas often allows one to read between the lines, to reveal the popular culture or "hidden transcripts" (Scott 1990) of early Iceland and medieval Scandinavia. Karras demonstrates (1992) that while accounts of the sexual exploitation of women are quite limited, comparison with other societies helps to illuminate the witness of the sagas and to specify some of the implications for Commonwealth Iceland. Using both the sparce saga accounts on the topic and ethnographic works from other parts of the world, she indicates the likely connections between servitude and the sexual exploitation of women, on the one hand, and, on the other, a high sex ratio, competition between chieftains, male violence, notions of masculinity, and the perceived danger of homosexuality. The reason for the lack of emphasis in the sagas on sexual relations between masters and servants is simply, she argues, that such relations were taken for granted and, unlike, for instance, feuds and warfare which are amply described, sexual exploitation largely took place within the household, beyond the view of wider society.

I will address the issue of authenticity later on, but if we regard the sagas as fieldnotes, as more or less reliable statements *about* medieval realities, a guided package-tour into the *past*, what can we do with them? Recent technological advances may be of some help. A computerized database which includes all the saga-texts has now been developed by scholars at the University of Iceland. This database, with its concordance and Old Icelandic dictionary, is likely to revolutionize saga studies. However, this data and technology are no substitutes for social theory, interpretation, and holistic reading. What *kinds* of analyses does our ethnography invite?

Just as anthropologists approach their fieldnotes with differing questions, so saga scholars bring differing perspectives to their texts. A general ethnographic view of the sagas allows for a number of problems and approaches and different authors are unlikely to agree on details. Some saga studies concentrate on the search for abstract semiotic systems, emphasizing ideational, normative codes ("culture") and mentalities (*mentalité*). Structural analyses of the sagas have been developed by some anthropologists, including Durrenberger (1982), Hastrup (1985), and Linke (1992). Many saga scholars have adopted a different approach, attempting to regain life from the text. There are important differences between saga and life, the written and the oral, and, of course, students of the Commonwealth and medieval Scandinavia do not have the advantage of the fieldworker who is able to arrive on the scene and participate in social life. We simply cannot "go back," as fieldworkers often do, to reexamine the praxis of the "natives." Nevertheless, the "world out there" presented in our second-hand fieldnotes, especially in the family sagas and *Sturlunga saga*, often gives the distinct impression of active persons, not of norms and rules.

It may be argued that a semiotic, structural, or "textual" approach in the social sciences which is informed by the cultural anthropology of Boas and Geertz, the structuralism of Saussure, and recent cultural criticism, necessarily operates with reified mental structures erected over the stream of social life. By this reasoning, the actors in the sagas are reduced to inmates, locked up in the asylum of medieval culture, a mental framework beyond their making. Praxis theorists emphasize that one must not lose sight of the actor, what people do, and how their activities shape the course of their own life and those of others. Despite the substantial tension between cultural analysis and praxis theory, however, their differences should not perhaps be overemphasized in saga studies. Different sorts of documents may invite different kinds of analyses. Thus, there is a stark contrast between the "mythic" texts (for instance, the *Poetic Edda*) and the social dramas of the family sagas, and it may not be wise to try to apply the same kind of analysis for both genres. Also, analyses of culture and praxis need not be regarded as mutually exclusive. Some successfully combine the two kinds of analyses.

The sagas are limited in many respects, but are they *all* we have got? As we have seen, an important theme in recent scholarship juxtaposes life and text. For some scholars writing in this genre, the sagas *constitute* medieval culture. Thus Meulengracht Sørensen suggests there is no Icelandic culture outside the sagas. For him "there are no longer any roads to reality outside the actual sagas" (1992:28). Such claims are overstatements informed by the linguistic turn. Research on other, normative and economic documents, combined with modern ethnography, archaeology, and economics significantly adds to latent contextual information in the sagas, for instance with respect to the reconstruction of the dynamics of production, exchange, and property.[3] Frye makes a useful comparison between saga studies and Biblical scholarship:

> we cannot get an inch further without new archaeological evidence, and such evidence would carry the authority that we have ceased to assign to the sagas themselves. Similarly, for the historian of the Biblical period, the primary historical authority is not the Bible but what (the written sources having been exhausted long ago) archaeology can still dig up in the way of acceptable evidence. (Frye 1982:43)

So far I have more or less assumed the "facts" of Icelandic literacy and literary production and the ethnographic and historical validity of the sagas. If we use the sagas as informative accounts we must inevitably face the question: what was the context of writing and reading and how good is the ethnography? To begin with, in most cases it has been difficult if not impossible to confidently identify the saga-author(s). And if we only know some of the names, we may never be able to establish the contextual nature of literacy. It seems that most "originals" were *thoroughly edited and revised in medieval monasteries by those who collected and* copied the manuscripts, and many of *their* works are forever lost. What we have does not, therefore, adequately represent what actually was produced.

We also know that most of the sagas (the family sagas in particular) were written long after the events they purport to describe. Scholars have debated on the relative importance of the pre-Christian period and the early Commonwealth, on the one hand, and, on the other, the later society of state hegemony and Christianity, the contemporary society of those who wrote the sagas. We have good reason, then, to doubt the value of our ethnography. To make things even more complicated, at times our ethnographers-informants have been deliberately cheating. Not only did they withhold information, they also invented or distorted the "facts," sometimes for the purpose of justification and entertainment. Inevitably, the rhetorical stamp of Plus X, mentioned in the third chapter, was added to the vellum.

This applies just as well to the near-contemporary sagas as those that purport to describe the more distant past. Grímsdóttir convincingly argues (1988) that *Íslendinga saga* was written to legitimize status quo, to vindicate chieftains' demands for compensation, to preserve their sources of wealth, and to maintain the present distribution of power. The saga's excedingly detailed descriptions of battles and its technical definitions of various kinds of wounds and slayings seem to be modelled on legal clauses, particularly those of *Vígslóði* in *Grágás* (1852). The Sturlung family seems to have encouraged detailed descriptions of the legal cases in which they were involved, for the purpose of securing their political and legal rights. While *Íslendinga saga* seems to be based on the accounts of witnesses and to be quite concerned with accurate and neutral "chronicles" and "description," the writers' motives and styles were somewhat different from those of modern anthropologists and historians, shaped by a different rhetoric. To borrow the substantivist argument in economic anthropology, the medieval world and the modern one represent quite different systems of literary production. Beside the obvious difference in technology between the "age of ink" (Averintsev, cited in Gurevich 1988:277f.) and the "computer era," there is a difference in concepts of historiography, writing, and literature as well as social relations of literary production.

The interpretive and methodological problems of authorship, validity, and representation have been discussed for decades by saga scholars. Understandably, many have advocated what has been called "book prose" theory, arguing that the sagas are pure fiction, written documents devoid of any ethnographic or historical value, although the opposite "free prose" theory, emphasizing the historical and ethnographic authenticity of the sagas as oral tradition, has also found some support. The modernist distinction between fiction and history, between rhetoric and scholarship, art and ethnography, would, however, have sounded strange to medieval Icelanders. While for the most part, medieval Icelanders regarded the family sagas and contemporary sagas as "true," since their vocabulary assumed another class of literary works more fantastic and imaginative, namely "lying sagas," they would not have subscribed to a "modernist" conception of truth and objectivity. For them, the word "saga" referred to both imaginative narrative and factual knowledge of the past. The *making* of history involves inventing the past and recording it. Durrenberger suggest that "the debates about historicity, foreign influences, influences of other literatures, and composition are couched in modern terms which are foreign to the conceptual world of thirteenth-century Iceland" (1992:101). Saga-writing was an activity very different from the historiography of modern scholars: "The boundaries between fact and narrative are repeatedly relocated over time" (Laxness 1965:67).

Clearly, our field-work in medieval Iceland is held back by acute problems of interpretation. Take, for instance, the issue of gender. Just as indigenous voices have spurred, perhaps obliged, students of "great men," "big men," and "chiefs" to emphasize the political leadership of male personalities, so the sagas have invited a biased, patriarchal discourse emphasising the notion of *goði* ("chiefs"). Thus, in Icelandic scholarship the term *goðaveldi* ("reign of *goðar*") is frequently used to denote the social system of the Commonwealth. Though the social life of the Commonwealth was not restricted to the world of males, many a saga, and, indeed, much saga-scholarship, is mute as regards women, in particular men's capacity to exploit them. Women and gender are subjects which now receive increasing attention.[4] Much of the emerging literature focuses on the "informal" political power of women, the credibility of the popular image of the strong and willful Icelandic heroine, and the influence of Christianity on both the reality of gender roles and the ways in which they are represented in the sagas.

Even though in one sense the sagas do *not* provide the kinds of analyses we now count as proper ethnography, there are sound reasons for juxtaposing saga "fiction" and ethnography. Some scholars suggest, as we have seen in earlier chapters, that the ethnographic present of field reports is a rhetorical construct, the orchestration of the anthropologist. By this view, the making of ethnographies is "creative" writing, a kind of "saga." Also, anthropological informants just as saga-makers tend to be left in the margin of the text. While western discourse has tended to emphasize the notions of authorship and ethnographic authority, and the corollary notion of the autonomous individual, details on the lives and identities of informants have not always been disclosed. From the colonial period onward "Orientalist" ethnographers have presented their "sources" as anonymous lives, to be appropriated and distorted at will. Partly for that reason, ethnographers have sometimes been deceived by their informants, just as saga-readers have sometimes been taken in by the sagas. For anthropologists, too, the fragmentary nature of the sources is a fact of life; losing notes in the field or on the way back home is quite common, almost a rite of passage. Edmund Leach lost much of his notes from the Kachin in Highland Burma during the Second World War (nowadays, recorders and computers break down and tapes and files are accidentally erased), yet he was able to produce an anthropological classic.

Much as saga scholars debate the rhetoric and reliability of their sources, social theorists debate the nature of ethnographic reports and what happens in the field during "participant observation." Empiricist scholars tend to regard ethnographies as objective representations of the realities encountered by the anthropological "observer," as fairly straight-forward statements about the world, while others question the faithfulness of fieldwork reports, arguing that the way one does the reporting inevitably depends on a host of personal, contextual, and historical factors. Carucci notes that the notion of "chieftaincy" may in some cases (in the ethnography of the Marshall Islands, for instance) have served as "a playable ideological construct," a construct that has as much to do with European ideas of the chief as indigenous understandings of social stratification (1988:33,40). Perhaps the most relevant demonstration of how the power of tacit political assumptions is writ large in scholarship is the "Icelandic school" of saga studies.[5] The "bookprosists'" distrust in the validity of the text is not just the result of a purely "objective" evaluation of the sources and their limits; various social factors, in particular Icelandic nationalism under Danish colonialism, the "struggle" for independence, and the ideological needs of an emerging state, helped to create an Icelandic paradigm which effectively banned the usefulness of the texts for historical and ethnographic analyses. Icelandic intellectuals sought to elevate the sagas from "simple" tradition and storytelling to literary monuments.

Even if events do not occur as written, nonetheless the assumptions of how the social context ought to work (how it is represented) is reflective of the writer's own history and reality. Every saga contains echoes from a distant discourse. By this reasoning, saga scholars need not be as terribly worried about the dating of their documents and the validity of their sources as they have usually been in the past. If the factual and fictive go hand in hand and any text or utterance is necessarily a collaboration of generations of writers and speakers, the boundary between literary studies and linguistics, on the one hand, and anthropology and history, on the other, is not as important as is often implied.

A FOREIGN COUNTRY?

Given that we think we are able to use the sagas as ethnographic documents, what does such a commitment entail. One source of disagreement among saga-scholars, historians, and anthropologists relates to varying views of otherness and difference. As already mentioned, the saga-writer and the modern scholar may not agree about concepts such as truth and historicity. To many literary scholars, however, and not only nationalistic Icelanders determined to find in the sagas solid evidence for a glorious era beyond the age of foreign colonialism, the idea of comparison is simply not on the agenda. Juxtaposing stories of the heroic deeds of medieval Norsemen and ethnographic accounts of simple societies, it is assumed, is a highly dubious exercise, if not blasphemy. Hallberg criticized the Soviet scholar Steblin-Kamenskij for regarding "medieval Icelanders and saga writers as strangely primitive people, with a bearing completely different from that of 'modern man'":

> they sometimes appear to belong, not to a period rather close to us, but to some mythical age... Icelanders were men with a keen, critical and sceptical understanding of human behaviour... There seems to be little reason to suppose that these men and their equals had "conceptions of truth" different in principle from those of "educated" people today. (1974:9)

What seems to have bothered Hallberg most of all is the notion that medieval Icelanders and saga writers may have been "primitives," not the idea of the primitive in general. His comment need not necessarily be read as a rejection of comparison, only a particular kind of comparison with a particular notion of "otherness."

On the abstract level, we may ask whether the people subject to scholarly analyses should necessarily be represented as the inhabitants of an exotic world. Anthropological understanding, it is often assumed, involves the "reading" of the alien worlds of other people, much like literary translation involves the "penetration" of a foreign text. Not only does such a discourse assume a world of humanity parcelled up into separate units, it also assumes a disengaged and culture-free observer, a fieldworker endowed with analytical powers denied to everybody else. This kind of privileging is particularly evident in works representing the "textual turn" in anthropology. Goody criticizes such a metaphorical extention of the notion of the text. For him, this is "to meet the 'other' not face to face but back to back; to force our history, our reading, on them is to abandon history, to see development and evolution (in all their complexity) as stopping with the apes. We are different, but are we so different?" (1991:95).

Similar theoretical problems are being discussed by historians with respect to projections of temporal distance and otherness. How strong, then, is the sense of otherness and difference that we encounter when reading the sagas? For Miller (1992), like Gurevich, the sagas provide "an Other," a distant world with particular notions of individuality and emotional life. Miller discusses the interpretive problems of recovering the emotions of Commonwealth Icelanders and objectivist claims about emotion universals. The sagas seem to be characterized by emotional emptiness, even though they provide detailed accounts of violence and feuds. Moreover, he doubts if the categories of English, rather than indigenous concepts, should have priority in representations of emotion universals. On the other hand, he finds plenty of evidence in the sagas on bodily reactions normally associated with emotions, the physical appearances of "surprise," "sadness," "joy," "anger,", etc.. While we cannot confidently label the emotions suggested by these bodily signs, we can guess what they feel like because of our intuitive knowledge of the "somatic semiotics" involved. Such an analysis echoes recent developments in literary studies and anthropology which challenge the western notion of understanding and communication which deprivileges somatic signals *vis-à-vis* the intellect.[6]

There are grounds, then, for resisting the popular claim that the past is inevitably a "foreign country" (Lowenthal 1985). O'Brien and Roseberry (1991) suggest that a form of historical theory which is based on the foundation of cultural relativism necessarily fetishizes the past, exaggerating its distance from an unproblematic present. If culturalist anthropology assumes a disengaged observer, a culture-free being armed with universal reason in a battle with the cultural boundaries that divide the rest of humanity, objectivist historiography assumes an equally paradoxical situation. An observer combating the boundary of time, and yet from the point of view of a temporal void. The claim to objectivity endows the observer with historical immunity, "an ability to step outside his historical situation that it must necessarily deny to the object he scrutinizes" (Patterson 1987:42). In colonial discourse, the colonized are frequently denied their knowledge of the past, as suggested by Wolf's analysis in *Europe and the People Without History* (1982). Indeed, the problem of how to give it "back" to them in the form of "history" is a central topic nowadays. Such efforts run the risk of applying modern state-embedded assumptions about time and narrative where they need not apply. History, in the usual understanding of the term, seems unavoidably caught up in politics. The *making* of the present inevitably presupposes a given past. How are we to represent the agency of "others" in colonial encounters? As Kaplan asks, "is it as *colonized* people with a status inherent in the relationship of colonizer and colonized that they make sense of their history?" (1990:3).

Evidently, in exaggerating difference and denying agency, the modern discourse of alterity, whether it be in history or anthropology, is just as ethnocentric as the earlier eurocentric view of the primitive. Perhaps we should refrain from indulging in the critical cold war of modern scholarship and adopt an intermediate position, assuming that something happened in history and questioning nevertheless any notion of privileged access to it. O'Brien and Roseberry forcefully argue that while "attempts to restrict history to 'what actually happened' result in gross forms of positivism and empiricism . . . attempts to restrict history to historians' discourses result in a bloodless nihilism and the neglect of the historical meanings of important categories of social actors" (1991:12).

THE SOCIAL AND COMPARATIVE CONTEXT

What kind of society do the sagas describe? Several terms have been suggested to describe the social formation of early Iceland, including the term "Free State" (or "Fristat") used by many Scandinavian students of the sagas, the concept of *þjóðveldi* generally preferred by Icelandic scholars, and the notion of the "Commonwealth." While the concept of the Commonwealth, employed here, is not without ambiguities, it seems more appropriate and ethnographically salient than either "Free State" or *þjóðveldi*. The latter terms both contain an anachronistic and misleading reference, to "state" and "nationhood," respectively.[7] The term "Commonwealth" has the advantage that it neither assumes a state formation nor a bounded and well-defined ethnic identity, nationhood. It only suggests a loose association of political assemblages, united by law and minimal agreement but without a centralized executive body.

Formally, the whole country was subject to a general assembly, *Alþing*. In practice, however, the "legal" institution of the *Alþing* was primarily an arena for testing political relations between local leaders and their supporters. In the Commonwealth, power was vested in particular local leaders, *goðar* (singular *goði*). While *goðar* occupied a formal position and there was a fixed number of political units or *goðorð* in the country (36 at first, 39 later on), the bond between a *goði* and his followers, *þingmenn* (singular *þingmaður*), was both personal and temporary. A *goðorð* did not necessarily imply authority over a well-defined territorial unit, nor was it necessarily associated with a single individual. Thus, the inheritors of a *goði* might share the power and responsibilities of a *goðorð*. Also, since *goðorð* could be bought and sold, a single *goði* might have more than one *goðorð* or "shares" in several different *goðorð*.

The political and economic role of the *goðar* was a central one. They would organize local assemblies (*þing*) on legal matters and set prices on imported goods. Most importantly, the *goðar* took an active part in settling disputes. In fact, most disputes were solved peacefully, by arbitration, despite frequent accounts of violence by both saga authors and modern saga scholars. In the absence of a centralized executive institution, managing minor conflicts that eventually might escalate into massive warfare was often a major problem. While the *goðar* were able to take a relatively neutral position in conflicts among members of other *goðorð*, as a third party in a dispute, in particular when giving advise to other *goðar*, in matters involving their own *þingmenn* they could not afford not to take sides. A *goði*'s power largely depended on his ability to assemble a group of local farmers, as potential fighters, in the case of armed conflicts involving other *goðar* or other *goðorð*. *Grettis saga*, for instance, tells of a *goði* named Þorkell krafla who rode to a meeting of the *Alþing* "along with sixty men" (16:972), a frequently mentioned size for a *goði*'s entourage.[8] "All of those belonging to his *goðorð*," the saga adds, "departed with him." The *goði* was also dependent on his *þingmenn* in an economic sense. Collecting taxes from his followers, he was able to meet the costs of luxurious consumption, including items such as grain (for brewing), clothes, wood, and weapons. Such consumption was important for a *goði's* image and reputation. In return for the support of his *þingmenn*, the *goði* provided protection in petty quarrels, for instance over witchcraft accusations and thefts of livestock.

Political leadership was not restricted to *goðar*, nor was it restricted to male personalities. Indeed, the sagas use several terms (including *höfðingi* ("headman" or "chief") *mikilmenni* ("great man") and *stórmenni* ("big man")) for leaders in general, for *goðar*, local people of influence and renown, and foreign earls and kings. *Grettis saga*, for instance, tells of a man who "had no *goðorð*" but was a "great *höfðingi* and fierce" (58:1043). Often, however, the saga account is vague as to whether an influential person is a *goði* or "simply" a man of considerable renown. There are many references in the sagas to "promising" (*efnilegir*) *höfðingjar*, men who "become" *höfðingjar*, and to the particular qualities of "good" *höfðingjar*, including honesty, generosity, and bravery. *Bárðar saga Snæfellsáss* tells of a young man named Oddur who was "a great man and promising. No one else in those regions was seen to be more promising for chieftainship" (10:57). The family sagas alone contain no less than three hundred references to *höfðingjar* and, significantly, in one case out of every three in association with the adjective "great" (*mikill*).[9] The brief sketch presented here hardly does justice to the question posed above, concerning the nature of the society of the Commonwealth. On the other hand, what we are after is a comparative view, not just the sociology and history of the Commonwealth. Detailed and useful accounts of Commonwealth institutions and practices and the development of medieval Icelandic society are available elsewhere.[10]

Unfortunately, saga scholars tend to restrict their analyses to the concepts of the Commonwealth and to ignore the rest of the ethnographic record, "going native," preoccupied with "their tribe," to use anthropological jargon. If they do venture beyond Iceland, it is likely to be to Norwegian society, the Germanic world, or the literary tradition of Medieval Europe. Equally, anthropologists engaged in comparative research elsewhere have largely ignored the comparative relevance of the sagas. Thus, the extensive anthropological literature on tribes and chiefdoms hardly mentions the Icelandic Commonwealth, although generations of scholars have referred anecdotally to the Oceanic "Vikings of the sunrise" in relation to the colonization of the Pacific (see Kirch 1984:1), in a mood no less nostalgic than that of many students of the Vikings of the north. This is rather surprising keeping in mind that few non-state societies have produced an extensive "ethnographic" literature such as the sagas. If, as Strathern points out, Melanesianists have been "curiously reluctant" (Godelier and Strathern 1991:xiii) to extend their own results to the Melanesian region as a whole, they have been even more curiously reluctant to extend their analyses to other parts of the world as well as other times, including the Commonwealth.

The comparative enterprise may take different forms. To simplify, at least two forms may be identified: ethnographically-oriented saga scholarship and saga-oriented ethnography. *Ethnographically-oriented saga scholarship* tends to emphasize the sagas and only seeks to understand particular aspects of culture and society, across the spectrum of social formations or in a given selection of societies.[11] While such comparison draws attention to social theory and, therefore, brings new insights to predominantly a-social saga scholarship, it is, by definition, restricted in scope. The other approach, *saga-oriented ethnography*, emphasizes the comparative record more than the sagas and seeks to identify and explore rather general questions. This approach not only contributes to saga studies, it may also bring new insights to "classic" areas of anthropological research. Thus while Turner and Durrenberger were drawn to the study of the Icelandic Commonwealth because of their ethnographic work on "similar" social formations in other parts of the world, in Central Africa (Turner 1971) and Southeast Asia (Durrenberger 1992), respectively, they continued to address larger anthropological issues, inspired by their acquaintance with the sagas.

If the former approach, ethnographically-oriented saga scholarship or limited comparison, moves from sagas to ethnography, the latter moves from ethnography to sagas. The two approaches should not, however, be seen as contradictory, but rather as complementary openings or emphases in a dialogic scholarship. Turner's use of the notion of social dramas, combined with the extended case method, apparently inspired by his reading of saga accounts of feuds and disputes, has received widespread currency in the anthropological literature. Thus, Rosaldo has found Turner's extended case method "especially instructive" (1980:17n) when dealing with Ilongot ethnography. Ilongot feuds, Rosaldo suggests (p. 61), move through particular phases resembling those outlined by Turner. Interestingly, such analyses later inspired saga scholarship (see, for instance, Miller 1990). Turner's notion of the feud as social drama has come full circle; moving from saga reading to anthropology, to ethnographies of other times and places, and, finally, to saga scholarship.

Given the approach of saga-oriented ethnography, our original sociological and historical question concerning the Commonwealth needs to be radically refashioned and broadened as a comparative query. What kind of social formation does the Commonwealth represent and what would be the closest ethnographic parallels? Traditionally, anthropologists have used several rather rigid "typological" schemes (Upham 1990:5) to deal with the multiple forms of political systems. One scheme distinguishes between bands, tribes, chiefdoms, and states; another identifies egalitarian, ranked, and stratified societies; and still another distinguishes between family-level groups, local groups (acephalous groups and big man collectivities), and regional polities (including chiefdoms) (Johnson and Earle 1987). Rigid typologies of this kind obviously have their drawbacks. In particular, they do not facilitate an adequate understanding of the processes of change, nor do they satisfactorily deal with "intermediate" cases and the range of variation found in the ethnography. And some schemes, ironically perhaps, as such schemes generally represent attempts to understand the so-called ethnographic record, have been challenged for their ethnographic hollowness, for shortage of actual cases or illustrations. Thus Carneiro claims that Fried's notion of "stratified non-state" society, a notion that may be applied to the Icelandic Commonwealth, is a "phantom concept" (Carneiro, cited in Gledhill 1988:11). Indeed, Fried himself suggested that "stratified societies lacking political institutions of state level are almost impossible to find . . ." (Fried 1967:185). Such doubts and criticisms are not sufficient arguments, however, for abandoning the comparative project. Some classification seems essential to identify similar social formations, to indicate what kind of comparison would make most sense. Whatever the Icelandic Commonwealth was, it was definitely *not* a collection of bands, an egalitarian society, a family-level group, or a state.

Some of the closest ethnographic counterparts to the Commonwealth are likely to be found in the richly documented pre-state social formations on Pacific Islands, in Southeast Asia and on the Northwest coast of North America. In his seminal essay on the political systems of Melanesia and Polynesia, Sahlins (1963) compared the personal authority of the big man and the ascribed, institutional power of the chief. To gain followers, he argued, the Melanesian big man has to build a name for generosity and bravery. In societies of big men, there is a flux of rising and falling leaders, each of whom is caught in a fundamental dilemma. The leader has constantly to try to secure his position to increase the number of his followers, but in doing so he risks alienating his supporters. He is under pressure to extract more goods and services from his followers, thereby delaying reciprocities. As a result, there is increasing defection among followers and, consequently, greater need for support. In contrast, the Polynesian chief is installed in a social position on top of a hierarchical, almost feudal, structure; his followers compose a permanent group, an army, and his power resides in his office, not his person.

While Sahlins may be right in his claim that the diverse social systems of Pacific Islands present to anthropologists an important analytical framework for examining cultural adaptation and the multiple forms of pre-state political systems, and his sophisticated model of the big man and the chief has generated much research, critics have drawn attention to its inadequacies. Sahlins, they point out, often misconstrues the ethnographic context and, moreover, few societies in Melanesia actually fit his description of the big man (see Lederman 1990). The "true" big man seems to be an exception in the region, not the rule. Probably the most telling critique is that of Godelier (1986), based on his extensive research among the Baruya in highlands Papua New Guinea. He argues that local leaders are not the bourgeois wealth-manipulators suggested by Sahlins's notion of big men, nor are Baruya leaders, it seems, hereditary "chiefs" in Sahlins's sense. Godelier, therefore, introduces a new term to translate Baruya notions of leadership, namely *great men*. Baruya leaders, some of whom are shamans, "simply" owe their position to their greatness, greatness, in contrast to the authority of big men and chiefs, having little to do with control of wealth. Following Godelier's lead, many Melanesianists have replaced Sahlins's original terms of binary contrast with the triangulation of great man, big man, and chief. On their reasoning, the three kinds of leadership represent radically different principles of political organization, with distinct practices of marriage, kinship, and exchange, each of which may entail a particular discourse on sociality, gender relations, and the public and private.[12] Sometimes, this scheme is conceived of in evolutionary terms, on the assumption that historically great-men societies predate those of big men and chiefs.

Sahlins's formulation has also been challenged for applying personified and gender-biased notions to the ethnography. While formal leadership is usually dominated by males, even though in some cases women may "choose to play the 'big person' game" (Lepowsky 1990:35), there are other avenues to power, some of which may be open to women. Arguably, the systems of the great man, big man, and chief, are not so much *political* systems (M. Strathern 1987, 1988) as social systems in a much broader sense. The great man, big man, and chief may not even represent different *kinds* of structures (whether social logics or evolutionary stages); the qualities of great men, big men, and chiefs, Whitehouse suggests (1992:120), "seem to designate *aspects* of leadership rather than distinguishable *types* of leader and, by extension, types of political systems." Whatever position one adopts in this somewhat excessively theorized discourse on leadership and sociality, it should be clear that the comparative potential of Melanesian ethnography, from the point of view of saga studies, extends far beyond personified "politics" and the confines of male power.

The criticism of Sahlins's model mentioned above draws attention to some of the pitfalls of cross-cultural comparison which students of Commonwealth Iceland may well keep in mind. Thus Godelier alerts us to the tendency to force established but inappropriate theoretical constructs upon the ethnography:

> the term *big man* and the portrait drawn by Sahlins have become such stereotypes, such a conditioned reflex that one even finds anthropologists applying the term *big man* to the great men of the society they are studying, and then wasting a great deal of time trying to explain that these big men are not like the ones found in the great societies of the Western Highlands who genuinely appear to be "true" big men. (Godelier 1986:172)

Ironically, a similar charge has been levelled against Godelier. Whitehouse points out (1992:112) that Godelier's own model of great men and big men seems strangely removed from local ideologies, from "any body of indigenous political theory," and that his theorizing about the great man seems primarily "to wrestle ... with the ghost of Marx" (p. 120), not so much with the ethnography as with

FIGURE 4.3   *Medieval sociality: from Jónsbók ("The Section on Dependency")*

theoretical preconceptions, deterministic models and evolutionary "logics."

Once again, however, rather than abandon comparison we should refine our analytical concepts, ensuring at the same time that we remain attentive to the reality of indigenous concepts and practises. While to some extent the "ethnography" presented in the sagas is bound to invite a set of concepts different from those which have emerged from comparative ethnography, it would undoubtably be productive to try to locate the Icelandic Commonwealth and indigenous concepts of leadership in the powerful analytical discourse developed by students of stratified non-state societies. Whether one thinks of the "great man-big man-chief" sequence as a triangular typology, an evolutionary ladder, different kinds of logic that sometimes go together, or different aspects of leadership is another matter.

There may be some grounds for associating the political leaders of the early Commonwealth with those of "great men" societies. The etymology of the term *goði*, it has often been pointed out, indicates the possession of religious powers, analogous to those of shamans in some great men societies. The term *goði* derives from *goð* which refers to some kind of magician, and several related terms, including *blótgoði*, *hofgoði*, and *goðorð*, clearly indicate pre-Christian religious practice. Also, there are some striking parallels between Godelier's saga (1986) of creation, gender relations, and symbolism of male domination in Baruya society and some of the accounts presented in the Icelandic sagas, particularly in poetic texts. As Linke shows (1992), Icelandic creation myths emphasize an original state of disorder and from which giants and humans emerged. Much of Icelandic mythology elaborates on the relative importance of male and female and Linke explores how it differs from and relates to that of many other creation myths from other parts of the world, including New Guinea.

While available evidence is too fragmentary to allow any firm conclusions, and we should certainly resist the "conditioned reflex" of Melanesianists identified by Godelier, it seems more reasonable given the ethnographic evidence of the family sagas and *Sturlunga saga*, to follow Turner's early lead and compare the Icelandic *goði* and the Melanesian leader pictured by Sahlins—granting political asylum, so to speak, to the big man:

> As in New Guinea today among the so-called "big men," a goði's influence depends on such things as physical strength, personal fame, and skill at arms, just as on birth and inherited wealth... The very attribute which gave him most fame, generosity in providing feasts for his own people and other neighbours, and helping them to pay debts and *wergild*, might be that which impoversihed him most decisively. Giving to win and keep followers depletes wealth and loses followers. (Turner 1971:364–5)

An interesting description of a big man is the self-account of Ongka, an Hagener of the Highlands region of Papua New Guinea (see A. Strathern 1979). Ongka and his colleagues were responsible for holding together a society that accepted no central authority, by managing disputes and conflicts, planning warfare and making peace. Their powers were not ascribed, although they often lead a life similar to that of their father; rather, as A. Strathern emphasizes, they had to *create* a position of leadership for themselves, largely by their skills in interpersonal relations:

> they must depend on the force of their arguments, their oratorical powers, and their ability to manipulate situations with reference to men's interests in exchanges of wealth... Exuberant yet dignified, boastful yet cautious, bold but canny, innovative and conservative at the same time, the big men, such as Ongka himself and a range of others both older and younger, are like the barometers of change in Hagen society. (A. Strathern 1979:xvii)

No doubt, there are important differences between the Hagen big man and the *goði* of the Icelandic Commonwealth, for instance with respect to kinship. Thus, political leaders in Hagen society were polygynists operating within the framework of clanship, identified with ancestral founders and a particular territory, whereas Icelandic leaders were monogamists working within a flexible network of kinship and loose territorial affiliations. As we shall see, however, judging from many saga accounts, the roles and powers of Commonwealth leaders, whether *goði*, *höfðingi*, *mikilmenni*, or *stórmenni*, were quite similar to those attributed to Melanesian big men.

While *goðar* sometimes inherited their position, their power-base was unstable and insecure. Generous and popular *goðar* were able to count on the support of their *þingmenn*, but arrogant free riders might always be overthrown. Not only might the *þingmenn* of a *goði* leave his *goðorð*, if they did not like him, and make an agreement with one of his competitors, lacking the necessry support a *goði* might simply be overthrown. *Laxdæla saga*, for instance, provides an accound of a confiscation of a *goðorð* (67:1637):

> Þórarinn was the name of a man living in Langadal. He had a *goðorð* and was not rich... His son's name was Auðgísl... Þorgils Hölluson seized their *goðorð* and, for them, that was an immense disgrace.

Occasionally angry farmers would even assemble and kill an unpopular *goði*. *Þórðar saga hreðu* discusses one such case:

> Össur was a great chief as he had a *goðorð* in the upper part of Skagafjörður... He was a troublesome man and he was not popular, nor was he greater or stronger than most other men. He was dishonest and treacherous. (6:2023-4)

Despite his potential power-base, a large *goðorð*, Össur is challenged by some local men of renown and in the ensuing fights he is killed.

Another example of violent fights with an unpopular *goði* is provided in *Gunnars saga Keldugnúpsfífls*:

> A man was named Þorgrímur... He... had two sons... both of whom were difficult and troublesome and particularly unfair in every possible way... Þorgrímur... treated his *goðorð* badly, appropriating farmers' possessions, both cattle and horses. All of this made him very unpopular. (1:1144)

On one occasion, Þorgrímur annoys local farmers by insisting upon setting the prices of foreign goods offered by a merchant ship. The merchant refuses to obey, but Þorgrímur responds by announcing that no one is allowed to engage in any kind of transaction with the merchant. Two young men, one of whom is Gunnar, the hero of the saga, challenge Þorgrímur's decision by inviting the merchant to their home, a local farm. A series of battles ensues and Þorgrímur's sons are killed and having lost his sons Þorgrímur himself dies of distress. According to the saga (8: 1157), Gunnar "took the *goðorð* that had belonged to Þorgrímur and everyone was pleased with such an arrangement."

To strengthen the bond between a *goði* and his *þingmenn*, the institution of friendship was particularly important. *Ljósvetninga saga* begins with an account of the close relationships between the "great chieftain" Þorgeir goði and some of his neighbouring farmers. According to the saga (1:1655), these farmers were both "the chieftain's *þingmenn* and friends." Relations between a *goði* and his followers were further strengthened by intermarriage and the institution of concubinage, by sexual relations with women from the families of the *goði's þingmenn*.

To be able to count on his friends, his *þingmenn*, and their supporters, a leader had to reciprocate with services. Political strength and support were constantly subject to reevaluation. A leader had to recruit supporters and maintain alliances through gifts, services and feasts. Among friends the gift was a particularly important mode of exchange. In Commonwealth philosophy,

> Friends should rejoice each other's hearts with gifts of weapons and raiment... That friendship lasts longest—if there is a chance of its being a success—in which friends both give and receive gifts...
> A man ought to be a friend to his friend and repay gift with gift. People should meet smiles with smiles and lies with treachery. (*The Hávamál* 1923:55, stanzas 41 and 42)

Exchanging gifts was not simply a matter of transferring "economic" valuables or assets from one autonomous individual to another. As Gurevich points out (1977:6), the wealth of a "rich man" (*ríkr maðr*) was "not seen as separate from its relationship with the particular qualities of the individual."

By giving and receiving gifts, people *shared* their personal and "magical" powers. "The objects bestowed were not regarded as inert and inanimate—they were supposed to contain a part of the person who bestowed them" (Gurevich 1992:180). Things had a social history of their own, much like people and their livestock. Various kinds of gifts were channelled through networks of friends, neighbors and affines, forming what Appadurai has called "tournaments of value" (1986:21). All this resonates with Melanesian notions of exchange and sociality. To paraphrase M. Strathern, we are "forced to collapse the conventional analytical difference between persons and relations. Put abstractly, we could imagine persons as relations, and vice versa" (1991:198-9). Perhaps, then, one could speak of the Icelandic *goðar* as "big men of the North," reciprocating the metaphoric association represented by the notion of the Oceanic "Vikings of the sunrise" mentioned above.

Much ethnography proper is rather dull reading. Such a claim can hardly be made with respect to the sagas, with their lively descriptions and social dramas, although some of them may be filled with scrupulous, distracting, and confusing detail. For some saga scholars, faithful to the dictum that "a thing of beauty is a joy forever," the pleasure of the text is always primary. Saga scholars trained in anthropology are likely to reverse the priorities, emphasizing the scrutiny. Their chief aim is to extract social information from the sagas to reveal the dynamics of early Iceland and similar societies elsewhere, in medieval Scandinavia or beyond. Having fun with the text and tearing it apart should not, however, be seen as mutually exclusive enterprises. Thus, it is quite possible to enjoy the "deconstruction" of a text. As Derrida remarks, "no deconstruction without pleasure and no pleasure without deconstruction" (1992:57).

There are many similarities between saga and ethnography. The saga-writers, I have suggested, may well be regarded as anthropological informants, bridging the temporal gap between their reality and ours, between the past and present. While neither sagas, ethnographic monographs, nor histories accurately depict reality, they must be somehow rooted in the interpretive community of their authors. But just as anthropologists do different things with their field-notes, so saga scholars do different things with their texts. It is both informative and theoretically useful to move from the sagas to other societies, with a series of limited comparative questions in mind, yet to proceed in the opposite direction, from other "primitives" to the Commonwealth, to address general questions of social formation and theory, is equally informative and useful. Comparative saga scholarship is a dialogic enterprise, not a one way street. As the comparative and social approach to the sagas gains momentum, perhaps the time is ripe for a "scientific revolution" in saga studies. This will involve new conceptions of academic specialization and cooperation, new definitions of what constitutes legitimate intellectual puzzles, and new ways of approaching them.

NOTES

[1] Saga scholars usually distinguish between *several* genres of sagas. The so-called "family sagas" or "the sagas of Icelanders," describe the period from the time of settlement, between AD 870 and 930, to sometime after the introduction of Christianity, in the year 1000. They comprise about one hundred sagas and shorter stories (*sögur* and *þættir*) that were compiled in one large manuscript sometime after they were written. *Sturlunga saga* (named after one powerful family) largely concentrates on near contemporary events from 1230 to 1262. The latter collection, fourteen sagas and stories, was arranged in chronological order and compiled in one manuscript from early on, around the year 1300. Other categories of medieval Icelandic prose include the kings' sagas, Fornaldarsögur or "Sagas of the Past," and legal texts, notably *Grágás* ("Grey Goose") and *Jónsbók*. Furthermore, there are extensive poetic texts, including the *Poetic Edda*.

[2] Gurevich (1968, 1977) elaborated on the Maussian insight with respect to gifts, exchange, and property relations; Wax (1969) explored changes in the world-view of early Icelanders; Turner (1971) forcefully argued for an anthropological reading of the sagas as social dramas; and Odner (1974) used the literary sources to understand the archaeology of Western

Norway. These pioneering works were followed by a thriving "anthropological" discussion of saga society; see, for instance, Hastrup 1985, Miller 1990, Samson 1991, Durrenberger 1992, Gurevich 1992, and Pálsson 1992.

[3] See, for example, Eggertsson 1992 and Ingimundarson 1992.

[4] See, for instance, Jochens 1986, 1991, Kress 1991, and Karras 1992.

[5] For an apt example, see Sveinsson 1959.

[6] See, for instance, Robinson 1991.

[7] Such misleading descriptions are abundant in Icelandic scholarship. Thus Einar Pálsson writes (1991:11): "With the establishment of the *Alþing* [general assembly], Icelanders are described as a separate nation within their own state-unit."

[8] Chapter and page references to the family sagas in both the present chapter and the following one are based on *Íslendinga sögur og þættir* (1987), except otherwise stated. All translations from the Icelandic editions cited are mine.

[9] See the analysis by Kristjánsdóttir (1992) of the frequency of the relevant words in the sagas.

[10] See, for instance, Durrenberger 1992, Miller 1990, Hastrup 1985, and Jóhannesson 1974.

[11] See, for instance, Amory (1991) on speech-acts and ritual insults, Bauman (1986) on the poetics of performance, Clover (1988) on infanticide, Hastrup (1985) on myth and world-view, and Miller (1986a) and Pálsson (1994b) on witchcraft and sorcery.

[12] See various contributions to Godelier and Strathern 1991, in particular that of Jolly.

CHAPTER FIVE

The power of words and the context of witchcraft

That is harmful witchcraft [*fordæs skapir*] when a man by means of words or magic [*fiolkyngi*] inflicts sickness or kills, whether sheep or humans.

Grágás, the medieval Icelandic law book

For the Word of God is living and active, sharper than any two-edged sword, piercing to the division of soul and spirit, of joints and marrow, and discerning the thoughts and intentions of the heart.

Hebrews 4.12

This chapter discusses a particular aspect of medieval society: the magical power of words and texts in the changing dynamics of Icelandic society. The powers of the word are particularly evident in the case of witchcraft. To be accused of using such powers might have deadly consequences for the accused. Anthropologists have produced a series of studies that show how accusations of witchcraft relate to the moral ambiguities and the tensions of social life.[1] Some have tried to specify the circumstances under which accusations are likely to develop or disappear, to explain why people are prone to witchcraft accusations in some societies but not in others. In the analysis of Commonwealth witchcraft presented below I shall draw upon these insights.

To early Icelanders, both the spoken and written word were imbued with potential power. Numerous saga accounts testify to the importance of the magical force of chants, gossip, libels, and insulting phrases in the everyday world of medieval Icelanders. The rich vocabulary relating to the importance of talk (*mál*, *orð*, *rómur*, *orðræða*, *tal*, and *umræða*, to mention only a few terms with various language-related connotations) indeed suggests a folk theory of speech acts—"doing things with words" (Austin 1975). Significantly, the term *goðorð*, a key term in indigenous political discourse, literally the "words of *goði*," both refers to the terrain or power of a *goði* (his sphere of influence) and his speech (his magic formulas).

The family sagas provide numerous accounts of sorcery and witchcraft, while such accounts are remarkably absent in the *Sturlunga saga*. This indicates, given the difference between the two genres of sagas in terms of temporal reference, that accusations of witchcraft were important during the earlier years of the Commonwealth period but not later on, during the age of the Sturlungs. I attempt to place witchcraft accusations in the social context of the early Commonwealth, using the *Eyrbyggja saga* in particular as an extended case, and suggest an explanation for their absence during the second period in terms of changes in social and political organization. The absence of witchcraft accusations in the *Sturlunga saga* is not due to the absence of thefts, since accounts of thefts are even more frequent in the *Sturlunga saga* than in the family sagas. Nor is it simply a result of the conversion to a Christian ethic as the saga writers sometimes lead us to believe. The ethnographic record shows that Christianity and witchcraft are not mutually exclusive systems of belief and that accusations persist in many societies despite the acceptance of Christianity. The saga writers themselves indicate that Commonwealth Icelanders did not take the doctrines of the church too seriously. I argue that accusations of witchcraft disappeared primarily as a result of increased social distance, that is, with the progressive development of asymmetrical power relations towards the end of the Commonwealth period. Mundane variables such as wealth and political force increasingly determined people's fortunes. Since social relations became less ambiguous than before, there was less need for secrecy and gossip. Force replaced negotiation and subtle manipulation. As a result, there were fewer witchcraft accusations than before. The idea of witchcraft did not disappear, but for the time being witches, sorcerers, and diviners became obsolete. Such a conclusion is consistent with Evans-Pritchard's interpretation for an African context. Witchcraft is a consequence of ambiguous social relations not clear ones.

It is important to point out that saga descriptions of witchcraft were, to some extent, rhetorical devices which had more to do with the constraints of storytelling by the time the sagas were written than the realities of the early Commonwealth. Some evidence suggests that such descriptions were modelled on accounts of shamanistic practices elsewhere in the world, among the pre-Christian Saami of northern Scandinavia and possibly further beyond, among Siberian groups.[2] The Norse merchants who travelled abroad may have returned with strange stories of indigenous practices involving trance-like sleep, magical acts that blunt weapons, runic inscriptions that affect the mind, etc.: stories that Icelandic writers would later exploit for "decorating" their sagas, in their attempt to make them suitably heathen and exotic for the pre-Christian and "foreign" past they described. Assuming that accounts of witchcraft are partly invented, in the sense that they modify or distort the realities of the early Commonwealth which they supposedly refer to, it may, indeed, be argued that they somehow reflect or mediate the ambiguities and tensions of the social world—that is, by the end of the Commonwealth. Saga accounts of witchcraft are unlikely to be simply literary inventions or the result of diffusion or borrowing. If this were the case, they would hardly resonate with accounts of the micropolitics of the non-state society of early Iceland to the extent they do. Generally, the accounts of witchcraft that are offered strike the anthropologist as ethnographically meaningful, given the information available about both the social context of the Commonwealth period and similar social formations elsewhere.

While it is difficult to establish whether or not witchcraft accusations declined towards the end of the Commonwealth period, due to the limits of saga texts and the interpretive problems they pose, we have solid evidence for their presence later on. With the Reformation, some three centuries later, witchcraft returned to the Icelandic scene, apparently with far more ferocity than ever before. Accusations became fashionable once again. Seventeenth century witch-hunts built extensively on earlier notions of magical power. They were different though and more along the lines of the witch-hunts of the European continent, importing the continental concept of *maleficium*. Every act of witchcraft (doing harm to other people *and* saving lives) was associated with the Devil. This time, witchcraft cases centered on the control of knowledge, in particular written texts.

THE MAGIC OF WORDS

For early Icelanders, runic inscriptions had a magical quality, with important consequences for the people involved, positive or negative, depending on the point of view. The word "rune" (*rún*) both referred to a letter of the indigenous alphabet and a secret symbol with magical qualities. The latter meaning is probably the original one. Thus particular symbols (*stafir, tákn*) were seen to influence fishing success, others would affect loss of livestock, and still others might ensure or prevent love relationships. In the beginning of writing, when the art of writing was only known to a few, the old Norse term "rune" was extended to embrace any kind of powerful "text." Theoretically, any piece of text might alter the course of events and, thereby, affect people's lives. For Icelanders, the text, whether it be a runic inscription, a work on grammar, a legal text, or a saga, had a force of its own.

The same applied to the formal genres of "love poetry" (*mansöngur*), defamation or libel (*níð*), and chanting or singing (*seiður, söngur*) as well as more informal talk, especially gossip. In the case of love poetry, the speaker typically attempted to hurt a man in control of a woman in a euphemistic manner, addressing the woman rather than the man. To make the poetry effective, the poet had to observe cetain rules of the game. Some poets, however, particularly the *kraftaskáld* ("power poet" or "magic poet"), were believed to be charged with greater powers than others; such an idea seems to have been entertained by Icelanders for centuries, until the nineteenth century.[3] As regards the defaming *níð*, another kind of ritualized performance, *Egils saga* provides this example:

> He took a hazel pole in his hand and went to a certain jutting rock facing the mainland. Then he took a horse's head and set it up on the pole.
> Afterwards he receited a formulary, saying these words: 'I here set up a scorn-pole, and I turn this scorn against King Eirík and Queen Gunnhild.' He then turned the horse's head inwards. 'I turn this scorn upon the landspirits

which dwell in this land, so that they all fare wildering ways, and none light on or lie in this dwelling till they drive King Eirik and Gunnhild out of the land.'

Next he jammed the pole down into a crack in the rock and let it stand there. The head he turned landwards, but he graved runes on the pole, and they state all the formulary. (*Egil's saga* 1960:151)

An example of magical chanting is provided in *Fóstbrœðra saga* (9:796). Here, a woman named Gríma is reported to have fondled the clothes of her slave Kolbakur, whereby he became "so charged by Gríma's chants that weapons did not hurt him." Quite possibly, such ideas were inspired by the Vikings' knowledge of systematic experiments in the Byzantine army with weapon-proof garments, protected by tar, asbestos and other materials.

The less formal genre of gossip is particularly interesting, if only because of frequent references to it in the sagas. As Kress (1991) has shown, the sagas are both based on and saturated with gossip. In the absence of any strict sociolinguistic rules as to who is to talk, when, in what manner, and about what, gossip had a potentially subversive power. It needed no authorization. Like the agents of the devil in seventeenth-century witchcraft cases, "bad tongues" might crop up anywhere, anytime, setting the stage for further talk, particularly about the deeds and social honor of males. At the same time gossip was practically the only source of power available to slaves, vagabonds, and free laborers and, above all, women who were normally denied access to other avenues to politics. The *Hávamál* poetry repeatedly warns agains the potential devastation caused by the irresponsible and careless "tongue," the "destroyer of the head" (*The Hávamál* 1923:63):

> I have known a man mortally hurt by the talk of a bad woman—a wily tongue brought about his death, through quite untrue accusations. (p. 73)

For the weak, gossip was an effective method of resistance, empowering the otherwise silent agenda of the mass *vis-à-vis* the noisy one of the wealthy and powerful. Because of its anonymity gossip might also be useful to those in power if other means of attack were considered too risky. The consulting of diviners, frequently used in legal disputes involving wrongdoings of one kind or another, was one way of spreading gossip. The mere fact that a victim consulted a diviner might force the wrongdoer to come out into the open. The diviner's statements might elicit responses from the community in general and direct the flow of gossip and discourse, making the community collectively responsible for an implicit accusation. Consulting a diviner was a way of spreading the risk of an accusation, reducing the responsibility of the accuser, an important safety valve in case the rumor, gossip, and accusation turned out to be either false or indefensible. Not surprisingly, Icelandic law books provide rather clear guidance in relation to speech and its potential misuses. Thus the authors of the medieval law book *Grágás* attempt to put restraints on threatening and dangerous words, advancing elaborate definitions of harmful talk—including slander, libel, love poetry, and, especially, evil witchcraft (*fordæðuskapur*) "by means of words" (*Grágás* 1852, Sect. 7:23). Significantly, the chief native term for witchcraft, *galdur*, is derived from *gala*, to "sing" or "shout."[4]

Although important, words were not the sole means of control and contest. The saga-authors often seem to be preoccupied with other aspects of politics, namely warfare and bloodstained weapons—or, if you like, how to do things with *swords* (see Figure 5.1).[5] However, very likely, warfare did not have quite the importance the sagas indicate. Detailed descriptions of battles, wounds and slayings may have been partly motivated by chieftains' demands for compensation. It also seems probable that the standard reading of some of the accounts of "heroic" violence have been both misguided and gender-biased. Some stories that reportedly provide an image of courageous deeds have simply been misunderstood by the patriarchal discourse of saga scholars. Scholars have missed much of the sarcasm and humor in the sagas. Much of what has been taken as admiration for the male hero should be regarded as parody of the phallic politics of the sword (see Figure 5.1). Some sagas, including *Fóstbræðrasaga*, have been classified as incomplete, since irrelevant or distracting descriptions and accounts (often they have to do with bodily processes and digestion problems) seem to have been inserted, almost by accident, in the main narrative, creating a certain tension within the text. This tension, Kress suggests (1987), drawing upon Bakhtin's analysis of laughter and carnivalesque in *Rabelais and His World*, is not simply to be regarded as evidence of a "primitive" heroic narrative, rather it serves to make fun of the warrior and the masculine ideal, as grotesque critique. Thus, the foster brothers Þorgeir and Þormóður, the key characters of *Fóstbræðrasaga*, usually kill their opponents in the middle of the night, catching them by surprise. Often, too, their victims are innocent people who just happen to be around when the "heroes" are passing by. On one occasion, Þorgeir encounters a tired shepherd who supports himself by a short walking stick, dropping his head in a moment of rest. Seeing his elongated neck, Þorgeir lifted his weapon and chopped the head of. Later when Þorgeir is asked why he had killed the man he responds: "He hadn't done anything to me, but, it is fair to say, I could not help it, he was so nicely positioned for the blow."

The sagas often give the impression of two spheres of politics, the "realpolitics" of warfare and related masculine activities and the politics of words and gossip, typically (but not exclusively) of women. These spheres were not necessarily independent of each other. Much like words, weapons were heavily loaded with magical qualities. Often the power of the weapon was seen to derive from the words of earlier owners or specialized magicians. In the *Brennu-Njáls saga* (30:157) a man named Hallgrímur hires someone to charge his spear with magic force (*seiða*). As Gurevich remarks, "a song . . . was quite as effective as a weapon" (1977:14). Swords

FIGURE 5.1   *How to do things with swords from Flateyjarbók*

and spears—important tokens of exchange and interpersonal relations—even had "personal" names, signifying the potency of the user and the donor. As the case of witchcraft demonstrates, the distinction between words and action may not have been a particularly salient one for early Icelanders. Thus, the term *sjónhverfingar*, frequently used with reference to witchcraft, combines sight and sound, action and word, meaning "ocular delusion by spell." *Brennu-Njáls saga* provides this example of such a spell:

> Svanur took a goatskin, swung it over his head and said: . . . Let there be fog . . . Shortly after so thick a fog fell over them that they could not see and they fell and lost their horses. (12:140–41)

The sagas, it is true, mention two aspects of witchcraft. The ritual act itself or the performance of witchcraft and the magical spell of the word. As regards the former, *Gísla saga Súrssonar* (18:871–72) provides an account of a woman who "walks a few times around the houses anti-clockwise, looking in every direction and pointing up her nostrils . . . whereby an avalanche of snow runs from the hill, hitting Berg's farm and killing twelve men." Many other accounts emphasize infliction through the act of speaking: chants (*söngvar, seiðir*) and libels (*ákvæði, áhrínisorð, níð*). Usually words and actions seem to have gone together. In some acts of witchcraft speech was dominant, in others not. The "ratio of words to action" (Tambiah 1968:175) varied from one case to another.

Some anthropologists argue that the concept of witchcraft needs to be recast or dissolved, just as the concept of "totemism," on the grounds that it is not a "separate topic" or "isolable problem" (Crick 1976:116). Comparative analyses need to be replaced by elaborate semiotic studies of particular systems of beliefs. While I do not share such a semantic and deconstructive enthusiasm, I would agree that an anthropological study of witchcraft must attend to the meaning of indigenous concepts, a point emphasized by Evans-Pritchard in his classic study of Azande witchcraft. The present account does not exhaust the implications of indigenous Icelandic terms. A further study would be necessary to reveal the complex semantics of witchcraft during the Commonwealth period.

THE CONTEXT OF WITCHCRAFT

A series of concepts in Old Icelandic translate generally as "witchcraft," for instance *galdur* ("magic"), *seiður* ("chant"), *fjölkynngi* ("multiple powers"), *fyrnska* ("old lore"), *forneskja* ("old heathen time"), *fróðleikur* ("knowledge"), and *margkunnindi* ("multiple knowledge"). Many of the relevant concepts refer specifically to the knowledge and power of the witch. One further aspect often mentioned is the ability to change shape, "not being single-shaped" (*eigi einhamur*), or to become berserk (*berserksgangur*). Some concepts (such as *galdur* and *seiður*) refer to what may be called "witch acts" (to invoke the language of pragmatism), the *use* of knowledge and abilities pertaining to witchcraft. There seems to be a conceptual distinction between two kinds of witch acts, sorcery and divination, but such a distinction is not a rigid one for sometimes a prediction is also a curse. To complicate matters even further, there are two kinds of divination, the prediction of future events (*forspá*) and the discovery of hidden knowledge (*eftirrýni*), particularly the discovery of thieves and other wrongdoers. *Eyrbyggja saga* mentions Spá-Gils who "foresaw the future and was clever in detecting thieves or indeed anything he wanted" (18:550).

In early Commonwealth Iceland misfortune was often defined as the result of human action. Sometimes no one claimed responsibility for a particular misfortune. For discovering the wrongdoer people sometimes carried out a formal investigation (*rannsókn*), based on direct evidence and "rational" procedures and specified by law (see *Grágás* 1852, Sect. 230). Other intuitive procedures, based on the hunches of diviners, were also employed. Some saga accounts suggest divination was used to discover freeloaders, to detect the abuse of the rule of reciprocity. In *Þorvaldar þáttur víðförla* (2:2322), Þórdís "the diviner" reveals the source of Koðráns's money. She accuses him of earning his money "with force and power as awards for settlements," and collecting it "by greed in debt and rent beyond fairness."

In some cases wrongdoing was itself an act of sorcery, in which case an objective investigation was unlikely to work. Sometimes a person practices sorcery in the service of someone else in return for some form of payment:

> Þóroddur hired Þorgíma the Witch to launch a snowstorm onto Björn when travelling over the moors. (*Eyrbyggja saga* 40:587)
> [They] hired Kjölvör and payed her a hundred in silver for killing the brothers ... by some kind of witchcraft. (*Víglundar saga* 12:1967).

How prominent, then, are witchcraft accusations in the sagas? The index of a recent edition has a particular section on "witchcraft and supernatural qualities."[6] According to this sample, which may not be exhaustive, seventy eight people are named witches in the family sagas. The sagas with the greatest number of witches are *Vatnsdæla saga* (nine people), *Eyrbyggja saga* (six), and *Bárðar saga* (six). Of the seventy eight people labeled as witches, fifty three are accused of using their powers. In fourteen cases the people involved use their power only to predict the future or to reveal some hidden truths. There are no less than forty one accounts of sorcery carried out for the purpose of manipulating persons, things, or states of affairs. Accusations of witchcraft sometimes relate to injuries, jealousy, and demands for exclusive affection, but most often they seem to be sparked by loss of property and untimely death. Many of the family sagas are rich with descriptions of thefts and forceful appropriation of hay, wood, land, and livestock. Much of the social tension reported in *Eyrbyggja saga* relates to claims of forceful appropriation. Thus, Arnkell goði is said to "unlawfully" appropriate wood belonging to Snorri goði (35:580), a claim that results in a killing and a lawsuit. Such accounts are rife with gossip, witchcraft accusations. "That summer," *Eyrbyggja saga* adds, "there was much defamation among men" (35:581).

The sagas provide scant information about both the people accused of witchcraft and their targets. Generalizations about their social identity are therefore difficult to make. In some cases the sorcerer and the target inhabit different countries: one in Iceland, the other in Scandinavia, as in the case of the libel from *Egils saga*. In most cases the accuser and the accused are neighbours. In one case a whole family is accused of practicing sorcery: "[Ingunn] . . . said that Kotkell and his wife and his sons made life difficult for her, that she was short of stock and subject to witchcraft" (*Laxdæla saga* 35:1585). Generally, however, individuals are accused, not families.

There may well be some difference between the kinds of witch acts performed by men and women, though gender does not seem to be a significant factor. Roughly the same number of men and women are labelled as witches—thirty nine men and thirty eight women (in one case gender is not specified). Males are accused of twenty acts of sorcery, females of twenty one. If one assumes that accusations of witchcraft are aroused by conflicts over property and power, it is somewhat surprising that women are equally likely as men to be accused since property and power was normally vested in the hands of men. The women accused of witchcraft are, therefore, likely to be "marginal" as heads of their own household. This is Miller's line of reasoning:

> . . . shift the nominal and real control over property and household power to a woman . . . and it [is] . . . the woman who [has] . . . to bear the burden of protecting her household from the depredations of her neighbours. She could be . . . accused, summoned, or killed . . . for sorcery. (1986b:115)

Of the thirty eight women labeled as witches, ten are identified as widows or heads of a household. In at least three cases the saga writer makes specific references to the woman's property:

> [Þórdís] . . . was wealthy. (*Gunnars saga keldugnúpsfífls* 1:1144)
> [Þorgríma] . . . became rich and powerful. (*Harðar saga og Hólmverja* 3:1254)
> [Esja was] . . . a widow and very rich. (*Kjalnesinga saga* 2:1437)

Among the remaining women described as witches there is one mistress, in *Vatnsdæla saga* (33:1884), and one vagabond, a "cheery, knowledgeable prophet" (*gleðimaður, fróð og framsýn*, *Víga-Glúms saga* 12:1923).

As for the men described as witches, there are some indications that ethnicity is involved. *Svaða þáttur og Arnórs kerlingarnefs* mentions (1:2253) Þórhallur "the diviner," a man of "Norse," non-Icelandic descent (*norrænn*). There are some slaves as well, for instance Gilli in *Draumur þorsteins Síðu-Hallssonar* (p. 2108). Most of the males, however, are native freemen. Their social status is quite variable; some are poor farmers, others wealthy chieftains. Not only is it difficult to generalize about the social identities of witches and their targets, it is even more difficult to establish the probabilities of inclusion. Ideally, we would have to check the relative sizes of different groups of people in the total population of the Commonwealth: the proportion of widows, concubines, outsiders, slaves, etc. That would be a difficult, if not impossible, exercise.

The discussion presented above indicates that witchcraft accusations and the practice of witchcraft were widespread in the medieval Icelandic community. The frequency of witchcraft accusations does not mean that the saga writers necessarily attached a heavily loaded, negative label to their witches. An important feature of early witchcraft is its dual nature in a moral sense; witches are described in both positive and negative terms. Some of the women who employ witchcraft do so to protect their sons, often foster sons, against enemy weapons, others are described as being wicked and seductive. One example, as we will see, is Katla in *Eyrbyggja saga*. The same applies to the men. Some of them are described in rather positive language as "great" men performing noble deeds. Egill Skallagrímsson cures a sick girl with magic runes, *rímgaldur* (*Egils saga* 73:482). Others are described as diabolic characters, as brutes, villains, and berserks.

About one third (twenty five) of all the people described as witches do not seem to use their powers. They remain inactive in the narrative but have the reputation for being competent, knowledgeable witches:

> Gríma was said to be knowledgeable and people spoke of her as a witch. (*Fóstbræðra saga* 9:795)
>
> There was a man named Dýri, one of the greatest chieftains... He is described as being big and strong, knowledgeable... doing many things with witchcraft. (*Hávarðar saga Ísfirðings* 19:1330)
>
> Many people were of the opinion that Esja was a sorceress. (*Kjalnesinga saga*, 2:1437)
>
> Stórólfur was the strongest of all men and in everybody's opinion he was a shape-changer. He was a knowing magician. For these reasons he was said to be a witch. (*Orms þáttur Stórólfssonar* 1:2189)

The reference to the reputation for being a witch may be part of the objective style of saga writing, a literary convention to increase the distance between the writer and the characters in the story. The number of potential but inactive witches may also be a rhetorical strategy. There may be more to the story.

Many of the family sagas may be regarded as medieval detective stories. The number of names associated with witchcraft appears superfluous, which may have served the purpose of eliciting similar responses among readers and listeners of the sagas as the diviner elicited in reality. Like the revelation of a divination or a dream, the act of naming invites responses from the audience, encouraging gossip about available evidence and plausible hypotheses about the wrongdoer's identity. The abundance of witch names also underlines the idea that the world is inhabited by people who possess magical powers, powers of potential use either for noble purposes or for harming others. In *Bárðar saga Snæfellsáss* a woman named Hildigunnur is accused of possessing the powers of witchcraft. Having been accused and summoned (*fyrir það var henni stefnt*, 6:53), she uses her knowledge to take revenge. The talk and gossip associated with such cases were the components of the social dramas of the sagas, the undercurrent that both resulted from and set the stage for other bloodier battles. Thus, the anthropology of the sagas is partly an exercise in contextualizing accusations and wrongdoings, in cross-cultural criminology.

EYRBYGGJA SAGA

An anthropological approach to witchcraft must go beyond etymology and the sociological distribution of accusations and situate accusations in the dynamics and relations among accusers and accused. *Eyrbyggja saga* provides an excellent opportunity for such an analysis.[7] Chapters 15 to 20 of the saga describe the unfolding of events that particularly affect three neighboring households: Mávahlíð, Fróðá and Holt. Gunnlaugur, the son of Þorbjörn at Fróðá, is found outside his home heavily injured and insane. His calamity causes a series of troubles which the saga describes in some detail.

Two women, Katla at Holt and Geirríður at Mávahlíð, seem to be somehow involved in Gunnlaugur's misfortune; Katla is said to be a "pretty woman but eccentric" (*fríð . . . sýnum en eigi . . . við alþýðuskap* (p. 547)), while Geirríður is described as a widow possessing the power of witchcraft (*margkunnig*) (p. 548). Geirríður, we are told, had been teaching Gunnlaugur her knowledge, but Katla wanted his attention too. At one point she complains jealously by asking Gunnlaugur whether he

> still intends to go to Mávahlíð to caress that old woman's groin . . . you seem to think that Geirríður is the only woman around but she is not the only woman possessing knowledge about witchcraft. (p. 548)

It is Oddur, the son of Katla, who first accuses Geirríður of being responsible for Gunnlaugur's misfortune. He says that Geirríður and Gunnlaugur "had parted" one evening "in an unfriendly manner" and, the saga writer adds, "that was the general opinion" (16:548). Þorbjörn then summons Geirríður for using witchcraft to hurt his son. As the case is opened at a local assembly (Þórsnesþing), the accuser and the accused receive the support of powerful and contesting *goðar*. Þorbjörn is supported by Snorri goði, his brother-in-law, and Geirríður by Arnkell goði, her brother. The case is dismissed, but the conflict is not resolved. It is no longer restricted to the three original households.

The household at Fróðá suffers from another misfortune, discussed in Chapter 18 of the saga. In the autumn, Þorbjörn searches in vain for his horses when he intends to drive them for slaughtering from the pastures in the highland. The saga account is typically objective. It makes no statement as to what happened to the horses; it only states that Þorbjörn was unable to find them. While the saga states that "many places were searched," it adds that "the weather was rather harsh" (p. 550), implying that Þorbjörn and his men did not search well enough and that the horses might not have been stolen at all. Þorbjörn sends Oddur to the diviner Spá-Gils assuming that the horses have been stolen. Oddur asks Spá-Gils whether the thieves were "foreigners or from other districts or his neighbours" (p. 550). Spá-Gils responds: "I think . . . [the] horses are not far from their pastures." Oddur returns and informs Þorbjörn about the verdict, adding that, according to the diviner, "those most likely to take horses were people who were themselves short of stock and still had added workers to their household beyond the usual." "For Þorbjörn these words pointed to the people at Mávahlíð."

By consulting the diviner, Þorbjörn threatens to accuse before making an accusation. He thereby simplifies the search for a thief and, perhaps, confirms his hunches. Having interpreted the verdict he resorts to an objective method of investigation. He goes to Mávahlíð and says to Þórarinn: "The purpose of our coming here, . . ., is to look for the horses which were stolen from me in the autumn. We want your permission to search." Þórarinn answers: "Is this investigation in any way in accordance with law or have you summoned any witnesses for observation . . . or have you investigated other places at all." The account of the fights that ensue states twice that Oddur is not injured since he is wearing weapon-proof clothes made by Katla, his mother.

During the fights someone cuts off one arm of Auður, Geirríður's daughter-in-law, which provokes further events. Oddur makes fun of Þórarinn, Auður's husband, implying that he is a poor womanly fighter, so poor that he manages to cut off his wife's arm in the middle of a battle. Later, Geirríður sends a message to her brother Arnkell goði, saying that she had discovered (*var þess vís orðin*, 20:558) that Oddur himself had cut off Auður's arm. Þórarinn and Arnkell then seek revenge. Katla uses her magic power to deceive them, hiding Oddur by transforming him into an animal, but Geirríður then uses her power to counteract Katla's. As a result, Þórarinn and Arnkell are able to find Oddur and hang him. Katla not only admits her defeat, but also claims responsibility for the first episode, the misfortune of Gunnlaugur. She puts a spell on Arnkell and is then stoned to death. As these events escalate, the tension between the major *goðar* of the story, Snorri and Arnkell, increases. Finally, Snorri's men manage to kill Arnkell, thereby ending the feuds. According to the saga, there is no revenge since the potential avengers are women.

In these episodes, sorcery is closely tied to the micropolitics of the community. Personal misfortune is defined as the result of the neighbours' malignancy, a diviner sets the gossip network going, and someone is accused and finally summoned or punished. In the process, a restructuring of social relationships takes place. A series of petty quarrels between neighbours escalates into larger feuds between competing goðar. As the participants in the events mobilize kin and dependents for support they are drawn into the political framework of Commonwealth Iceland. At the same time, the episodes summarized above may be considered as sociological allegories about particular kinds of social relationships and household structures, in particular the disruptive nature of sexual relationships and the instability of female-headed households.

THE ABSENCE OF WITCHCRAFT ACCUSATIONS FROM THE *STURLUNGA SAGA*

A computerized count of words relating to witchcraft shows that in all the family sagas there are no less than 116 references to witchcraft; the most common word, *fjökynngi*, appears on 62 occasions.[8] The sagas of the *Sturlunga saga* are a different matter altogether. Here references to witchcraft are virtually nonexistent; the word *fjölkunnigur* appears only twice (in Chap. 50 of *Sturlu saga*) and in relation to the same person, the thief Þórir the fjölkunngi (*Sturlunga saga* 1988:58). The word *seiður* occurs a few times, but, significantly, as a metaphor, that is, not specifically in relation to witchcraft. Other witchcraft-related concepts do not appear at all.[9] This contrast between the family sagas and the *Sturlunga saga* is a striking one.

It is true that the two classes of sagas represent somewhat different kinds of documents or genres, by both our standards and those of the saga writers. The family sagas emphasize family relationships and local events, including witchcraft accusations, whereas the *Sturlunga saga* emphasizes larger scale ones. More important, perhaps, the two classes of sagas describe different periods. The former describe events from the 2-300 years past while the latter discuss near contemporary events. Accounts of witchcraft accusations in the contemporary sagas might be very real accusations with serious social and political concequences for the saga writers and others involved. On the other hand, many of the family sagas, as we have seen in the case of *Eyrbyggja saga*, *do* describe events af regional significance and, conversely, there are plenty of localized events in the *Sturlunga saga*. Also, in the contemporary *Sturlunga saga* people are accused of many *other* misdeeds and sinister acts, so why exclude witchcraft?

Perhaps witchcraft events are invented as part of the narrative structure of the family sagas. But, clearly, *if* we take the two classes of sagas as representative of the social realities of the earlier and later years of the Commonwealth respectively there are significant discontinuities between the two periods in terms of sorcery and witchcraft accusations. The differences in emphasis and time reference between the two classes of sagas do not adequately explain this stark contrast. Witchcraft accusations are abundant in the former sagas but more or less absent in the latter.

In some respects, the apparent decline of witchcraft accusations during the latter period is rather surprising. Durrenberger (1990) shows that there is a significant contrast between the family sagas and the *Sturlunga saga* in terms of accounts of economic transactions and dispute settlements. His analysis suggests that during the early Commonwealth period objects were typically exchanged by negotiation and purchase. On the other hand, disputes were frequently resolved by violence. Judging from the *Sturlunga saga* the reverse was the case during the later years of the Commonwealth. Objects were taken by force, but disputes were typically solved by arbitration. If witchcraft accusations develop in disputes over missing property, as we are led to believe by the family sagas, and thefts were more frequent than before, which also seems to be the case, we would expect a *greater* number of accusations during the latter period. There is indeed more anxiety and tension in the *Sturlunga saga* than the family sagas, as we would expect given the amount of violence and insecurity. Comparative evidence suggests this is likely to raise the level of witchcraft accusations, not reduce it.

The explanation offered by the saga writers of the apparent decline of witchcraft emphasizes the conversion to Christianity, comparing the Christian present with the heathen past. *Grettis saga*, for instance, provides this account of an old woman named þuríður:

> As a young woman, in heathen time, she knew much about witchcraft. Now
> it seemed that she had lost everything. But even though Christianity had come
> to the country many heathen sparks still remained. (78:1071–2)

Eyrbyggja saga similarly attributes the decline of witchcraft to Christianity: "[þrándur stígandi] . . . was said to be a shape-changer when he was heathen but in those days people lost their power when baptized" (61:615). The reference to Christianity in the folk theory of witchcraft has more to do with ideological constraints than ignorance. Turner's argument that whereas the saga-writers are good informants they need not be "sociologically" conscious (1971:358) is therefore somewhat beside the point. Given their position in the power structure, their aim was not to produce a sociological account of witchcraft.

It is true that during the second half of the eleventh century onwards some of the clergy were much opposed to witchcraft and heathen customs. And no doubt the conversion to Christianity did have some impact. *Eiríks saga rauða* (4:523–24) tells an interesting story of a diviner, Guðríður, caught between Christianity and heathen customs. While in Greenland during a harsh winter, she is asked to use her knowledge to foretell local weather conditions. Guðríður, resists at first, saying that she is "neither a witch nor a knowledgeable woman" (*hvorki fjölkunnig né vísindakona*) and that her knowledge is of no use since she is "a Christian." She is persuaded to stage a performance and surrounded by a group of women she sings "a poem so wonderful and so well" (*svo fagurt og vel*) that no one present had heard anything like it. Her chanting is interpreted by another diviner, the news get around and, as a result, Guðríður is asked to provide her service elsewhere.

Significantly, one of those involved would not be present "while such a heathen act was performed" (*meðan slík heiðni var framin*). The Christian ethic, indeed, was backed by law. *Grágás* states that people shall abandon heathen rituals and "believe in one god" (1852, Sect. 7) and then goes on to say that attempting to use sorcery or hiring someone to do so is to be punished by temporary banishment (*fjörbaugsgarður*). The successful use of sorcery was to be met with outlawry (*skóggangur*). Much evidence indicates that in real life people bypassed the legal code with impunity. What mattered at court was less the legal principles relevant to the case than the number of allies and supporters of the parties involved. While there is clearly a conflict between two codes of conduct in the episodes from *Eiríks saga rauða*, the heathen one is hardly on the losing side. In some respects the conversion to Christianity seems to have been a matter of formality. Well into the thirteenth century many priests and bishops led a way of life, for instance in sexual matters, that had more to do with heathen customs than Christian canons. As we have seen, the saga account is morally diverse—some sorcerers and diviners are described in neutral terms, others are praised, and still others condemned. The sagas, after all, were copied in monasteries, and all the accounts of witchcraft we have witnessed would hardly have survived had those who copied the family sagas subscribed to a worldview very much opposed to heathen customs. As we shall see later on, the idea of witchcraft never fully disappeared in medieval Iceland.

If we reject an explanation for the decline of witchcraft accusations in terms of the role of law and Christian ethics, how should we explain it? I suggest an explanation in terms of radical organizational changes that Icelandic society underwent from the earlier to the later years of the Commonwealth. The apparent decline of witchcraft accusations in Iceland was a consequence of inherent contradictions in relations among chieftains and followers. Such an explanation resonates with much of what anthropologists have said about witchcraft in other contexts. As political structures change, the arrows of accusation may point in new directions, or simply become irrelevant.

It may be tempting to regard the Commonwealth as a permanent structure. After all, it seems to be sealed in the poorly-dated or undated "ethnographic present" of the sagas. Turner argues that "sagas treating of both the earlier and later periods can be regarded equally as models of and for social life as it lasted over several centuries" (1971:358). He may be partly right, but there were considerable social and political changes from the earlier to the later years of the Commonwealth. Our informants, at least, the saga writers, seem to be conscious of marked differences between the two periods for there is a stark contrast between the family sagas and the *Sturlunga saga* with respect to witchcraft. Any social system is necessarily a product of history, representing a particular moment in time. We know for sure that the Commonwealth underwent important changes before it eventually "collapsed." Not only was there important ecological and demographic change and, as a result, mounting pressure on land, access to resources was increasingly determined by the political manoeuvres and battles of competing *goðar*. According to the near contemporary *Sturlunga saga*, the battles between contesting leaders involved an ever larger number of men: no less than two thousand fought in the biggest one, at Örlygsstaðir in year 1238. To increase the number of followers, each *goði* had to maximize his fund of power at the cost of competitors. Feasts and gifts, a measure of the generosity of the *goði*, and the display of imported luxury goods, must have been an additional burden to the household, at a time of economic decline. One saga describes a large wedding feast extending through a whole week (*Sturlunga saga* 1988, 3, Chap. 17:22). The only way to meet the costs involved was to collect taxes, hire additional labor, and seek further support from followers. With the Tithe Law, the tax law enacted in 1096, the ownership of churches became an important source of wealth and power. Furthermore, slavery seems to have disappeared early, probably because recruiting freemen who had insufficient land was less costly than maintaining slaves. This meant that soon there was a reserve of labor. On one occasion, in 1208, a group of more than three hundred unemployed people, many of whom were strong and healthy, followed a travelling bishop in the hope of some sustenance.

From the beginning of the Commonwealth there was inequality. Despite the constraints of reciprocity and fairness, the idea of accumulation was always present. Sveinsson aptly describes early Commonwealth society as "aristodemocracy" (1959:49). During the later years of the Commonwealth, however, power relations became increasingly asymmetrical. Some of the *goðar* became *stórhöfðingjar* (literally, "big chieftains": more like Polynesian "chiefs" in Sahlins's characterization (1963). As a result, the bond between chieftain and followers became less personal than before. *Eyrbyggja saga* seems to compare these different political systems. As Ólason points out (1971:19–20), the struggle between the two goðar, Arnkell and Snorri, reflects the changing times. Arnkell signifies the reality of the early Commonwealth. He is a heroic fighter who mobilizes support by personal charms, and his obituary is full of praise. In his "age," competing chieftains had to establish their reputations by personal deeds. As a result, they were likely to claim responsibility for their actions. According to the saga, Arnkell was "a great loss to everybody, an expert on old lore, ..., good tempered, brave and determined" (37:584). Snorri, on the other hand, represents the reality of the chiefs during the thirteenth century. He is a clever politician who controls an army but does not fight himself. From the twelfth century onwards, especially during the Sturlung period, a few families managed to control all the *goðorð* in Iceland. Increasingly the *goðorð* became territorial units; the most powerful chiefs sought to consolidate their position, appropriating land and property on a large scale. Durrenberger suggests (1990:77), citing Fried (1967), that saga-accounts of the political development of the Commonwealth add to the general credibility of the sagas. They indicate precisely the kind of history one would expect from the ethnography and dynamics of stratified societies without states.

FROM RUNES TO BOOKS AND WITCH-HUNTS

During the seventeenth century, witchcraft once again became an important element of the social life of Icelanders. This reflected the general trend of early modern Europe. This time, however, the issue of witchcraft appeared in a somewhat different form. For one thing, written texts played an even more central role than during the Commonwealth period for both the practice and accusation of witchcraft. Also, the official reactions and the punishments were more extreme. During the sixteenth and seventeenth centuries, witchcraft manuscripts (*galdrabækur*) and "magic sheets" (*galdrablöð*), originally written or translated by learned magicians some of whom had been trained abroad, achieved widespread circulation in Iceland. Originally such texts were studied and distributed at Cathedral schools, but after the Protestant Reformation in the middle of the sixteenth century they were strictly banned. Writing or using manuscripts containing magic runes or formulas was a deadly sin. To *own* a manuscript was itself sufficient evidence of a malicious contract with the Devil.

No less than twenty one people were burnt for witchcraft between 1625 and 1685: a significant figure in a country with roughly fifty thousand inhabitants. Understandably, few of the relevant manuscripts have survived to the present day. Books of magic were too dangerous a possession and many of them were burnt with their owners. Fortunately, one important manuscript has survived: the so-called *Icelandic Book of Witchcraft*. This book, which is a disorderly collection of rather different texts, was written by three Icelanders and one Dane over a period of several years during the first half of the seventeenth century. The surviving manuscript came into the possession of a Swedish scholar in Copenhagen in 1682. It is a remarkable testimony about heathen Iceland and Catholicism in Northern Europe, a mixture of magical runes, figures, and formulas as well as Christian symbols and prayers. One example of the magic tricks mentioned in the book is the icon known as the "sun symbol" (*sóltákn*) used to locate and catch thieves by means of the powers of vision and the sun.

If *The Icelandic Book on Witchcraft* is an important source on the witches' point of view, another seventeenth-century document, the autobiographical *Píslarsaga* (Nordal 1967) of a certain Jón Magnússon, provides interesting information about the world of the accusers. Magnússon, a priest in a constituency in the isolated Western fjords, declared that one day in 1655 during a priestly visit to a neighboring farm he was attacked by a "devilish spirit." When he returned to his home he was again haunted by the Devil, and overcome by a strange, deep sleep. The priest assumed from the beginning that a relatively prosperous peasant and his son whom he had visited were responsible for his troubles, as they had quarrelled with him during his stay. He complained about their assault during a sermon and afterwards he said that the guilty expression shown on their face confirmed his charges against them. The attacks continued and the priest felt compelled to take the matter to court. The court established that a book of witchcraft and magic sheets had been discovered in the house of the accused, father and son were consequently found guilty of collaborating with the Devil and sentenced to death, half a year after the priest began his accusations. The priest received compensation (the equivalent of twenty cows) from the relatives of the convicted men for the distress he incurred and, apparently, the case was closed.

The Devil returned, however, and this time the priest accused a woman, the daughter and sister of those already sentenced, for "embodying" the Devil and continuing assaults on him. "A successful accusation," on the other hand, as Douglas emphasizes, "is one that has enough credibility for a public outcry to remove the possibility of repeating the damage" (1991:726). In the latter case, the accused managed to clear her name, with the help of her parishioners and the wife of an influential priest in a neighboring constituency. The accused woman sued the accuser for unfounded allegations and he was sentenced to pay her a fine. These cases illustrate the risky politics of seventeenth-century witchcraft and the narrow line between innocence and guilt, between life and death. In the former instance, the accused had no chance since magic texts were found in their house. In the latter, the balance of power tipped in favor of the accused. According to local rumor the priest had lost his wits and gone too far.

Commonwealth Icelanders entertained a complex set of ideas of witchcraft; about magical powers (*fjölkynngi*), multiple knowledge (*margkunnindi*), shape changing (*hamskipti*), the biting force (*bit*) of words and texts, etc. The seventeenth-century witch-hunts adapted such ideas to foreign concepts of *maleficium* and devilish acts. With the Reformation, indigenous ideas therefore aquired a new meaning, largely informed by European demonology. Most importantly, every form of magic became a sign of the Devil, in other words, "black" magic. Whereas Commonwealth society made a distinction between beneficial and evil witchcraft, presenting witchcraft as a relative matter, seventeenth-century demonology subsumed everything magical under the latter category, as immoral mischief (*fordæðuskapur*). Magical acts performed for protection or healing were no more noble or justifiable than those of the misfit and the murderer.

Thus, in 1667 a man was sentenced to death for writing magic symbols on a piece of wood for the purpose of curing a sick girl. Not only had his efforts been in vain, the girl had died after the "treatment." The man was found guilty of "worshipping the Devil" and engaging in "unlawful healing by means of runes."[10] Earlier he had been regarded as a trustworthy and knowledgeable person, always ready to lend a helping hand to neighbors in need. Now his character was radically redefined as that of a dangerous agent accountable for any kind of evil and misfortune. Although there certainly was significant continuity in Icelandic concepts of magic and witchcraft before and after the Reformation, there was an important shift in both practice and frame of reference. The witch-craze that swept over Iceland during the seventeenth century was far more diabolical in character than the "primitive" witchcraft of the early Commonwealth period, given the evidence of the family sagas. Also, witchcraft became gender-related if not gender-specific. Hastrup's assertion that "the generic term for witch in Iceland was masculine" (1990b:237) adequately describes the seventeenth century but not the early Commonwealth.

It is by no means easy to explain the form and upsurge in witchcraft accusations in seventeenth-century Iceland. In any case, a full account is beyond the scope of the present work and I shall only offer a few remarks. Hastrup has attempted to develop a "structural explanation" (1990b:247) in primarily mentalistic terms, based on cultural classification, categorical association, and "conceptual danger." Although such an account may contribute to the ethnographic description of seventeenth-century witchcraft, it only raises new questions about history and social context. Nor does Christianity on its own adequately explain the transition, as Morris implies comparing early medieval Iceland and the European continent: "The central problem is why . . . demonization of the sorceress took place on the continent and did not take place in Iceland. The answer is Christianity" (1991:2). An alternative hypothesis suggests the image of the Devil developed in response to the intensification of imperial tensions, the political economy of seventeenth-century Iceland, the Danish colonial empire, and the larger world. Much like European imperialists brought the Devil to the South American miners studied by Taussig (1980), Danish colonialists brought the idea of *maleficium* to Iceland. This is not simply a matter of implanting new ideas from abroad. In both Iceland and the New World, the idea of the Devil served to mediate temporal and imperial tensions, between the pagan past and the colonial (and Christian) present. Thus, the idea of the Devil gave expression to the needs of the oppressed in the face of alien forces, helping them to comprehend the "fetishization of commodities and devitalization of persons" (Taussig 1980:227).

The notion of the Devil also gave expression to the fears and tensions of the larger world, providing Icelanders with a means for understanding the radical Other they were confronted with as a result of sporadic foreign travel and migration. There are several seventeenth-century accounts of the travels of Icelanders in distant lands. One of the best known is that of Jón Ólafsson, who spent more than a year in India from 1623 to 1624. His account includes relatively detailed observations of indigenous rituals and customs, for example the treatment of sacred cows, and the burning of corpses (Ólafsson 1946[1661]:Chap. 17). Ólafsson's manuscript seems to have been quite popular, for there are many copies of the original version and one Danish translation. More importantly, in 1627 several hundred Icelanders were captured as slaves by North African pirates and transported to Algiers. Some wrote letters back to their families and some managed to return seven years later. At least one of them wrote a detailed description of his travels and his stay in the Arab world (Egilsson 1969[1628]). His descriptions were copied and widely read in Iceland. For seventeenth-century Icelanders, the Maghreb world became known by the term *barbarí*, derived from the name of the Berber tribe (an almost identical expression—*barbari*, from the Greek—was used to refer to all kinds of savages). Icelanders were shocked to learn of the "absurd customs" (*fáheyrða siði*, see Egilsson 1969:151) of the Arabs (the "Turks," as they called them) and to discover that fellow Icelanders were defined as *bestian* by their masters. For his consolation one of the slaves wrote, "but we know better thanks to our God" (Egilsson 1969:147). In an otherwise isolated society, preoccupied with fears of foreign powers, such accounts tended to conflate the exotic and the satanic.

It may not be legitimate to speak of a *general* witch-craze in early modern Europe (as there were significant variations in form and intensity from one region to another), but where it *did* occur the poor were usually the target of attacks. Also women tended to be the majority of the accused (the figures varied from 57%, in Aragon, to 95%, in the Bishopric of Basel; see Levack 1987:124). We also know that the association of witchcraft with women in the continental witch-craze emphasized their seductive power. While the Icelandic witch-hunts had much in common with those on the European continent, there were important differences as well between the two contexts. Differences in political economy and the imperial context may help to explain why seventeenth-century witchcraft in Iceland differed from that of contemporary Europe. Sabean's analysis (1984) of witchcraft in village life in early modern Germany is useful to illuminate both the contrast and the parallels. In German discourse, Sabean argues, witchcraft often expressed inherent tensions and hierarchies in the relations between the village and the state, "between the culture of the local community and that of the religious establishment" (1984:110). What was primarily at stake in the German witch-hunts was control over the *spoken* word, an issue that became central with the Reformation. "Just as God's Word was capable of creating the Christian with sudden force, so the words of the witch were capable of corruption with lightning speed. The witch craze of the seventeenth century can be seen as part of the dialectic between state and population . . ." (Sabean 1984:210).

The Icelandic witch-hunts similarly reflected political hierarchies and the tensions of the colonial state. On the other hand, there was a significant difference with respect to social stratification. Icelandic witches were not typically from the bottom of the social scale, a vulnerable lower class, as was the case on the continent, for those who were better off were just as likely to be accused as the poor. Also, whereas in Germany witchcraft accusations tended to draw attention to women, in Iceland female witches were in the minority. Only one woman was burnt for witchcraft compared to twenty men. Icelandic witchcraft, in contrast to that of the continent, had less to do with sexual corruption and body politics than textual power. Textual knowledge typically belonged to males, and, if anything, to the wealthy more than the poor. Outside monasteries very few women learned to write and read. Women may have engaged in the subversive practice of gossip but what mattered in the Icelandic witch-craze was the written text, not the spoken word. The authority of the state was channelled through the church (the priest) to the individual household, usually the male head of the domestic sphere, the *húsbóndi*. His authority was codified in law and reinforced when the witch-craze was over. To realize the goal of domestic discipline and moral upringing, confirmation, catechism, and individual literacy were seen to be highly important. At first, however, literacy was not aimed for the general public (an unrealistic objective, given the sparsely distributed population, the absence of general schooling, and the esoteric nature of available printed texts). The important point was to ensure that every household had at least one adult who could be trusted with reading aloud important religious texts.

It is true that Icelanders assumed, just as Christians elsewhere in Europe, that carnal lust was an important aspect of the body, particularly women's bodies. The Icelandic and Danish authorities, both state and church, took strong measures to suppress the sexual sins of women, punishing them for adultery, for seducing men, and for giving birth to illegitimate children.[11] Witchcraft, however, was mainly about something else, namely the control of knowledge and, above all, written texts. The majority of seventeenth-century witchcraft cases relate to writings of one kind or another, runes, books of witchcraft, and magic sheets. Icelandic textualism and European demonology went hand in hand.

NOTES

[1] For some examples, see Marwick 1970, Baxter 1972, Taussig 1980, Galt 1982, Douglas 1991.//
[2] See Ellis Davidson 1973.
[3] See Hastrup 1990b:239, Jochens 1992, and Bauman 1992.
[4] Much saga material in fact calls for the application of speech-act theory. Amory (1991), for instance, has analyzed violent saga-language in terms of the theories of Austin and Searle, using the sociolinguistic work of William Labov on ritual insults in contemporary America for comparison.
[5] There is a growing anthropological literature on violence and "primitive" warfare; see, for instance, Rosaldo 1980 and Haas 1990. It may be quite revealing to examine the sagas in the light of this comparative literature.
[6] See *Íslendinga sögur og þættir* 1987, III:xxii–xxiv.
[7] The case that follows has been discussed by several scholars; see, for instance, Ólason 1971, Miller 1986b, and Odner 1992.
[8] For this purpose, Örnólfur Thorsson kindly made available his data on word frequencies in the family sagas. The words searched were *fjölkynngi* (and the related expressions *fjölkunnigur, fjölkynngilega*), *seiður (seiða, seiðskratti, seiðstafur, seiðlæti, seiðmenn), galdur (galdra, galdrakona, galdramaður)* and *margkunnindi (margkunnandi, margkunnigur)*. The computer is a truly magic or *fjölkunnig* machine, discovering wrongdoers in seconds.
[9] I am grateful to Bragi Halldórsson, who helped search the computerized version of the *Sturlunga saga*.
[10] See Sæmundsson 1992:27.
[11] See Hákonardóttir 1992.

PART THREE

Lives, Texts and Modern Realities

CHAPTER SIX

Fetishized language, symbolic capital, and social identity

> Of necessity, a commodity-based society produces ... phantom objectivity, and in so doing it obscures its roots—the relations between people. This amounts to a socially instituted paradox with bewildering manifestations, the chief of which is the denial by the society's members of the social construction of reality. Another manifestation is the schizoid attitude with which the members of such a society necessarily confront the phantom objects that have been thus abstracted from social life, an attitude that shows itself to be deeply mystical. On the one hand, these abstractions are cherished as real objects akin to inert things, whereas on the other, they are thought of as animate entities with a life-force of their own akin to spirits and gods. Since these "things" have lost their original connection with social life, they apppear, paradoxically, both as inert and animate entities.
>
> Michael Taussig, *The Devil and Commodity Fetishism in South America*

The analysis presented in this chapter of the textualization of speech and culture and the relationships between language and society draws upon the theoretical insight of Marx with respect to the fetishism of commodities. The starting point is the famous formulation that relations between humans sometimes assume "the fantastic form of a relation between things ..." (Marx 1976:165). The concept of the "fetish" is somewhat problematic and it has been used in many ways, some of which are not particularly revealing. While fetishism suggests some basic cognitive processes, notably the attribution of living organisms, a fetish need not be an object at all since sometimes it is merely an abstraction which is treated as if it were a thing.[1] Language, I argue, is one such abstraction. The linguistic parallel to fetishism in the domain of things is exemplified by what Volosinov identified as "philologism," language disassociated from social life.

What is peculiar to the linguistic fetishism of Icelanders is precisely the phantom objectivity of language, the social life of words and sounds, not of things.[2] Icelandic folk philologism, I argue, allows us to study the social relations of Icelanders by looking at their language. Much as the past is sometimes inscribed in commodities—including luxurious goods and *kula*-objects—the social life of Icelanders is inscribed in speech and its cultural representations. The social relations between Icelanders assume the fantastic form of a relation between particular ways of speaking. Language appears as an autonomous figure endowed with a life of its own. Although indigenous views on language should not be represented as a unified voice, the scholarly approach which emphasizes the static, thing-like and authoritative character of Icelandic has for a long time held a hegemonic status. I examine some of the relevant writings of Icelanders, particularly the linguistic "experts," and the metaphors and assumptions of the language policy of recent decades. The folk linguistics, dominant in Iceland, assume a resemblance between particular utterances and particular social groups. Many Icelanders like to believe that inequality is minimal, that opportunities are equal, and that existing differences in terms of resources are due to personal rather than structural differences. In a situation like this, where an explicit account of class differences is unappealing if not unacceptable, but where class differences nonetheless do exist, a euphemistic theory of inequality is likely to develop. The end product of labeling particular utterances as deficient is the reproduction of social differences within the speech community. While social and economic inequalities are denied, inequality is projected onto language use.

Three kinds of evidence contradict the asocial conception of Icelandic. First, recent empirical studies demonstrate a correlation between both socioeconomic status and gender and particular aspects of language use. Contrary to prevailing assumptions, the social use of Icelandic is not, and has not been for quite some time, a "free" phenomenon. The second kind of evidence for a relationship between language and social class is provided by statements made by native linguists regarding language policy. Even though policy makers claim that nonstandard language is a property of the individual and not some particular social groups, it is clear that the lower classes are the target of their policy. Finally, ethnographic evidence and creative writings testify to speakers' growing awareness of language differences. The fact that we are able to establish statistical correlations between linguistic and social variables and that we can adduce ethnographic evidence to this effect is not a trivial matter. On the other hand, it is important to go beyond the mere discovery of empirical details regarding the social context of language to address larger theoretical concerns.

THEORETICAL REIFICATION

In Western discourse, language tends to be seen as an objective external entity, as a "thing-in-itself." During the eighteenth century, some linguists took this idea to its extreme, seriously entertaining the idea of language as being literally a natural organism. Franz Bobb argued that languages must be regarded as "organic bodies, formed in accordance with definite laws; bearing within themselves *an internal principle of life* ...."[3] Due to the impact of Darwinian theory, however, linguists discarded the organismic view of language, at least for the time being. For if the principles of natural selection applied to languages no less than organic stuff, their chances of survival had to depend on their internal properties, and linguists reasoned this was not the case. Perhaps the idea that a dead but "classic" language like Latin was just a maladaptive dinosaur in the Jurassic language park was simply too much to take.

More than anyone else, it was Saussure who established the influential idea that language is best understood as an autonomous entity. According to him, language (*langue*) is an independent system of inherent relationships. Such a position was underlined in the well known remark: "The true and unique object of linguistics is language studied in and for itself" (Saussure 1959[1916]:232). For Saussure, language is "outside the individual" for it "exists perfectly only within a collectivity" (ibid.:14), while the act of speaking (*parole*) is accidental, belonging to the individual. The individual speaker simply draws upon a collective inventory belonging to the speech community. This suggests a natural model of the speaker, analogous to the Durkheimian model of the individual. As I have argued elsewhere, there are several parallels between Saussurean theory of language and Durkheimian theory of production:

> Speaking ... is for Saussure what production is for the Durkheimians—an activity taking place in nature. In both cases autonomous, natural individuals extract what they need from the resource-base available to them. If, for Durkheimians, production is a series of isolated events in the metabolism of nature, for Saussureans speaking is a series of individual acts in the metabolism of the symbolic. (Pálsson 1991:9)

The Saussurean notion of the natural speaker was reinforced by Chomskyan linguistics. Not only has Chomsky suggested the concept of language as a "mental organ" (1980:39), in his approach speaking is reduced to the obeying of abstract cognitive rules, independent of social context. Speaking becomes "a string of words with the sound turned off" (Harris 1980:18). While the utterance may be a point of departure, it does not constitute language. It merely demonstrates the systemic properties of grammar. To apply a "natural" metaphor to language does not, however, necessarily suggest the image of an autonomous speaker. Indeed, the modern concept of ecology may well be applied to emphasize the embedded nature of language, to place language in its social context. Haugen uses the term "ecology of language" (1972:xiv) as a synonym for sociolinguistics, for the study of the interactions between language and society. The utterance is a contextual phenomenon, the product of the household of human life.

Charles Frake, Einar Haugen, Dell Hymes, William Labov and many others added an important dimension to the study of language. Collectively they challenged the narrow Chomskyan idea of grammar and the ideal speaker. Drawing upon a range of ethnographic studies of language in different contexts, pioneering the "ethnography of speaking" (Bauman and Sherzer 1989[1974]), anthropologists pointed out that communicative competence necessarily involves the ability to produce culturally acceptable utterances. Since mastery of grammatical rules is no guarantee for competence, and "correct" sentences may be totally irrelevant or out of place, the notion of grammar, they reckoned, had to be transcended so as to include culture. For this purpose, Hymes suggested the notions of "ways of speaking" and "speech economy." Undoubtedly, the ethnography of speaking has sharpened our understanding of language and its social context, particularly relationships with ethnic identity, social class, and gender.

The disembedded written word has a curious hold on the modern, western imagination. Representations of language are characterized by the fetishism of signs and sounds. Anthropology, as McLuhan suggested years ago (in a rather polemic response to anthropological critique of his *Gutenberg Galaxy*) has had its share of textualism:

> One of the more unfortunate features of the entire anthropological enterprise in the twentieth century is that its practitioners are almost entirely and unconsciously literate. They approach structures of nonliterate and oral societies with many of the expectations and patterns which they have acquired from their own literate society ... The anthropologists of our time have been extremely guilty of importing, uncritically, literate assumptions into nonliterate areas of study; of using models of perception that have no relevance to their materials. These models are constructed of literacy, visual points of view. (McLuhan, in Stearn 1967:272–3)

McLuhan's critique is even more valid now than in the past. Not only is there a tendency to focus on language but also to textualize speech, as if our utterances were visible icons or material inscriptions.

Some scholars have claimed that oral language has received too much attention, relatively speaking, in academic discourse. Thus Goody suggests that written language has been treated as "a purely derivative phenomenon" (1987:261). I suggest the opposite argument, namely that there is a tendency to think of speaking *in terms of scripts*, to treat the former as if it were a derivative of the latter. Linguists have invented an idea of language which has very little to do with the notions that most people have about their activities in their capacity as speakers: "To be able to do this, they have to 'stand back' from the current of discourse, focusing on speech *as* speech whilst the rest of us concentrate on what other people are telling us *in* their speech" (Ingold 1993c:457). The fetishism of language is, no doubt, less common in folk linguistics than among students of *foreign* languages and professional linguists. The latter, in contrast to ordinary native speakers, typically position themselves outside the flow of everyday discourse, focusing on language as an abstract, objectified system. Indigenous fetishism of language, however, has its own social logic, rooted in a colonial past, in a context of alienation and engulfing foreign threat: "One is led to take an objectified, externalized view of one's way of life that would hardly be possible if one were simply *living* it" (Keesing 1989b:33). The case of Iceland is one example.

THE ETHNOLINGUISTICS OF ICELANDERS

The reification of language in the social discourse of Icelanders, evident in the objectivist vocabulary of language policy, has partly been informed by the larger western discourse on language discussed above. Not only, however, have Icelandic views of language assimilated general theoretical constructs; more importantly, they are rooted in a specific local history, the textualist discourse of Icelanders with its ancient emphasis on sagas, manuscripts, and written texts, colonial resistance, and the social policy of the modern class system.[4] With the nationalist agenda of the independence movement, language became one of the most important, if not *the* most important, means of social identification.

Inspired by nationalist politics and rhetorics, the Icelandic school of saga studies usually emphasized the deep historical roots of the Icelandic nation. "This was a special and independent nation, with a special kind of social system, and it was quite conscious of it" (Sveinsson 1959:33). It seems, on the other hand, that the early settlers in Iceland did not identify themselves as Icelanders. Nor did they regard their language as "Icelandic."[5] The first evidence for the identification of Icelandic as a separate language is provided by *The First Grammatical Treatise*, a manuscript which provides a detailed description of Icelandic phonology, a remarkable document showing significant similarities of methods to those of modern structural linguistics. The author repeatedly refers to "our language" (*vor tunga, vort mál*) as opposed to "Danish language" (*dönsk tunga*, a term that was commonly used for "Norse language" or *norræna*). While Icelandic was identified early on, direct attempts to preserve it came much later. *Crymogea* by Arngrímur Jónsson, which is the oldest written record of linguistic purism, dates back to 1609. The author discusses the "danger" of linguistic change, the "threat" of Danish and German influence or "imitations," and the necessity of preserving the "purity" of Icelandic.[6] The main thrust, however, was Danish. In particular, the linguist Rasmus Rask (1797-1843) fostered the purist movement in Iceland. Not only was he the founder of the highly influential Icelandic Literary Society (*Hið íslenska bókmenntafélag*), he was also the key person behind the movement for the "resurrection" of the Icelandic language.

By approximately 1780 linguistic purism had become an established doctrine. Purism became a useful ideological weapon for the nationalists who argued for independence from Denmark, emphasizing the literary heritage of Icelanders, and the sagas. Not only did the sagas provide a symbol of national pride and unity, they also exemplified Icelandic language and heritage in their "purest" form. In the 1940s, new editions of the sagas using modernized Icelandic spelling caused heated debates in the country. Some of the leading intellectuals and politicians angrily asserted that modernized spelling violated the purity of Icelandic and the true spirit of the saga literature. Laxness, who was responsible for some of the new editions, was accused of "translating" the sagas to a new language, "the language spoken by the degraded part of the nation."[7] Generally, purism sought to revive "uncorrupt" Icelandic, to uproot Danish influence, and to modernize the Icelandic vocabulary. Finnbogason, one of the most influential native intellectuals of the first half of the twentieth century, compared Icelandic to a great polluted river: "During periods of thawing many brooks have joined it from far away, carrying clay and mud, but they have never succeeded in polluting the deepest channels ... gradually the dirt has sunk and disappeared" (Finnbogason 1971:82–3). In recent decades Icelanders have not worried so much about the danger of corruption from abroad, although there has been some discussion during the last years of the growing influence of English.

Icelanders continue to show great interest in their language and its purity. Their attitudes to language, as Thomas points out, are characterized by "extremist, xenophobic purism" (G. Thomas 1991:117). One element of the ethnolinguistics of Icelanders is the notion of language as an "instrument" for the enrichment of culture and the cultivation of thought. The instrument-analogy appeared, for instance, in the works of the writer Einar Benediktsson who suggested that Icelandic represented a "powerful instrument" or "weaponry" (1952[1932]:338), capable of enhancing spiritual and intellectual life. Finnbogason similarly suggested (1943:285) that Icelandic was analogous to a musical instrument—a harp. The aim of policy is to prevent the speakers from doing harm to their language. One of the policy makers has written: "Language cultivation is similar to the conservation of nature, the protection of plants and the soil ... Frankly speaking, the Icelanders are somewhat sloppy in their pronunciation" (Jónsson 1978a:4).

To some extent Icelanders have entertained the opposite idea, namely that their language is an *extension* of themselves, reflecting their spiritual characteristics. Finnbogason suggested, for instance, that the national language (the "harp") was "tuned from time to time because it is living people" (1943:285). He also implied that some of the properties of modern Icelandic reflected an "Aryan" or "Viking" spirit. Earlier, Finnbogason had invoked the "science of eugenics" to argue for the purification of the Icelandic race to preserve its spiritual and physical asset. While the "original race," he suggested, was "exceptionally good" and, fortunately, Icelanders had largely avoided "mixing with foreign blood" (1922:202), there were some signs of "racial pollution" (*kynspell*). Even worse, the law of natural selection might no longer be operating in modern society:

> Previously, nature itself took care of racial hygiene. The weakest would die and only the fittest would survive. For a long time men would not forcefully resist this natural selection; often they employed themselves the same harsh method, practicing infanticide in the case of the weak, killing criminals, castrating vagabonds, and ignoring lunatics and idiots, and, as a result, such natural outcasts would only minimally reproduce themselves. Now humanism,

medicine, and educational institutions preserve all of this as much as possible.
(Finnbogason 1922:198)

These ideas were largely informed by the Euro-American genetic discourse which foreshadowed the racial hygiene of the Nazi regime. An Icelandic physical anthropologist, Eiður Kvaran, trained in Germany between the two World Wars, developed racial ideas along these lines to suggest that the literary heritage of Icelanders had a genetic basis. Similar attitudes were expressed in German (and Italian) scholarly journals during the Second World War (see Newmeyer 1986:37). Many accounts mixed aesthetics, genetics, and nation worship, trying to identify the characteristics of a particular language with the presumed physical and spiritual properties of its speakers and to show its superiority as a medium of expression.

Another element of the ethnolinguistics of Icelanders is the belief that Icelandic is a particularly eloquent or noble language. Bishop Guðbrandur Þorláksson suggested in his book of prayers, from the sixteenth century, that Icelandic was "more honorable than many other languages."[8] Finnbogason cites (1971:87), with obvious approval, several Icelanders who have suggested that their language is particularly rich, fertile, pure, transparent, beautiful, soft, strong, and eloquent. Einar Benediktsson also remarks that the Icelandic language (or rather its history) is "perhaps more noble than that of any other nation," adding that "the greatest linguist of the world" (Rasmus Rask) placed Icelandic "on top of all languages" (1952[1932]:336). This position was motivated by a romantic image of Icelanders as a tiny nation maintaining a strong literary tradition over centuries and preserving the purity of their language in spite of extreme hardship, natural catastrophes and colonialism. Such an idea was not just an indigenous invention. It was firmly established in nineteenth century European discourse on language and national identity. In a correspondence regarding frequent complaints about the "miserable" latinization of English, Marx explains "as a consolation that the Dutch and Danes say the same thing about the German language and that the only chaps not corrupted by foreign language are the 'Icelanders'" (Marx 1979[1855]:100).

Because Icelanders have tended to see their language as a noble instrument, even above themselves, they usually represent linguistic change as a result of the internal dynamics of language itself and not the product of social or "extralinguistic" factors. Accounts of the honorific usage called *þérun* and pronominal dual are a case in point.[9] Several Icelandic scholars have commented upon the linguistic properties involved, the evidence for the change involved, their chronology and geographical distribution. None has systematically related changes in meaning and usage to social structure, even though some have remarked that honorific usage underlined the inequality between parents and children, particularly in the families of clergymen and other prominent people. This is rather surprising, since, as Haugen points out (1975:330), the pronominal dual is "ideally suited for treatment from a sociolinguistic point of view." While Haugen is slightly misinformed about the nature of Icelandic society prior to the development of honorifics (he remarks (p. 329) that there was "no class structure, only a kin structure"), he rightly insists "there must have been something special about the seventeenth century in Iceland to make *vér* and *þér* unusable as plurals." He draws attention to the analysis of the non-reciprocal power semantics of honorifics in other societies and suggests that in Iceland honorific usage developed in response to Danish colonial power and increasing stratification. In recent decades, honorifics have largely disappeared again, safe perhaps as ritual insults, analogous to the abusive forms of address described by Parkin (1980) for some other contexts.

A further element of Icelandic ethnolinguistics is the application of a primarily geographical model of variability. Students of the Icelandic language agree that there are geographically distributed variations in speech, or "dialect" differences. The existence of *social* variations in the use of Icelandic is more problematic. Most scholars have assumed that in Iceland social variations in language are negligible or even non-existent. Some have stated quite categorically that speech is not an indicator of occupation or the economic and social position of the speaker. Some foreign scholars, on the other hand, have drawn attention to "some facets of the Icelandic language which do not fit well in the picture of the language that knows of no differences between standard and substandard." Groenke hastens, however, to add that the "facts presented . . . must be seen . . . in the right proportions of their linguistic significance" and that "the 'unity of the Icelandic language' is not just an obsolescent *Schulmeinung* —it simply must be taken with the famous grain of salt" (Groenke 1966:229–30). Similarly Jones, while arguing that "substandard" Icelandic has been almost entirely neglected by serious students of the language (1964:63), gives the impression that *götumál* ("street language") only reflects the temporary predilections of teenagers in the capital, who read trash books and watch bad movies. Such an emphasis on the homogeneity of the language community is an extreme version of what Bourdieu refers to as the "illusion of linguistic communism" (1991:43).

THE LANGUAGE OF PURITY

Even though people may perceive social differences in language, they do not necessarily make much fuss about them. If people can devote full attention to the meaning of an utterance, then the form may be said to be standard for them, an established way of speakig. If attention is diverted from the meaning because it sounds "posh," then the utterance is superstandard, and if attention is diverted from the message because the utterance sounds like poor language then the form is substandard or impure. What do these terms stand for in an Icelandic context?

The confusion of *i* and *e*, and *u* and *ö* in pronunciation has frequently been cited as an example of substandard Icelandic. This is reflected in the labels attached to it, *flámæli* ("slack-jawed" or "open" speech) or *hljóðvilla* ("sound mistake"). Whatever the linguistic properties, the sound mistake clearly had strong social connotations. People whose pronunciation showed some signs of it had a particular label, *hljóðviltir* or "those with mistaken (or wild) sounds." One of the policy makers has stated that in language classes in primary schools "the correction of sound mistakes should have priority" (Halldórsson 1971a:92). In some schools in Reykjavík children were tested and subjected to particular training if their pronunciation was incorrect in this respect. Children from particular "sound-mistake-families" (*hljóðviltar fjölskyldur*) received special attention. The sound mistake was clearly a substandard phenomenon. In 1945 a member of the *Alþingi*, who was known for being *hljóðviltur*, interrupted one of his colleagues during a session in Parliament. The colleague responded by referring to the language of his opponent, saying that he should "learn to speak" and that he was a shame to Parliament.[10] What mattered was the form, not the message. The sound mistake is probably extinct by now in the language of the younger generation, in Reykjavík it is certainly very rare.

It is possible to isolate several stigmatized phonetic, morphological and syntactic features. Many of these have frequently been mentioned in popular radio programs on "everyday language." The syntactic phenomenon of dative substitution or "dative disease" (*þágufallssýki, mérun*) is particularly interesting. A frequently stigmatized version is *mér* (dat.) *hlakkar til* ("I am looking forward to"), instead of *ég* (nom.) *hlakka til*.[11] Generally, the policy makers have rejected tive substitution without attempting to account for its emergence and distribution. It is simply classified as "wrong" (Guðfinnsson 1967:60). Some regard it as a "violation of established grammatical rules" (Halldórsson 1975:197,173), others see it as a serious "deficit" belonging to the "street" (Halldórsson 1976). Á. Svavarsdóttir points out (1982:12) that expressions, which are generally known by the term "dative disease" have been used in several recent novels to underline the low social position of particular characters. In some recent translations of foreign novels, dative substitution is used as a symbol of Black English and lower class language.

The proponents of language policy in Iceland tend to use the language of purity when talking about nonstandard language. Often they express their attitudes by employing a metaphor of pathogenic organisms. Standard language is regarded as "pure" (*hreint*) language, while non-standard language is seen to be pathological or the result of some kind of contamination. Dative substitution, for instance, is usually referred to as "dative disease." The "confusion" of particular sounds, *hljóðvilla*, has even been equated with "lice living on people's heads" (Halldórsson 1978). The fact that variations in language and linguistic changes are interpreted in such terms raises an interesting question. Why is the metaphor of contamination and organic life employed in native theory of language? I suggest the language of health and purity is "good to think" in the sense that, much like totemism, it presupposes a resemblance between "two systems of differences" (Lévi-Strauss 1963:77), one linguistic and one social. Differences in language provide a convenient euphemistic metaphor for talking about social differences, about social class. A closer look at the dualistic language of purity and its application will reveal its social nature.

The opposition of the pure and healthy and the impure and contaminated is related to a series of other oppositions. One is the opposition between good and bad thought. Pure language is assumed to exhibit "clear" thinking, and impure language is assumed to represent "unclear" thought. In this scheme, there is no room for the possibility of using "good" language to express muddled thought, or using "bad" language to express clear thought. Thought and language are somehow identical:

> I am aware of the fact that a mob language, which reaches to the lowest cultural strata of society, is emerging . . . But it is important that the language and, therefore, the thought of the intellectually gifted does not become influenced by the unenlightened. (Halldórsson 1964:157)

One commentator suggests (Gylfason 1973:155) that the cultivation of language ("thinking with Icelandic") is the same as the cultivation of thought ("thinking in general").[12]

Another opposition is that of clever and stupid. Utterances which are classified as bad are not only expressions of muddled thinking, they are also a sign of intellectual inferiority:

> . . . it cannot be denied that the level of intelligence varies within the population and that the structure of Icelandic is complicated. I doubt if all Icelanders are or have ever been able to master the structure of Icelandic. (Halldórsson 1971b)

Furthermore, the civilized, mature, and the sane is contrasted with the savage, childish, and the insane. This is reflected in some of the terms used for nonstandard language: *skrílmál* ("mob language"), *málfar götunnar* ("street language"), and *húsgerska* ("the language of the back-street"). The term *villa* (in *hljóðvilla*) has the connotations of the wild, the savage, and the ignorant. Still another contrast suggests that there are two kinds of Icelanders, real ones, who speak good language and false ones who speak poor language. There are those who "know how to sing" and those who "sing out of tune." "Although everyone doesn't speak beautifully, we should not surrender. Some people can never learn to sing, but no one would think of using the worst singer as a reference . . ." (Jónsson 1978a:5).

This series of contrasts boils down to a major opposition between order and disorder. It is assumed that there are two alternative policies of language, laissez-faire and a strict public policy. The former will inevitably lead to a chronic state of language disease. Left to themselves diseases would become plagues. Only by rigidly applying the publicly "established" rules of language is it possible to bring thought and language under control and divert the danger of pollution. As some anthropologists have argued, pollution behavior often maintains some kind of order. Douglas remarks (1966:47) that if we abstract pathogenicity and hygiene from notions of dirt we are left with an old definition of dirt as "matter out of place." Similarly, the Icelandic notion of dirty talk emphasizes a contravention to order. "Deficient" language is seen as a threat to the stability and hierarchies of the school system and the labor market. This helps to explain why fishermen and laborers sometimes take pride in using stigmatized language. For them, it is both a means of deliberate subversion—a challenge, in the form of a verbal carnival, to the intelligentsia and those in power—and a means of social identification, a sign of "toughness" and belonging.

The pervasiveness of the distinction between the pure and impure is reflected in its forceful imposition of gender relations during the Second World War, when Iceland was occupied by British and American troops. Women who dated foreign soldiers were regarded as impure and contaminated, in other words, fake Icelanders. The most extreme violation of Iceland's holiness was for an Icelandic woman to bring a foreign soldier to þingvellir, the national shrine, the center of the *Althing* during the Commonwealth period, and the "real" home of the "Mountain Woman" (*Fjallkonan*), a late nineteenth-century national symbol of Germanic origin. This was a common theme in Icelandic post-war literature (Björnsdóttir 1989). The image of the Mountain Woman (see Figure 6.1), an important element of Icelandic nationalist and feminist thought, nicely captures the complex association between nature, gender, nationalism, and purity in Icelandic discourse. It emphasized the uniqueness of Icelandic history and cultural heritage, drawing upon Herderian ideas about the links between nature and culture. Icelandic language and culture were seen to be rooted in a particular natural environment, an environment different from that of the Danish colonizers. The natural forces shaping Icelandic heritage were controlled and protected by a moralizing mother-figure, the Mountain Woman. Located on the boundary between nature and culture, the Mountain Woman was the guardian of purity, of Icelandic nature, language and tradition, especially the sagas. When Vigdís Finnbogadóttir was elected as President, in 1980, such ideas surfaced once again. The maternalistic and protective notions of the Mountain Woman were symbolically embodied in her Presidency, a unifying motherly institution preventing dangerous polluting effects from abroad.

Whom does it serve to label particular utterances as impure and what are the significant social boundaries? Most policy statements are vague regarding the meaning of the terms used for those who speak nonstandard language: the "lowest cultural strata," the "mob," etc. Some, however, make it quite clear that the lower classes are

134 THE TEXTUAL LIFE OF SAVANTS

FIGURE 6.1   *The image of the "Mountain Woman"*

the target. Surprising as it may sound, the policy makers argue that language policy reduces the differences between socioeconomic categories. Clearly, the language of purity represents a middle class device. It labels expressions that come to prevail among the lower classes as deficient:

> The chief purpose of language cultivation is to *raise* those, whose mother and father's language use is deficient, above the level of their parents . . . Its purpose is . . . to teach the underprivileged a language which is considered to be superior. (Halldórsson 1971b)

This strongly suggests that the modern language of purity is one element of the ethos of cultural reproduction where people are assigned to class positions through the production and allocation of what Bourdieu (1991) calls "symbolic capital," in this case, "proper" ways of speaking and thinking. One of the policy makers states that "language cultivation . . . (represents) the morality of language. This morality is applied to . . . many other issues . . . It is expressed, for example, in civilized appearance and good manners in general" (Jónsson 1978a:14). As Donaldson (1978), Willis (1978), and many other have argued for different contexts, one can speak of the convenience of having educational failures. The class bias of language policy is also evident in the combat against foreign slang. Thus, the lexical paraphernalia of the University and the policy makers much of which is of foreign origin, for instance words denoting academic rank, i.e. *lektor*, *dósent*, and *prófessor*, has largely been left in tact while lower class slang has been systematically attacked from above. Words like *troll* (from "trawl") and *hol* or *hal* (from "haul"), popular in the everyday language of fishermen, have generally been rejected by the policy makers who insist (sometimes unsuccessfully) upon more "Icelandic" expressions.[13]

One is Icelandic to the extent that one speaks *pure* Icelandic. Some are more Icelandic than others. Icelandic society may be exceptional in its reliance on linguistic concepts for cultural reproduction. The explanation, I suggest, is to be found in the nationalist movement and its emphasis on social equality. During the first half of this century, the nationalist movement encouraged cooperation and consensus among Icelanders. As a result, Icelanders tend to minimize the differences among them. The idea of equality is one of the key values of Icelandic culture, as popular ideologies testify. Sometimes an image of equality is even projected onto the distant past, the stratified society of the Commonwealth period. Guðmundsson partly explains the unity of Icelandic in terms of the absence of social divisions in earlier times (Guðmundsson 1977). One observer (Haugen 1975) suggests a similar explanation for the relative absence of honorifics.

Because of the value bestowed upon equality among Icelanders, accounts of existing differences in terms of resources have to be formulated *implicitly* in euphemistic language. Explicit accounts are neither acceptable nor convincing.

Inequality is therefore reproduced under the cover of an individualistic ideology which suggests that people are very much different but that the differences among them have nothing to do with social structure. Even racism, strangely enough, is sometimes the consequence of egalitarianism (see Dumont 1972:51). When humans are regarded not as hierarchically ranked in various social species but as equals, the differences between them are sometimes reasserted as proceeding from somatic characteristics. Although Icelanders tend to deny the existence of inequality and language differences, they freely admit that there *are* nonstandard varieties of Icelandic and that those who use them are somehow deficient. A similar paradox characterized Swedish culture in the 1950s and 1960s, when a new ideology of classlessness replaced the aristocratic ideology of earlier decades. "On one level class differences did not exist, on another level they permeated even the most trivial details of everyday life. During this period the language of class became much more indirect and metaphorical" (Löfgren 1987:8). There are interesting parallels, too, with the elitist ethnolinguistics of modern Greece. As Herzfeld has shown, "the elite reproduced internally the pattern of domination that it both resisted and exploited externally; . . . this combination of circumstances reinforced the authority of linguistic purism and eventually made language the primary focus of all cultural debate, popular and academic alike" (1987:112).

OTHER VOICES: INDIGENOUS CRITIQUE

Most of the Icelanders cited above who have shaped or contributed to the "public" view of Icelandic are linguists and intellectuals, and it is important to keep in mind that there are other indigenous views with alternative interpretations of language and its social context. If this is the dominant scholarly view, what is the impression of the general public? Such a question invites two kinds of approaches, one quantitative and statistical, the other qualitative and ethnographic.

In a survey in 1986 a representative sample of Icelanders were asked about language use and attitudes to language (Pálsson 1987a). The results revealed some interesting aspects of the folk model of language differences. For one thing, the survey indicates that there is far more opposition to the dominant discourse of linguistic homogeneity than Icelandic linguists would like to believe. Although most Icelanders (61.3%) think there is "little or no" difference in language in terms of social class, no less than 29.9% believe there is "considerable" difference, and an additional 8.8% believe there is "very great" variability from one socioeconomic group to another. These responses turned out to be unrelated to social class, gender, and education. On the other hand, the survey indicated a statistically significant relationship with age. The younger the respondent, the more likely he or she is to emphasize the existence of differences.

In the survey just mentioned, respondents were asked about dative substitution, which case form was proper (*rétt*) in the sentence *Ég/Mig/Mér hlakkar til að fara* ("I look forward to going"). One way to explore linguistic traditionalism, the degree to which attitudes conform to established norms, is to examine variance in the responses to such a question. In this case there was a significant relationship with social class. The higher the socioeconomic position of the speaker, the more traditional the attitude. Some observers have stated quite categorically that dative substitution is simply an individual characteristic unrelated to social variables (Halldórsson 1983). The survey of 1986 also asked about the individual speech of the respondents, in particular, which case form *they* would use in the sentence "I look forward to going." The responses, it must be emphasized, do not so much represent actual usage as *reported* language, what people say about their language use. Nevertheless, the results should be informative. The survey indicates that statistically the higher the socioeconomic status of the speaker the less is the likelihood of nonstandard usage, i.e. dative and accusative. The "proper" (nominative) case form "*ég*" is far more frequent in the responses of people of upper class status than those of lower class status, or 71.7% compared to 41.6%. A recent empirical study of children's language also indicates there is a relationship between the frequency of dative substitution and social class (Svavarsdóttir, Pálsson, and Þórlindsson 1984). The latter study clearly demonstrates that dative substitution does not occur without regard to socio-economic background.

It is often difficult to reconstruct the history of language differentiation. But while data on everyday language at different points in time are rather limited, we do have some interesting information relevant for such a task. In the 1940s Björn Guðfinnsson, Professor in Modern Icelandic Language, conducted a comprehensive survey of dialect differences in pronunciation, interviewing almost all eleven to thirteen year old children in the country. Guðfinnsson's survey, based on formal reading, found "surprising differences" in language *within* the same dialect-region (Guðfinnsson 1946:128). However, although he did examine the relations between language and gender, and in that respect he was ahead of his time, he never examined the relevance of speakers' social characteristics for understanding local variation in language use. Like many of his contemporaries, both in Iceland and abroad, he seems to have regarded variations in language which could not be accounted for in terms of regional affiliation as being "free" or unrelated to social divisions. My tentative reanalysis of a representative sample of Guðfinnsson's data for Reykjavík indicates that pronunciation was in fact related to social class. Many of the children in the expanding capital had parents who had migrated from other dialect areas and, as one would expect, statistically the linguistic variables were related to the geographical background of the family. Further analysis revealed, rather surprisingly, that there was a significant relationship as well, even if a weak one, with social class and, in some cases, even when controlled for geographical background. By this evidence, admittedly a limited one, Icelandic had some signs of differentiation already before Iceland's independence.

As to the qualitative and ethnographic evidence regarding language attitudes, both my experience during recent fieldwork in a fishing community on the south-west coast and my general impression as a native speaker of Icelandic indicate that many Icelanders approach their language with far more imagination and playfulness than the dominant prescriptive linguistics would suggest. Those who fail to conform to the standards of the educational system, including the criteria for the proper use of Icelandic, need not, for instance, accept the notion of purity. Many people, as the survey of 1986 indicates, are well aware of their use of nonstandard language such as the "dative disease." It seems that the common person is much less worried about language correctness than the public view would indicate. When I interviewed fishermen, fish workers, and boat-owners and followed informal discussions during face to face interaction ashore or on the inter-boat radio during fishing, language purity was very rarely an issue. Attention was rarely diverted from the meaning for the single reason that the utterance in question was impure or poor language.

A popular autobiographical novel significantly derives its title, *Ég um mig frá mér til mín*, from a grammatical formula often associated with the struggle with case forms. The author remarks, with reference to the obsolete and alienating language policy of the post-war years, that "the soil from which the language has grown has been eroded, language remains like a heap of rubbish" (Gunnarsson 1978:56). Another recent novel partly about the predicament of lower class children in the school system comments:

> The Icelandic teacher was great. He called us 'poor ones' and those of us who had difficulties with the difference between nominative and dative trembled with fear when in class. (Haralds 1979:49)

Such views are not, however, very outspoken, nor are they combined in a full-blown, counter-theory of Icelandic. They remain a relatively silent discourse, "hidden transcripts" in Scott's sense of the term (1990). Interestingly, the survey of 1986 indicates that "linguistic insecurity," defined as the *discrepancy* between attitude and reported usage, turned out to be quite variable. Only 2.2% of those who use the standard nominative regard *another* case form as proper, whereas 9.5% of those who use accusative regard something else as proper, and no less than 23.3% of those who use the substandard dative.

The claim that modern Icelandic contains significant class and gender-based differences was first expressed in 1978, by the present writer, in a brief newspaper article, and repeated the following year in a semi-academic journal (Pálsson 1979).

This claim was hotly debated in the academia, especially among linguists, and some newspapers. One of the most influential linguists at the time observed in an international academic journal (*Word*) that

> most of those taking part in this dispute supported purism. Yet there were exceptions: a young sociologist, for example, who out of ignorance thought that there were sociolectic or professiolectic language differences in Iceland. Many linguists maintained that this was not the case .... (Halldórsson 1979:84)

"Icelandic", Halldórsson went on, "is—in the social sense—free from dialects" (ibid.:85). Some of the younger Icelandic linguists (many of whom, unlike their older colleagues, have been trained at foreign universities) readily accept the idea of class and gender-based differences in modern Icelandic. Some are even willing to reverse the current establishment evaluation of nonstandard language. Thus Rögnvaldsson argues (1983) that dative substitution may be regarded as a beneficial defense-reaction preventing more radical changes in the case-structure of Icelandic. By this view, some of the "diseases" that have plagued the language of Icelanders in recent decades are healthy signs of strength. Such a claim would not have been tolerated by the academic community one or two decades earlier.

TRANSLINGUISTICS

While for Icelanders language remains a contested issue, the center of debate is shifting. Contrary to the assumptions of many native intellectuals, modern Icelandic is not devoid of social differentiation. While appreciation of this fact is important for the ethnography of language, for the understanding of the social context of speech, Icelandic ways of speaking, and indigenous policy of language, it it essential to move beyond both descriptive sociolinguistic and the sociology of policy making and academic scholarship. To some extent, the discourse of sociolinguistics, preoccupied with correlations between linguistic and sociological "variables," is no less objectivist and normative than the public discourse on modern Icelandic. In fact, both (or perhaps one should say *all*) sides in the debates on the social aspects of modern Icelandic have been trapped within the same textual discourse, a discourse modelled on writing. Speech is merely an appendage to norms and rules (linguistic *and* social), an expanded but reified Saussurean *langue* given to the speaker in advance.

The early ethnography of speaking necessarily maintained a normative textual emphasis, not only to establish the important point that communicative competence is more complex than the advocates of autonomous linguistics normally assume but also to compel the latter to address the "extralinguistic," social factors of language.

Speaking, therefore, remained a normative exercise, the execution of abstract grammatical and cultural rules. The competent speaker draws upon a complex intuitive knowledge about social context, besides the rules of "grammar" in the narrow sense of the term. This theoretical innovation did not reverse the priority of rules over action, the description of language only became a little more complicated. The ethnography of speaking was only one aspect of a complex of related theoretical developments, one of which was the so-called "new ethnography." One of the advocates of the latter suggested that ethnography should provide descriptions of behavior which "succinctly state what one must know in order to generate culturally acceptable acts and utterances appropriate to a given socioecological context" (Frake 1980[1962]:14). Much like the notion of the culturally competent speaker, the notion of the "culturally acceptable" performance reduces the individual to an instrument of culture.

Some anthropologists took the programmatic perspective to ethnographic description quite literally. For them anthropology was an exercise in artificial intelligence, the writing (or discovery) of programs for cultural automata. Keesing, on the other hand, questioned the ability of the new ethnographers "singlehandedly to write cultural grammars of everything the 'natives' knew" at a time when artificial intelligence researchers were "beginning to write simple 'cultures' for robots with enormous difficulty" (1987:384). Given the size of the programmers' task, the writing of cultural grammar is a major methodological headache for the ethnographer. The very idea of such an exercise should give rise to theoretical concerns as well, and for informants no less than ethnographers. It might be argued that the theatrical metaphor of roles and scripts endows the actors with *some* element of creativity, in the sense that the script is necessarily interpreted in each case and, hence, performed in different ways by different actors, but the logic of the computer analogy allows no freedom at all. If culture is analogous to a silicon chip or a computer program, people have no say in what they do and they cannot behave differently. Recently, the ethnography of speaking has begun to reexamine the notion of the normative cultural context, partly from the perspective of language as a means for action.[14] Inspired by the views and vocabulary of speech-act theorists and the perspective of praxis, Frake seems to have revised his earlier notion of the culturally acceptable, adopting a notion of language as an element of action and human agency, embedded in a social context: "The ethnographer in the field, unlike the linguist in his office, cannot escape the fact that people do not just string words together in an idle game of solitaire. People mean things, intend things, and do things with words. And they accomplish these deeds in concert with other people in social situations" (1980:334).

One related current of thought draws upon the early works of the Russian philosopher and literary critic Mikhail M. Bakhtin. This approach, sometimes referred to as translinguistics, not only offers a powerful critique of the abstract objectivism of autonomous linguistics, the notion of the natural speaker, and the single-speaker-single-listener model of the ideal conversation, it also seeks to readdress the social nature of language, giving primacy to the interactive nature of speech and practical engagement. For Bakhtin, language is not an independent tool that can be freely used or discarded by the individual speaker, rather it is embedded in the stream of life, the community of speakers: language is "social throughout its entire range and in each and every of its factors, from the sound image to the furthest reaches of abstract meaning" (1981:259). This does not suggest a return to the notion of language as a collective dictionary, a "storehouse of sound images," as Saussure had it, embodied in the brains of individual speakers. Abandoning the radical separation of the individual and social, *parole* and *langue*, Bakhtin suggests that every word in language the dynamic, cumulative result of the prior experiences of the speaker and his or her interactions with the speech community: every word is "half someone else's" (ibid.:293–4). In a very real sense, then, the speaker is constitutive of social relations, immersed in a sea of collaborative practices. Such an approach, recently popularized in western scholarship, has much in common with Malinowski's notion of language as a mode of action, Wittgenstein's concept of the "language game," the social theory of pragmatism, and, of course, Volosinov's idea of language as a stream of utterances.[15] The Heideggerian perspective of "dwelling" is also representative of this increasingly commanding current of thought: once we "stop dwelling in it and listen to it as occurrent, language, ... appears to us as a stream of mere sounds ... Only dwelling in our linguistic practices reveals their sense" (Dreyfus 1991:219).

Field studies of the folk linguistics of non-western societies may help to dispel ethnocentric scholarly speculations on the nature of language and speech, providing useful ethnographic correctives. Thus, taking an ethnographic perspective, Ochs and Schieffelin have developed the argument that standard accounts of "white middle-class caregivers" of language acquisition and socialization represent just one "developmental story."[16] Comparing this story with the developmental stories of Kaluli (Papua New Guinea) and Western Samoan, they suggest, reveals striking differences. Apparently, among Kaluli and Samoans, a situation of a single speaker and a single listener, modelled on Saussurean lines, would be highly exceptional, an indication of bizarre eccentricity. For them, ideal communication necessarily involves perpetual mutual collaboration, multiple speakers and listeners. Such a view nicely resonates with Bakhtinian translinguistics.

The dominion of language and texts in western academic discourse has much to do with the development of scripturalism, the deployment of literacy in religion. The mysterious power of writing endows it with a particular prestige. Given this historical background it is not so surprising that western scholars tend to speak of language in essentialist terms and to assign it a privileged standing as the gist of culture and world making. As Henry James put it:

> All life ... comes back to the question of our speech, the medium through which we communicate with each other; for all life comes back to the question of our relations with each other. These relations are made possible, are registered, are verily constituted, by our speech.... (James 1905:10)

Many anthropologists are likely to retain James's emphasis on social relations. Much evidence, however, including ethnographic fieldwork, neurophysiological experiments, and primate research, indicates that we are well advised to reject the essentialist position of autonomous linguistics, the prison house of language, and to assume instead that language is the result of a cognitive engagement with the world, an engagement that *precedes* language.[17] Increasingly, anthropologists seem to be coming to the conclusion that the theoretical hegemony of language is ethnocentric and, therefore, untenable.

NOTES

[1] For a useful review and commentary on the use and theoretical significance of the concept of the fetish, see Ellen 1988.

[2] Some students of things and commodities have drawn attention to the objects themselves and their "social life" rather than the Maussian sociology of their transactions, adopting a "minimum level of ... methodological fetishism" (Appadurai 1986:5).

[3] Cited in Newmeyer 1986:23, emphasis added.

[4] Speaking Icelandic has been an important ethnic marker as well among Icelanders abroad, in particular among those who settled in Canada from the end of the nineteenth century onwards. The linguistic "retentiveness" among Canadian Icelanders has been attributed to "a fierce pride of national culture" (Haugen, cited in Bessason 1967:118).

[5] See Karlsson 1988 and Hastrup 1990b:76.

[6] See Jónsson 1985:96–105.

[7] See Laxness 1942:324.

[8] See Finnbogason 1971:83.

[9] In the grammar of Old Icelandic, the personal pronouns of the first and second persons had three numbers—singular, dual, and plural (*ek, vit, vér* respectively for the first person in the nominative, and *þú, þit, þér*, for the second person). From the seventeenth century onwards the old dual was usually used as a plural and the old plural only in high formal style. Nowadays, the concept *þérun* refers to the use of honorific terms of address. Apparently, Icelanders dropped the dual category later than most other Europeans. Icelanders tend to look at this change from a strictly linguistic point of view.

[10] See *Alþingistíðindi*, 1945D:371.

[11] It is typical in impersonal sentences in modern Icelandic to put the simultaneous "subject" in either accusative or dative case-form. The choice between accusative and dative used to depend on the case-government of the verb involved, and often the choice seems to be arbitrary: *mér* (dat.) *líkar* ("I like"), *mig* (acc.) *lystir* ("I like"). Recently, there have been

attempts to account linguistically for the phenomenon of dative substitution.

[12] Incidentally, such a position contradicts recent discoveries pertaining to the neurological basis of language and the autonomy of grammatical form (see Newmeyer 1986:143). It seems that the form of language exists independently of its content. If this were not the case it would be difficult to account for the fact that there are people whose syntax is fluent but who cannot convey a coherent thought, and others whose intent is obvious but cannot phrase that intent grammatically.

[13] See Halldórsson 1953.

[14] See, for instance, Duranti and Goodwin 1992.

[15] See Volosinow 1973[1929], Malinowski 1923, 1937. On Wittgenstein's idea of the "language game," see Rose 1980. A useful work on the social theory of pragmatism is Joas 1993.

[16] Citation in Duranti 1988:215.

[17] See, for instance, Ingold 1992, 1993c.

Chapter Seven

Beyond environmental Orientalism

> Humans struggle to interpret the human-environmental relationship in familiar terms, or, . . . human beings treat the environment of earth in much the same way they treat other human beings. One should therefore expect to find most of the frames of reference in the field of environmental philosophy that one finds in general humanistic scholarship . . ..
> John Bennett, *Human Ecology as Human Behavior*

This chapter discusses the application of textualist approaches in the context of environmental issues, focusing on practical knowledge, resource management, and property regimes, moving from the discourse on language and cultural identity to more mundane aspects of Icelandic nation building, namely fishing. While the dominant discourse on language explains variability in everyday speech primarily in terms of individual deficiencies at the bottom of the social scale, the discourse on fishing tends to emphasize outstanding personalities and individual efficiencies at the top. In both cases Icelanders tend to deny structural and economic inequalities, projecting difference onto the autonomous person. Whereas the language issue, as we have seen, has largely been constructed from above (by the local intelligentsia, the colonial elite, and western theoreticians) during most of the twentieth century the discourse on fishing has been developed from below, grounded in the practical knowledge and the grass-roots of Icelandic fishing communities. Recently, however, the pattern has become more complex. Discussions on fishing are increasingly textual and hegemonic, dominated by marine scientists, resource economists, state officials, and boat owners.

In this matter, Iceland follows a well-known example. In many fisheries, resource management is largely informed by professional scientists and public regulations. Such management often assumes that the extensive knowledge that fishermen have achieved, after years of practical experience, is of relatively little use. Indeed, in many cases there is very little attempt to utilize such knowledge in ecological research and in the process of decision-making. The textual position of bio-economics and resource management, typical for the modernist paradigm of science, suggests that the current crisis in many fisheries is due to their open-access nature. This paradigm tends to assume that marine ecosystems are characterized by linear relationships, that establishing the relevant ecological "facts" is a relatively straight-forward task (albeit mainly for "experts"), and that only a "market" approach, emphasizing private ownership of resources (usually privileging capital rather than labour), will ensure stewardship and responsible resource-use. I argue that while the modernist approach to environmental science assumes human responsibility, it does operate with Orientalist assumptions about the relationship between nature and society, similar to those of the irresponsible paradigm of resource exploitation which it seeks to replace, the assumptions of othering and human mastery. Thus, one may speak of "environmental Orientalism," the projection of "resource" use and management as monologic, technical enterprises.

Increasing empirical evidence and a growing body of theoretical scholarship questions those assumptions. An alternative approach abandons the radical distinction between nature and society, an historical product of the Renaissance and the Age of Discovery, and between science and practical knowledge, integrating human ecology and social theory. Such an approach sees humans as belonging to nature, engaged in situated, practical acts. Given the uncertain (if not chaotic) nature of marine ecosystems, practitioners' knowledge, knowledge gained on the spot, in the course of production, is of key importance. There are good grounds, therefore, for exploring how fishermen acquire knowledge about the ecosystem within which they operate, how their knowledge differs from that of professional biologists, and to what extent the former could be brought more systematically into the process of management for the purpose of ensuring sustainability.

If nature and social life are impossible to separate, the "textual" metaphors of irony, tragedy, comedy, and romance, may be relevant for a discussion of resource appropriation and human-environmental relations. Donham argues, following Hayden White and Northrop Frye, that even though the attempt to construct typologies with such metaphors "is bound to result in a certain crudeness, questions of rhetoric nevertheless appear to delineate . . . the manner in which all social theories proceed from particular moral assumptions" (Donham 1990:192). Such metaphors, indeed, have appeared in a wide range of fields and contexts at different points in time. One example of the extension of the metaphor of tragedy to the sphere of human-environmental relations, is the theory of the "tragedy of the commons" (Hardin 1968) which assumes a moral universe of asocial, individualistic villains who left to themselves, in the absence of both government control and the institution of private property, will inevitably drive the ecosystem beyond its sustainable limits. To render the morality of the abuse of natural resources and its impractical consequences, many scholars have found such a metaphoric extension a useful one; there has been an exponential growth in the literature on the subject. I argue, drawing upon Donham and McCay, that if we adopt a metaphor from classic rhetorics to describe human-environmental relations, the metaphor of romance is far more appropriate than the one of tragedy. The former allows for contingency, mutualism, and uncertainty, relaxing the modernist assumption of predictability and human mastery emphasized in the ecological project of sustainability.

FAST FISH AND LOOSE TALK

In many societies, fishing grounds have been appropriated by national or regional authorities which divide the total allowable catch for a season among producers, often the owners of boats. In some cases, such systems become the foundation for a property regime. The Icelandic case discussed below is one example. Before proceeding it may be useful to ask what textual claims to property entail and why they are important. Such questions seem to be pressing ones, for both practitioners and social theorists.

In his classic novel *Moby Dick*, Herman Melville addresses the issue of property by contrasting "fast" and "loose" fish:

> What is Fast Fish? Alive or dead a fish is technically fast, when it is connected with an occupied ship or boat, by any medium at all controllable by the occupant or occupants,—a mast, an oar, a nine-inch cable, a telegraph wire, or a strand of cobweb, it is all the same. Likewise a fish is technically fast when it bears a waif, or any other recognized symbol of possession; so long as the party waifing it plainly evince their ability at anytime to take it alongside, as well as their intention to do so. (Melville 1962[1851]:422)

Does a whale become fast fish as soon as the whalers invest their labor in the chase or, later on, at the moment of capture? How, exactly, do they "invest" their labor in their prey? For Melville and his fellow whalers such questions were of great importance, since sometimes after the capture of a whale the body would get loose from the ship and be retaken by a another whaler. Melville himself seems to have opted for a labor-theory of appropriation, much like the one of Locke, suggesting that one appropriates a thing by mixing ones labor with it. A whale stops being "loose" and becomes "fast" long before the moment of capture. Melville's questions concerning the ways in which title to fish is acquired may seem a silly, academic question, but the analogy of the wild animal often shows up when people have to make decisions on a nonstatutory basis about "fugitive" resources that are being appropriated for the first time. The problem continues to intrigue hunters, gatherers, and fishermen as well as students of human-environmental relations and property institutions.[1] Access to fishing is often restricted, but there remains a disagreement as to how to interpret such restrictions, in particular, how to define and account for what Melville called "fast fish."

Some scholars have attempted to apply the perspective of textualism to the issue of possession and property. Carol Rose, a legal scholar, has developed the idea that people become property-holders by making their intention to appropriate clear to others. Given such a perspective, Rose argues, a claim to property "looks like a kind of speech with the audience composed of all others who might be interested in claiming the object in question" (1985:79). "Possession as the basis of property ownership," Rose goes on, "seems to amount to something like yelling loudly enough to all who may be interested" (ibid.:81). Rose seems to think of social life in terms of the Boasian notion of autonomous individuals informed by cultural constructs. For her, a claim to title or an act of possession is a hermeneutic phenomenon, a cultural text. The speaker must make his or her intention in a "language" the audience understands. If they are to understand each other's claims and to interpret cultural artifacts, including declarations of intent and acts of possession, in the same way, speaker and audience must inhabit the same symbolic universe:

> The point... is that 'acts of possession' are, in the now fashionable term, a 'text,' and that the common law rewards the author of that text. But, as students of hermeneutics know, the clearest text may have ambiguous subtexts. In connection with the text of first possession, there are several subtexts that are especially worthy of note. One is the implication that the text will be 'read' by the relevant audience at the appropriate time. (Rose 1985:82)

Rose cites an eighteenth-century court-case about contesting claims to landed property, between an Indian tribe and the United States government, as "an example of the relativity of the 'text' of possession to the interpretive community for that text" (ibid.:87). The Indians lost the case partly because they did not "play the approved language game" (ibid.:85).

In reducing property to a consideration of symbolic systems, texts, and interpretive communities, Rose, I think, removes the issue of possession from the context of social relations. A speech-act theory that radically separates the superorganic (whether "culture" or "society") and the autonomous individual is not really about "doing," about purposeful acts or world-making, but rather about the obeying of rules. Given such a scheme, the appropriator is simply an instrument of culture. Another approach is needed which assumes human agency, responsibility, and individual sociality. Claims to property should be seen as modes of action firmly embedded in the social relations, not as a text, a "stationary rainbow" arched *over* the stream of social life (Volosinov 1973:52). Given such a model, the act of possession derives its power not from an "external," superorganic script but from the momentum of social life itself.[2]

If claims to property rights are not to be regarded as "texts," nor are they to be treated as a unified category. The property notions of the "modern" Icelandic fisherman and the "primitive" hunter are not identical. The latter's notion presupposes social obligations, sharing and reciprocity, while that of the former concept emphasizes the right to have or retain. There are basic differences as well in concepts of human-environmental relations. While in both cases a claim to possession may be based on the rule of capture, the hunter and the fisherman do not hold identical views of what "capture" is all about. In the hunter's case to kill an animal is to engage in a dialogue with an inhabitant of the same world. Thus, Inuit and Cree think of themselves as being in communion with nature, animals, and fellow humans.[3] In their view, there is no fundamental distinction between nature and society. Animals are regarded as social persons. The fisherman, in contrast, appropriates his prey in the sense of removing it *from* the natural domain, a world separated from that of humans.

While a textual approach to the issue of appropriation will not get us far, texts on property, including those of resource economists, have often been powerful instruments of appropriation. Eonomists tend to argue, emphasizing the efficient and sustainable use of resources, that privatization is the only alternative to environmental problems. The arguments for such systems are seductive in the modern world and often they effectively silence the "loose talk" of indigenous producers.[4] In several fisheries in different parts of the world, fishing stocks are being turned into private property. First, the resource is appropriated by regional or national authorities and later on the total allowable catch for a season is divided among producers, often the owners of boats. At a still later stage, such temporary privileges are turned into a marketable commodity. While in the early stages, quota systems only imitate private property rights, later on true property rights, similar to those found in western agriculture, may develop. As Scott points out, such an evolution of appropriative regimes "can be expected to continue until the owner has a share in management decisions regarding the catch; and, further still, until he has an owner's share in management of the biomass and its environment" (1989:33).

Scientific knowledge is often conceived as an "objective" representation of the external world. In reality, however, the scientific enterprise cannot be fully separated from its social environment. Thus, a scholarly model of nature and resource-use is no more a straight-forward or "factual" representation of reality, independent of the social context in which it is produced, than the "folk" models of indigenous producers. McEvoy argues, for instance, that Hardin's thesis of the tragedy of the commons represents a "mythology" of resource use, a model "in narrative form for the genesis and essence of environmental problems" (1988:214).[5] In this sense, the tragic theory of the commons is an important means for *making* history, an authoritative claim with a social force of its own, and not simply an attempt to understand the world. Indeed, the argument of the tragedy of the commons has been forcefully used by governments, companies, and individuals when pressing for fishing quotas or for leasehold or freehold rights to be granted to individuals on areas formerly used by the local community. I shall argue that the appropriative regime of Icelandic fishing has been transformed in a public discourse informed by both scientific rhetoric and class interests.

FROM COMMONS TO QUOTAS

From the time of settlement to the beginning of the twentieth century, subsistence production on the Icelandic coast included the exploitation of marine resources. In some cases, where cultivable land was plentiful, fishing was of minor importance, while in others, where good land was scarce, fishing was the mainstay of the economy. Fish formed a staple of the Icelandic diet, together with the milk of cattle and sheep and soon after the union with Norway in 1262, fish replaced woollens as the island's main export. The importance of fish for foreign powers as well as Icelanders themselves can be seen from the fact that ten cod wars have been fought on the fishing grounds around Iceland, the first one starting in 1415 when the Norwegian king charged English fishermen with "illegal" trading with Icelanders. The Icelandic peasant economy, however, always put some kind of ceiling on production. Fishing was a seasonal activity practised in conjunction with other tasks, particularly animal husbandry. Peasant fishermen had neither the motivation nor the technology to explore distant fishing grounds. Handlines, operated by one man, were the typical fishing gear. Access to foreign markets was limited because of Iceland's status as a colony. People could have invested in boats, but capital accumulation was negligible due to colonial relations and restricted markets for fish. In addition, the periodic worsening of the climate reduced the size of livestock holdings and limited opportunities for making fishing trips, leading to scarcities of food and periods of starvation. Fishing effort, then, was limited by a series of ecological, social and technical factors.

From early on, at least from the thirteenth century onwards, the pressure on land was subject to systematic collective control by the local "commune" (*hreppur*) to prevent overgrazing. The early laws of *Grágás* (compiled in the twelfth century) and later *Jónsbók* address the problem of overgrazing in fairly modern terms:

> The criterion for optimal usage of an afréttur appears to predate, with modest success, the marginal revolution in economics: the arbitrators were instructed to find the maximum number of sheep that could use the pastures without affecting the average weight of the flock—"let them find that number, which in their judgement does not give fatter sheep if reduced but also fills the afréttur," says *Grágás*. (Eggertsson 1992:433)

The ocean, on the other hand, was generally regarded as a boundless source. Rights of access to fishing nevertheless depended upon a range of factors, the occupation of coastal areas, the type of resources exploited and the method of extraction. In the old Icelandic law books, no simple clauses were applied to the resources of the sea. The early laws seem to have been developed gradually when particular conflicts demanded some sort of solution and, as a result, clear-cut definitions are often missing. The resources of the beach, however, belonged to the owner of the land. The landowner was also given privileged use-rights in relation to resources of so-called "net areas" (*netlög*), defined in terms of the depth at which a net of 20 meshes could be located. Beyond that, the rule of capture applied. If a prey was caught further out and brought ashore by boat it belonged to the hunter. Particular areas were defined as "commons" (*almenningar*) and in general they began at the point where a flattened cod could no longer be seen from land, this being the criterion used to define the "fishing limits" (*fiskhelgi*).

Collective rights did not imply ownership of unharvested resources. The resource could be claimed as property only when it had been found, as in the case of dead whales, or, in the case of hunting, when the animal had been caught. The legal clauses concerning the commons seem to have applied only to the collective "right" (*ítök*) to *use* particular resources. A look at the etymology of Icelandic concepts of property relations suggests that the Icelandic verb *eiga* (to "own" or "have") was applied in the old law not to direct ownership, but only to limited usufruct rights. But while most of the seas were conceived of as not ownable, in early Icelandic history access to the sea was often controlled by ownership of sites in the bays where boats could land. Landing a row-boat on the coast was risky, especially during the winter season, and access to the ocean therefore depended upon the availability of good landing sites. Access to the fishing grounds was largely controlled by inhibiting others from gaining access to landing sites.

During the "struggle" for independence late in the nineteenth century the leading Icelandic nationalists encouraged peasants to increase production and acquire new technology and knowledge. Such efforts encouraged innovation which thereby increased productivity of labor. However, further development would not have been possible without structural changes in the colonial economy. With the relaxation of Danish trade monopolies in 1787 Icelandic merchants replaced the Danish ones and invested in boats and fishing gear. In the nineteenth century new markets for Icelandic saltfish were developed, especially in Spain and England. Fishing villages grew and there emerged an expanding market economy. With the development of the market economy early in the twentieth century, fishing catches multiplied. Fishing became a full-time occupation and a separate economic activity, and boats and fishing gear became ever more efficient. At the same time, foreign fleets fished extensively on Icelandic fishing grounds. After independence in 1944 and the end of the Second World War, the fishing sector rapidly expanded. While the so-called "Cod Wars" with Britain and West Germany in the 1970s, during which Iceland claimed national ownership of the fishing stocks in coastal waters (within 200 miles), put an end to large-scale foreign fishing, the Icelandic fleet continued to grow.

As a result of these developments, some of the most important fishing stocks were heavily overexploited. In the expansive, competitive fishing of most of this century, Icelandic attitudes to the ocean and its resources were characterized by an aggressive stance, by environmental Orientalism. The chief criterion used for evaluating the social honour of a fishing skipper was the relative size or the volume of catch, not the relative value of what was landed. The hero of expansive fishing was the brave skipper who might risk the crew for extra tonnage, not so much fishing "by diligence" (*af lagni*) as "by force" (*af krafti*). During this period, the sea represented a gigantic, continuous mass of energy to be actively and offensively worked upon by humans, "by force"—more specifically, by daring males almost at war with the ecosystem. There was minimal recognition of either reciprocity in human-environmental relations or the need for "theoretical" ecological expertise. The aquatic world was simply a source of energy to be extracted for human purposes by the most efficient technical means.

In 1976, the Icelandic government extended the national fishing limits to 200 miles to be able to prevent overfishing of its major stocks, particularly cod. This marked the end of the last Cod War. The domestic fishing fleet, however, continued to grow and catches, relative to effort, continued to decline. The first serious limitations on the fishing effort of Icelandic boats were temporary bans on fishing on particular grounds. By 1982 politicians and interest groups were increasingly of the opinion that more radical measures would be needed to limit effort and prevent the "collapse" of the cod stock. In 1983 the total annual cod catch was even less than the amount recommended by fisheries biologists, and the forecast for 1984 was bleak. The government decided to reduce the cod catch for 1984 to 220 thousand tons, from an estimated catch of around 290 thousand tons. At the annual conference of the Fisheries Association, most interest groups were rather unexpectedly in favor of a individual boat-quota system suggested by the Union of Boat-Owners, a system that would divide this reduced catch within the industry itself on the basis of previous catches or "fishing history" (*aflareynsla*). The precise allocation of catches was debated, until it was agreed late in 1983 that each boat was to be allocated an annual quota on the basis of its average catch over the past three years. This meant that some boats would get higher quotas than the rest of the fleet, a fundamental departure from traditional policy.

The quota system has been revised several times, but with the changes in the fisheries legislation in 1990 the "experimental" period of the system had a rather formal ending: the system was extended into the distant future. Quotas became a fully marketable commodity, independent of boat ownership. Furthermore, the quota system was applied to most species of fish and every kind of fishery (with the exception of "sport fishing"). The new fisheries laws, moreover, state quite categorically that the aim of the authorities was *not* to establish private, government-protected ownership. It seems increasingly clear, however, that the new laws represent a significant step in the evolution of private property rights and that boat owners have become *de facto* owners of the fishing stocks. Thus, the tax-authorities have decided that quotas are to be reported as "property" on tax-forms and that the selling of quotas involves a form of "income." This should not be surprising, given that the economic rationale for the establishment of such systems was precisely that they would involve the establishment of property rights. Árnason, an influential Icelandic economist, suggested that "individual harvesting rights or catch quotas may constitute an adequate substitute for private property rights in fisheries. Provided such quotas are permanent, transferable and perfectly divisible they constitute true property rights . . ." (1991:410).

THE GRAND NARRATIVES OF SCIENCE

To understand the fundamental shift in fisheries management represented by the quota system, we have to look at the increasing role of textual knowledge, of fisheries science. In Iceland, some marine biological research already occurred at the beginning of the twentieth century, but full-time research started later. Fishermen and the general public regarded the first marine biologists as strange and eccentric people. The disrespect seems to have been mutual. In the beginning, the relationship between fishermen and biologists was characterised by shared ignorance. Each group tended to view the discourse of the other as entirely irrelevant. Fishermen, however, had much more say in the running of the industry than marine biologists.

The recognition of the voice of fishermen in management and law making during earlier decades, especially in the 1930's, can be illustrated by the institution of "rowing time" (*róðrartími*), the synchronization of departures in line fishing. Since the lines of each boat could stretch several miles, and different boats left the harbour at different times, competing for locations that had proved to be highly productive on the day before or the previous days, lines often got chopped and intermingled, in particular when currents were strong. Skippers sometimes tore the gear of their competitors apart, claiming that they had been the first to visit the location in question. After years of territorial arguments and rivalry, local skippers agreed that in order to prevent "chaos of lines" (*lóðaþvarg*) on the fishing grounds it was necessary to bring competition under control. The agreements which followed were meant to regulate the conduct of fishing by specifying both the point or line of departure and the timing of trips, the "rowing time." In this episode we see recognition of a common problem and a collective but informal solution that later attained the status of law. It shows the ability of fishermen to translate common interest into common rules sanctioned and enforced by the state.

With threats of overfishing, the Cod Wars, and the increased involvement of the state in the management of the industry, fishermen and biologists confronted each other, armed with their competing theories and rationalities. The growing importance of biological and economic information for resource management meant that fishermen became less powerful than before. At the public level of fisheries management, the rationality of fishermen was replaced by the more "plausible" rationality of marine scientists, a "harvesting" orientation which assumed that humans were in total control of the ecological situation. Fishermen complained that all initiative was being taken from them, that everything was "being banned," and that they were increasingly dominated by techno-scientific knowledge and the agencies of the state. From their point of view, management became increasingly the business of wise men who spoke a "strange" language. Confronted with the details of biological research, fishermen became powerless, in their words "mute" (*klumsa*). One issue in management debates involved the relative importance of emotions and rationality. Marine scientists liked to think of themselves as the "conscience of the nation," as a sensible force, essential for matching emotional and irrational impulses.

Recent campaigns of environmental and animal welfare organizations against the hunting of whales and seals have very much brought the issue of science and emotions to the fore. Several foreign organizations, including Greenpeace International, have effectively opposed the hunting of marine mammals by Icelanders with international campaigns for the boycotting of Icelandic fish products, especially in the United States and Germany. While Icelandic fishermen tend to disagree with the "conservative" prognoses of the biologists when the cod stock is concerned, in the case of whaling and sealing fishermen and scientists have tended to agree. Both groups emphasise that the marine mammals in question are not endangered species and that giving in to the pressures of the international environmentalists would invite an emotional and therefore highly-dangerous fisheries policy, surrendering to the authority of sentimental, self-appointed guardians of the ecosystem. The campaigns against Icelandic whaling were part of a larger battle which had an important legal impact on the international scene. In 1985 the International Whaling Commission imposed a ban on whaling which affected Iceland as well as other whaling nations; the only exceptions were "indigenous" groups of "subsistence" hunters in the Fourth World. Seal hunting was a significant part of the Icelandic household economy, but whaling has always been of minor economic significance. Most of the larger whales landed in Iceland in recent decades have been caught by the vessels of a single company (by capitalist producers, not "subsistence" hunters, according to the definitions of the International Whaling Commission) and, traditionally, smaller whales, including minke whales, were seldom hunted, partly because people considered them to be "good" whales protecting humans against larger and more "wicked" species. Despite the minimal economic interests involved, Icelanders would rigourously defend their right to hunt sea mammals, risking some of the foreign markets for their far more important fishing products. What mattered most were the values of independence and sovereignty, the symbolic control of Icelandic territory.

Marine biologists have been careful not to enter public debates on *how* to divide access to fishing stocks, emphasizing that their expertise only allows them to define the upper limits, the total allowable catch (TAC). This was important in order to establish the credibility and legitimacy of scientific discourse among fishermen. Given the political importance of marine biological knowledge and the close co-operation between the Ministry of Fisheries and the Marine Research Institute, a radical distinction between advice and responsibility, between science and politics, is hard to accept. The scientists have defined the terms of discourse, setting the stage for a "rationally" managed biological regime. This was evident, for instance, during one of the Cod Wars, in 1975, when the Marine Research Institute issued its "Black Report." That report which offered depressing predictions with respect to the state of the most important fishing stocks, suggesting that the fishing effort should be drastically reduced to allow for maximum sustainable yield in the future, not only had quite an impact on domestic discourse, it also provided substantial arguments in negotiations with Britain and West Germany about the extention of the fishing limits and foreign fishing within Icelandic waters.

While marine science restricted the scope of fishing operations, setting the limit of the total allowable catch for a fishing season on the basis of "precise" measurements and "informed" estimates of stock sizes and fish recruitment, the science of resource economics was to play an even more important role, providing the theoretical framework and the political rationale for a quota system, and, by extension, private property. In many ways, in fact, resource economics has replaced marine biology as the hegemonic discourse on Icelandic fishing. While the original, formal demand for the quota system came from within the fishing industry, it would hardly have been instituted if it had not been advocated by influential Icelandic economists. Not only did they play a leading role within political parties as well as on a series of important committees that designed and modified the Icelandic management regime, their writings, in newspapers, specialized magazines, and scholarly journals, paved the way for the "scientific" discourse on efficiency and the "rational" management which the quota system represents.[6] Some of the economists argued, with reference to the "tragedy of the commons" that overfishing was inevitable as long as the fishing grounds were defined as "common property," i.e. where access was free for everyone, and that the only realistic alternative—euphemistically defined as "rights based" fishing, as if rights were something new—was a system of individual transferable quotas. Assuming a sense of responsibility among the new "owners" of the resource (the quota holders) and a free transfer of quotas from less to more efficient producers, economists argued, a quota system would both encourage ecological stewardship and ensure maximum economic efficiency.

The initial quota system was largely the result of the joint efforts of boat owners and economists. Nowadays, however, there is no consensus among them, nor is there agreement in either camp about some of the most debated issues in Icelandic politics. Because of growing public awareness of the inequalities produced by the system, some basic assumptions about the allocation of fishing quotas and the privileged rights of owners of boats and capital have increasingly been reconsidered. One of the most hotly contested issues concerns resource rents, and here the most serious challenge to the dominance of the boat owners in the political arena has come from economists favoring state auctions of fishing licences. The selling of access in the form of licences on an open market, they have argued, would ensure that the rents produced by the quota system are returned to the community and distributed among the public, the real owners of fish and other national resources. This argument, on the other hand, has not received extensive public approval. For one thing, an important counter-argument has been offered by rural politicians who fear that in the future power and economic resources will be increasingly concentrated in the capital city, and, possibly, with European integration, even abroad. A fully free market, they claim, where the right to fish in Icelandic waters would be sold to the highest bidders on international markets, would mean that the trawlers of multinational companies that were expelled during the Cod Wars would be allowed to return to Icelandic waters. Another reason has to do with the rhetorical use of language in debates on management. The opponents of a free market solution (the privileged boat owners, in particular) have emphasized that selling licences would in effect represent a "resource-tax" (auðlindaskattur). This of course reflects the general dislike of taxes of all kinds and the dangers of the "socialist," authoritarian state. Why should the extraction of fish, traditionally a "free" enterprise, boat owners say, now be subject to taxation and governmental control, in an age of bankruptcies and general economic difficulties?

With the quota system, capitalist production in Icelandic fishing has been subject to stringent regulations and "scientific" control. At the same time, the discourse of fishermen has been suppressed or silenced. Indeed, one of the strong arguments for the quota system is that it obliterates the complex kind of politicking illustrated by the institutionalization of the rowing time discussed above, making it possible to circumvent local debates and everyday discourse, assuming that once the system has been instituted the machinery of the market will take care of "the rest." Several anthropologists and economists, however, have raised doubts with respect to the neoclassical preconceptions of economic theory and the general attempt to separate economics from politics, ethics, and culture, emphasizing the insufficient attention of orthodox economics to empirical realities, its individualistic biases, and its androcentric assumptions.[7] Some economists argue for an expanded, "provisioning" definition of economics, a definition that considers humans in relation to the world. "Economics", Nelson suggests, "could be about how we live in our house, the earth" (1993:33).

"PROFITEERING" AND "FEUDALISM"

The quota system in the cod fishery attempted to redress the ecological balance by dividing access among those who happened to be boat owners when the system was introduced. Leaving aside for a moment the economic and biological rationale of the system, it is important to examine the broader social implications of textual knowledge, what it means to the "house." In particular, how do people talk about the new system, how are quotas distributed, and what changes in distribution have occurred over time? In an attempt to answer such questions, I revisited the fishing communities that I worked in a couple of years before the system was established, focusing on a range of new issues, including the issue of quotas and inequality.

When the quota system was first applied there were heated debates about what to allocate and to whom. Boat owners argued for a "*catch*-quota," to be allocated to their boats, claiming that as owners of capital they alone were entitled to the rents produced by the quota system (a tacit assumption, it seems, in standard economics). A "rational" use of resources, they suggested, can only be expected as long as the ones who use them are dependent upon them as owners. Some fishermen, on the other hand, advocated an "*effort*-quota," to be allocated to skippers and crews, insisting that they were the "real" producers of wealth.[8] In fishing, they argued, value was created through the application of their expertise and labor-power and not that of capital and equipment, the boat and the fishing gear. Not only would the allocation of quotas to the owners of capital be grossly unfair, since the "best" skippers and crews would be assigned the same quota as the "bad" ones, much effort would be pure waste. Under a system of effort-quotas, in contrast, successful fishermen would be rewarded for their exceptional contribution to the economy by an extra catch.

Discussions with fishermen reveal that they continue to challenge the privileging of capital over labor. This is sometimes expressed in a radical critique of the notion of "fishing history" which defined original quota allocations on the basis of previous catches. In the words of one fisherman:

> It's a shame that quotas were only allocated to boat owners. Originally, allocations were based on "fishing history," but that history has nothing to do with companies and boat ownership. It's the men on board the boats who have created the right to fish.

One skipper similarly raised the following question:

> who has more rights concerning quotas, the man who hires crew-men, the one who finds the fish and brings the catch ashore, or the boy who inherits the boat of his father but has never been at sea?

The present debate on fisheries management, then, is not so much concerned with the technical details of quota allocation as with the larger social and political consequences of the system. The most serious criticism of the system is that it transfers immense resources into the hands of a relatively small group of people, comprised of the owners and managers of the biggest fishing companies. Many people have questioned the privileged access of the large quota-holders, the "feudal lords" or the "princes of the sea" (*sægreifar*), as the latter are frequently called. In a popular phrase from recent political campaigns, the quota system represents "the biggest theft in Icelandic history."

Not only has the quota system given permanent rights of access to an exclusive group, but this right has been turned into a marketable commodity. Many people expressed concern with increased inequality due to the concentration of quotas. One skipper who had a bigger quota at his disposal than most of his colleagues claimed that the apparently increased concentration of quotas in only a few hands was "totally unacceptable": "It scares me to think of the possibility that four or five companies might gain control of the entire national quota." With some companies holding more than they are capable or willing to fish and others with less than they actually need, some companies temporarily rent a part of their annual quota. In public discourse this is frequently referred to by a loaded and fuzzy term, "quota-profiteering" (*kvótabrask*). The standard rental price payed by the "recipients" in such transactions can be quite high, or 40% of the value of the catch. For the companies "donating" the rented quota, then, "quota-profiteering" may represent a lucrative business transaction. By renting a part of its permanent share, a company can free itself from the expenses of actually catching the fish, while still procuring much of the value of the resulting catch. This state of affairs has led many fishermen to describe the quota system in feudal terms, with the "quota-kings" (*kvótakóngar*) controlling most of the quota and profiting from renting it to "tenant" enterprises (*leigulidar*), who actually do much of the fishing. As one "tenant" skipper put it in an interview:

> we fish vigourously while fishing our own quotas. After that we end up in the tenancy-system, a system which gives us no earnings. All the profit goes to those who own the quota, the quota-kings.

In the "tenancy" system it is the "quota-kings" who make the rules; not only do they own most of the permanent quotas, they also control many of the plants that buy the catch. Thus, quoting the same skipper again: "One must give in to almost every demand. The quota-king makes all the rules, sets the price and everything."

Results obtained through ethnographic fieldwork were strengthened by statistical conclusions regarding the distribution of quotas. I constructed a data base for this purpose with detailed information on quota allocations from the beginning of the quota system, during a whole decade. It is impossible, in the present context, to go into the details of the use of the data base. These have been presented elsewhere.[9]

One simple way, however, to look at distribution and inequality in the Icelandic fishery is to examine changes in the number of quota owners. The statistics show that there have been radical changes in the total number of quota holders, a reduction from 535 to 391 (27%), from 1984 to 1994. Another measure is provided by examining the relative holdings belonging to different groups of quota holders, heuristically defined as "giants," "large" owners, "small" owners, and "dwarves" (those who own more than 1% of the total quota, 0.3–1%, 0.1–0.3%, and less than 0.1%, respectively). If quotas are changing hands, with full transferability, and the total number of quota owners is decreasing, where are the quotas going? To cut a long story short, the proportion of the quota-holdings of the "giants" has rapidly increased in only one decade, from 27.9% to 49.7%. During the same period, the proportion of the quota belonging to the "dwarves" has decreased from 12.5% to 8.7%. Thus, quotas are increasingly concentrated at the top.

We need to keep in mind that some, if not all, of the "giant" companies are owned by a large number of share-holders. One could argue, therefore, that concentrations of quotas mask a more egalitarian distribution of access and ownership. But, for one thing, it is quite possible that some individuals own shares in several different companies; thus, the distribution of ownership of quotas may be even more unequal than the raw figures on distribution indicate. Also, the distribution of holdings within the biggest companies may be very uneven, with few individuals controlling the majority of the shares. Finally, even though share-holders turned out to be more numerous than before, in actual practice a small group of managers have immense powers in their hands. They are the ones who control access to the resource, how the resource is used, what happens to the products, and how the benefits are distributed. Currently, only twenty six companies (the "giants") own about half of the national cod quota.

As we have seen, with the growing importance of the science of fisheries biology and the establishment of a quota system based on economic theorizing, a highly modernist management regime has been instituted in Iceland; a regime that reverses the roles of laypersons and scientific expertise. Some humans, it is assumed, are able to bring nature and the rest of humanity under control. This regime generates increasing unrest. Significantly, fishermen went on a national strike in January 1994, protesting against "quota-profiteering" and the "tenancy" system, leading to a two-week stand-still in the fishing industry. The government put an end to the strike by passing temporary laws to force the fishermen back to work. The statistical results summarized above, concerning the distribution of quotas, were presented in a few newspaper articles, co-authored with Agnar Helgason, one of which was published at the time of the fishermen's strike. We argued that in focusing on economic efficiency, economists, policy makers, and fisheries managers generally failed to consider issues of equity and distribution, issues of great concern to the general public. Interestingly, some economists challenged our arguments by suggesting that our position was situated in public protest and that we were guilty of using value laden terms, the feudal metaphors that kept appearing during fieldwork and interviews. While efficiency was a legitimate subject, deserving full attention, "inequality" and "feudalism" were questionable "ethical" concepts beyond modernist reasoning and the proper vocabulary of serious academics.

The main stated objective of the quota system was to control the total annual catch of the most important species (cod, in particular) and to make fishing more economical. While the cost side of the economic equation may have been reduced, there has been little success as regards the ecological objective. According to biological estimates, the cod stock is still overexploited and stock recruitment is poor year after year. During the last years, some skippers have even had difficulties in catching what they have been entitled to, always considered too small. Sometimes they have given up mid season because there has been "too little fish" relative to fishing effort. The proportion of immature cod in the reported catch has been increasing and yet, under the present system, fishermen tend to dump immature fish, as well as low-price species and excess catch for which they have no quota. Recent surveys indicate that great quantities of dead fish are dumped into the sea during fishing operations, and much greater than Icelanders generally like to believe. Illegitimate discarding of fish creates many problems in relation to the policing of the seas. To make sure that all the catch is landed is both expensive and technically difficult. Alternative management schemes continue to be actively discussed by fishermen, politicians, and the general public. There are demands for a return to the prior system of temporal closure of particular fishing areas. Such a development, however, is unlikely, given the inadequacies in economic and ecological terms of the previous system. There are also demands for communal quotas where local authorities would be given a certain amount of autonomy as regards the allocation of quotas in their areas, a limited revival of the grass roots politics of earlier decades. Similar debates are taking place in many other fisheries beside the Icelandic one, including those of Norway, the Faroe Isles, Canada, and the United States.

The history of the quota system in the Icelandic cod fishery indicates some of the potential political implications of a narrowly technical or "scientific" approach to the problem of management, even in a relatively democratic system. A discriminatory but seemingly fair and neutral policy has been adopted. The fear of environmental disaster has not so much resulted in successful attempts to redress the ecological balance; rather it has instituted a policy which radically alters the balance amongst social groups. No doubt, analyses that present the politics of advanced capitalist states as automatic, functional responses to "class" interest often fail to deal with the complexities of particular historical realities. This is not to say that social discourse is immune to capitalist interests and that class politics are irrelevant for the understanding of state policies; only to allow for important contextual differences in forms of discourse and the function and design of institutional structures. In the Icelandic fishery, a small and well-defined class has managed to appropriate a highly important national resource for themselves, through skilful lobbying *vis-à-vis* the state, intervention in party politics, and firm control of public discourse.

The rhetorical metaphor of irony may be pertinent to capture the problems of the Icelandic quota system and scientific management. While the managers naïvely expect to be solving all the major problems they face, the results of their "solutions" allow no optimism after a whole decade of experimentation. Moreover, in the process they have generated a huge problem of inequality, ethics, and political unrest. To act in terms of concepts and theories that have such unintended consequences is, indeed, rather ironic.

PRACTICAL KNOWLEDGE

The relative failure of the quota system and scientific management of recent years to deliver the goods they promised and the severe social and ethical problems of inequality they have raised, suggest that it may be wise to look for alternative management schemes emphasizing the practical knowledge of the fishing industry, in particular the people who are directly engaged with the ecosystem. In Icelandic fisheries management, there is very little attempt to utilize the knowledge that skippers have acquired in the course of fishing, although there are some signs of change in this respect. Skippers frequently complain that marine biologists tend to treat them "as idiots," reducing practical knowledge and local discourse to mere trivia, and that despite all the talk of "collaboration" (*samráð*) there is no real dialogue between fishermen and marine biologists. Those who have come to know the fishing grounds around Iceland, during a lifelong career in fishing, they say, must remain silent when the "wise men" (*spekingar*) announce their precise measurements of the stocks. One reason for the lack of collaboration is the fundamental difference between the knowledge of biologists and fishermen; the former is largely normative and textual, preoccupied with theoretical ways of knowing, while the latter, often tacit, is tuned to practical realities in the ever-changing sea.

The contrast between the approaches of skippers and biologists is nicely illustrated by the so-called "trawling rally" (*togararall*), introduced a few years ago by biologists at the Marine Research Institute, and skippers comments upon it. In an attempt to bridge the gap between science and practical knowledge and to use the latter to supply detailed ecological information on the state of the seas and the fishing stocks, the Institute hires a group of skippers to regularly fish along the same, pre-given trawling paths on their own vessels. Such efforts are not only diplomatic endeavours to reduce the tension between biologists and fishermen and to improve the image of the Institute. No doubt, the trawling rally yields much information that the biologists could not possibly gain otherwise, given the few research vessels at their disposal and their limited funding. Skippers, however, frequently point out that, fixed to the same paths year after year, the rally fails to respond to fluctuations in the ecosystem, providing unreliable estimates. Also, the reliance on trawling is likely to produce biased results, for often those fishing with gill nets on nearby grounds offer a very different picture. From the skippers' point of view, a more dynamic and holistic approach, allowing for different kinds of fishing gear and greater flexibility in time and space, would make more sense. Indeed, skippers discuss their own strategies in such terms, emphasizing constant experimentation in the flux and momentum of fishing, the role of "perpetual engagement" (*að vera í stanslausu sambandi*), and the importance of "hunches" (*stuð*), intuition and tacit knowledge.

Generally, both marine scientists and economists have presented the coastal ecosystem as a predictable, domesticated domain. While they may qualify their analyses and predictions with reference to some degree of uncertainty, the "margin of error," they often act as if that margin is immaterial. Fishermen question their basic assumptions, arguing that knowledge of fish migrations is still very small. Knowledge of the ecosystem, they claim, is too imperfect for making reliable forecasts. "Erecting an ivory tower around themselves," one skipper argued, "biologists are somewhat removed from the field of action; they are too dependent on the book." Like their colleagues in other parts of the world, biologists have usually focused on one species at a time, modelling recruitment, growth rates, and stock sizes, although recently they have paid increasing attention to analyses of interactions in "multi-species" fisheries. This means that fisheries policy is often literal and rigid in form, unable to respond to changes in the ecosystem. It is understandable that skippers, aware of the discrepancy between reality and the "pessimistic" forecasts of the past (the predictions of the "Black Report," in particular, turned out to be off the mark), fail to be impressed with the rhetoric of the scientists.

Elsewhere I have argued, emphasizing the theory of practice which focuses on whole persons, master-apprentice relations, and the wider community to which they belong, that skippers' extensive knowledge of the ecosystem within which they operate is the result of years of practical enskilment, the collective product of a community of practice.[10] Formal schooling is essential for skippers, but they all seem to agree that most of their learning takes place "outdoors," in the course of fishing. This is emphasized by frequent remarks about the "bookish," "academic" learning of those who have never "had a pee in a salty sea" (*migið í saltan sjó*). It is largely in the role of an apprentice at sea that the novice skipper (the mate) learns to attend to the environment as a skipper. Working under the guidance of a skipper gives the novice the opportunity to develop self-confidence, and to establish skills at fishing. The role of the mate institutionalizes a form of apprenticeship that allows for protection, experimentation, and varying degrees of skill and responsibility. This is not a one-way transfer of knowledge as the skipper frequently learns from the co-operation of the mate; mate and skipper—in fact, the whole crew—educate each other.

Much evidence indicates that a multi-species coastal ecosystem like the Icelandic one is highly unpredictable, with constant fluctuations in interactions among species and between species and their habitat. If this is the case, those who are directly involved in resource-use on a daily basis are likely to have the most reliable information as to what goes on in the sea at any particular point in time. It is essential, therefore, to pay attention to the practical knowledge of skippers, allowing for contingency and extreme fluctuations in the ecosystem. Such arguments have recently been developed in the scholarly literature on fisheries management. Wilson and his associates suggest, for instance, that the "numerical" approach of current resource economics and marine biology, emphasizing linear relationships and states of equilibrium, fails to account for the "chaotic" aspects of many fisheries. Their empirical work shows that while fisheries are deterministic systems, because of their extreme sensitivity to "initial conditions" even simple fish communities have no equilibrium tendency. As a result, management faces forbidding problems when trying to explain the noise in ecological relationships, for example the relationship between recruitment and stock size, often a key issue for managers: "the degree of accuracy and the completeness of knowledge required for prediction are far beyond any capabilities we might expect to achieve in a fisheries environment" (Wilson et al. 1994: 296). Therefore, it becomes impossible to know the outcomes of management actions such as quotas. It does not mean that governance is impossible; it suggests, however, a finer spatial and temporal scale, a scale that only the skilful practitioner is able to apply. Self-governance in fishing may be a practical necessity, strange as it may sound to those accustomed to the notion of environmental Orientalism implicit in the theory of the "tragedy of the commons." In some fisheries, including the lobster fishery of Maine in the United States, fishermen have an important role to play in fisheries management. The relations of power between local fishermen and experts in marine biology typical for many fisheries in the western world seem to be reversed.

I have argued for the importance of practical knowledge and for decentering the study of learning and human action. Such a perspective, I think, provides a useful antidote to both the practical project of modernist management and the theoretical project of Cartesian dualism. The proper unit of analysis is no longer the autonomous "expert" but rather the whole person in action. Learning by doing, as Harper remarks for a mechanic in a small shop, entails the development of "working knowledge," a fine kinesthetic sense that "infuses" all of the work. "Married to the knowledge of materials, it produces a working knowledge that stands in stark contrast to the working knowledge produced by formal education" (Harper 1987:131-2). This is precisely the kind of skill attributed to Pastor Jón Primus in Laxness's novel *Christianity at Glacier* discussed earlier. The priest applies his diverse skills with ease and patience, he "can do everything" (1972:41), "such an excellent man to have near the road, always ready to shoe a horse at any time of the day or night, a veritable artist at patching up people's worn-out engines so that everything goes again like new" (ibid.:13-14). When confronted with theological questions about the Creator and the universe, Pastor Jón himself responds with a down-to-earth reference to the routine tasks of everyday life: "Primuses are repaired here" (ibid.:144). Pastor Jón is a wise person well tuned to the issues of the practical world. For him, the practical is more important than anything else.[11]

Much of the scholarly discussion of resource use, fisheries management and property claims, both in Iceland and elsewhere, hinges on what is meant by terms such as "individual." Among students of European history, there is a tendency to adopt fairly recent definitions, viewing such concepts "through a nineteenth-century —that is, bourgeois—lens, defining them as essences rather than relations" (Roseberry 1991:21). Williams points out that the term "individual" originally meant "indivisible," that which cannot be divided, like the unity of the Trinity. The change in meaning, he suggests, the adoption of the modern meaning emphasizing *distinction* from others, "is a record in language of an extraordinary social and political history" (1976:133). The concept of the "commons" has been through a similar treatment. While in medieval Europe it was associated with "community property subject to community control" (Hanna 1990:159), nowadays it is frequently associated with "tragedies" and "open access."

The relationship between nature and society is another thorny issue in both environmental debates and social theory. On the one hand, westerners increasingly think of themselves as situated *in* nature. Interestingly, a critical commentary on the idea of "sustainability," focusing on the history of fisheries management, suggests that it may be "more appropriate to think of resources as managing humans than the converse" (Ludwig, Hilborn, and Walters 1993:17). Guðmundsson's powerful image of the "Mountain," reproduced on the cover of this book and in Figure 1.2, captures the modern sense of belonging to the ecosystem, emphasizing the unity of the natural and the social. Humans are an integral part of a larger context, a context that allows no radical distinction between *habitus* and habitat. While such an idea has probably always been around in Iceland in one form or another, it has usually been suppressed in modernist, public discourse. Pre-Renaissance thought similarly emphasized the interrelatedness of nature and society, the "individual" nature of human life, in the original, unified sense of the term. As Gurevich shows, in medieval societies "man thought of himself as an integral part of the world ... His interrelation with nature was so intensive and thorough that he could not look at it from without; he was inside it" (1992:297). In the modern (or "postmodern") view, humans have a particular responsibility to meet, not only to other humans but also to members of other species, fellow inhabitants of the animal kingdom, and the ecosystem of the globe. Some of the key issues of current environmental discussion focus around ethical questions, on human responsibility.

On the other hand, the inhabitants of the industrialized world often continue to present themselves as masters of their environments, as godly beings *removed* from nature. We need not elaborate on the tragic consequences of this anthropocentric and expansionist world-view. In line with this reasoning, we tend to project an image of the "management" of the environment as a technical, a-political enterprise (the rational application of mathematical equations independent of social discourse) assuming at the same time that the optimum use of resource-bases necessitates that they are parcelled up and privatized. Some scientific communities stubbornly stick to Baconian notions of scientific method and the domination of nature. Economists, biologists, and policy makers often remain firmly committed to a positivist and modernist stance, curiously innocent of recent developments in social theory, presenting themselves as detached observers, as pure analysts of the economic and material world. A pertinent example of this kind of scientism in the discourse on resource management is the preoccupation with individual transferable quotas and the market and the suppression of the issue of inequality and social distribution, an issue frequently pushed to the margin in economic thought.

One avenue out of the modernist project and current environmental dilemmas is to reject the radical separation of nature and society, object and subject, and the notions of certainty and monologue. This is not to return to the medieval world but rather to emphasize contingency, dwelling, and dialogue—in Dewey's words (1958[1929]: 295), "to restore connectedness and unity." The need to develop an "ecological" theory along such lines, an approach that fully integrates human ecology and social theory, is often recognized nowadays. Unfortunately, the ecological theory that informs radical environmentalism, including the animal rights movement, tends to reproduce the distinction rather than resolve it. While the concern with the welfare of animals represents charitable motives, it has much in common with the ethnocentric discourse of the colonial past. Trapped in objectivist, western discourse on science and the Other, animal rights activists make a fundamental distinction between "them" (indigenous hunters) and "us" (Euro-Americans), nature and society, animals and humans. Humans, however, whatever their mode of production or subsistence, are simultaneously part of nature and society. Modern policy on animal rights and the environment should be based on *that* premise, and not on the idea that humanity, or some part of it, is suspended above nature. The outline of such a theory was proposed early on in the writings of the young Marx who insisted that humans could not be separated from nature, and, conversely, that nature could not be separated from humans: nature, he argued, "taken abstractly, for itself—nature fixed in isolation from man—is *nothing* for man" (1961[1844]: 169).

Discourses on the natural environment, translation, and ethnographic practice have much in common, including the "textual" language of rhetorics and theatre —the metaphors of comedy, tragedy, and romance. If people are aware of the ecological consequence of their actions and they seek to organize themselves to redress the "balance," the metaphor of the comic plot may seem an appropriate one. The metaphor of comedy has, in fact, been used by several scholars to draw attention to the potential of collective action for corrective environmental purposes, to capture the narrative style of anti-Hardinian, economistic approaches to the question of the commons, including those informed by game theory. While such approaches represent an important shift in economistic assumptions about human nature, the comic plot is still modernist in the sense that it fails to seriously address the larger contexts of history, power, and culture. Given the contingent (if not chaotic) nature of social life, the overly optimistic plot of comedy is hardly the appropriate theatrical metaphor for capturing the human condition, nor is the excessively pessimistic plot of tragedy a convincing one. The members of the human household are not simply greedy "Robinsonades" (to borrow a Marxian label) who inevitably destroy the systems of which they are a part, nor are they necessarily able to work in harmony for a well-defined common good. McCay suggests the metaphor of romance: "In romance, conflict drives the narrative and is not overcome in the manner of neoclassical analyses. . . . Romance implies . . . complex development of character, situation, and plot and hinges upon the tension of not knowing what the outcome will be, but hoping for the best" (1993:22). "As a literary metaphor," she goes on, "it comes closer to the anthropological endeavor." Such a metaphor seems, indeed, a befitting one for describing the essence of what I referred to earlier as the "living discourse," allowing for some degree of future hope, in a world with contesting perspectives, conflicting interests, and unexpected turns.

NOTES

[1] See, for instance, Rose 1985 and McEvoy 1988.
[2] Adopting a constitutive model of the person, I have argued elsewhere (Pálsson 1991), allows one to locate the roots of title and possession in the community of persons.
[3] See Wenzel 1991.
[4] See, for example, Neher et al. 1989.
[5] See also McCay and Acheson 1987 and Hanna 1990.
[6] The economic arguments are summarized in some of the articles in Helgason and Jónsson 1990.

[7] See, for instance, McCloskey 1985, Marglin 1990, Dilley 1992, Gudeman 1992, Nelson 1992, and England 1993.

[8] The authorities temporarily conceded to such criticism when revising the regulatory framework of the quota system in 1985. Boat owners were offered the right to choose between effort and catch.

[9] See Pálsson and Helgason 1994. The technical work on the construction and statistical use of the data base (the "Quota base") is largely that of Agnar Helgason. The basic unit applied in our calculations, and the one that is used in all quota allocations, is that of "cod equivalents" (*þorskígildi*). A boat owner may have access to several species with different market values (cod, haddock, saith, etc.), but the overall size of each individual quota is measured in terms of a single unit, cod equivalents.

[10] See Pálsson 1994a.

[11] To the extent that one may regard Jón Primus as a philosopher, his attitude echoes the pragmatism of, say, John Dewey and Richard Rorty (see, for example, Joas 1993). Jón Primus has much in common with the heroes of Veblen's *The Instinct of Workmanship* (1964[1941]), Polanyi's *Personal Knowledge* (1958), and Pirsig's *Zen and the Art of Motorcycle Maintenance* (1974).

CHAPTER EIGHT

Conclusions: towards a theory of living discourse

> Undue participation of the subject in the object is never more evident than in the case of the primitivist participation of the bewitched or mystic anthropologist, which, like populist immersion, still plays on the objective distance from the object to play the game as a game while waiting to leave it in order to tell it.
>
> Pierre Bourdieu, *The Logic of Practice*

The discussion in earlier chapters of social theory and Icelandic ethnography has focused, in one way or another, on the relevance of texts and textualism for the comparative project of anthropology. The nature of the fieldwork encounter and anthropological representation generally are obviously highly pertinent issues in this context. How we bring life into text, I have argued, depends upon our relations with our hosts. Ethnographies are not only informative with respect to the societies they reportedly describe, they often provide much information on ethnographers as well. In concluding, two general themes discussed in previous chapters need to be developed: the relative importance of monologues and dialogues for the anthropological enterprise and the limits of the textual approach to social life and cultural boundaries.

MONOLOGUES AND DIALOGUES

Summarizing some of the arguments developed in earlier chapters, we may distinguish three modes of anthropological representation, each of which is characterized by particular relations of ethnographic production. One approach, that of the colonizers or Orientalists, typically employs the vocabulary of objectivism and universalism. This approach has much in common with the patriarchal discourse of literary translation, emphasizing aggressive appropriation, the "penetration" of texts. In both cases, "translation" is represented as a one-way street. The power-laden Orientalist encounter is nicely illustrated by the "ethnographic" journey of the Bishop's emissary (Embi) in the novel *Christianity at Glacier*. The main problem with the Orientalist approach is the detached stance it takes with respect to the object of study, the epistemological and social break it assumes with action and the world. Just as psychologists "conduct" experiments with their subjects in their laboratories, anthropologists "observe" their natives in the field. Some indigenous voices are silenced, others tend to be mystified, distorted, and objectified. Objectivism, as

Bourdieu remarks, is a viewpoint "taken from high positions in the social structure" (1990:52). Given that anthropology was the offspring of colonialism, the predominance of the objectivist and Orientalist extends over a long period in the history of the discipline.

Another and more recent approach to anthropological representation emphasizes subjectivism, reflexivity, and relativism. This is the approach advocated by the textualist, the linguistic turn. Although, at first glance, the reduction of all difference to culture and text suggests a reversal of the relations of ethnographic production characteristic of the colonial mode (the apparent replacing of dominance with submission), on closer inspection the Orientalist and the textualist turn out to have much in common. Stretching the limits of a discourse already saturated with labels, one may say that just as colonialism was replaced with neo-colonialism, with new relations of dependency, Orientalism was replaced with neo-Orientalist ethnography. In the neo-Orientalist fashion, the anthropologist tends to essentialize his or her informants, disempowering and "canonizing" their voices, refusing them the right to speak.[1] Some examples which have a bearing on the ethnography of Iceland are provided by the works of Kirsten Hastrup. Her works on ethnography and modern Iceland, as we have seen, tend to emphasize cultural boundaries, ethnographic privileges, and the inherent "violence" of fieldwork.

Both approaches mentioned so far assume a hierarchy of power relations and a rigid division of "academic" labor. The arrogant position of privilege and superiority taken by both Orientalist and neo-Orientalist ethnographers—informed by the rhetoric of modernism and postmodernism, respectively—is not based on any logical grounds; rather it is constitutive of the same relations of power and dependency as the larger world. Keeping in mind the inadequacies of both of these approaches, it is important to search for other possibilities. One emerging, alternative approach may be called the mode of the "living discourse." In this case, anthropologists engage themselves in a serious ethnographic dialogue with the people they visit, forming an intimate rapport or communion and representing the experience as a moment in the stream of life, not as sundered pieces of text. In fact, an emphasis on symmetry and mutualism, the living discourse, is far more appropriate than the discourse on mastery and control dominant in the past, given the present intellectual climate. Most importantly, ethnographic authority is increasingly being challenged and on several fronts, among both natives and anthropologists. While the triad of colonization, textualization and living discourse is a rather simplistic formulation, such a scheme promotes appreciation of the role of power and asymmetry in fieldwork and anthropological practice generally.

A good example of the mutualism of the ethnographic mode I have identified as the living discourse is the work of Gudeman and Rivera on Colombia, a work that underlines the need for expanding the "community of modellers" (1990:190).[2] For them, to engage in fieldwork is to participate in a continuous conversation that allows no boundaries in either time and space, extending from the distant past to the present and from the local community to the larger world. Fieldwork, Gudeman and Rivera emphasise (1995), is a cooperative enterprise; the anthropologist does not produce his or her ethnography in contemplative isolation but in the company of others, *with* a responding people. Their work, significantly a joint venture of a foreign and native anthropologist, refuses to acknowledge the persistent anthropological dualism of inside and outside, native and observer, and the hierarchy of knowing which it inevitably suggests. This is post-Orientalist scholarship, an egalitarian discourse that presents anthropologists and their hosts as the inhabitants of a single world, engaged in a meaningful, reciprocal enterprise, having a "good conversation." It seems important to explore the potential of such an approach, to move from the genre of the ethnographic autobiography to the notion of fieldwork as a cooperative enterprise, rejecting any fundamental distinction between experts and laypersons. In earlier chapters, I have outlined the implications of the living discourse with respect to the ethnographic encounter and the study of language and practical knowledge.

Fieldwork has often been likened to apprenticeship. "The relationship between informant and anthropologist," Bourdieu remarks, "is somewhat analogous to a pedagogical relationship, in which the master must bring to the state of explicitness, for the purpose of transmission, the unconscious schemes of his practice" (1977:18). When in the field, anthropologists usually see themselves as apprentices and their "informants" as their mentors, but often the relations seem reversed. Not only do our tutors (our hosts) sometimes symbolically reverse the status relationship, for instance by means of hospitality (see, for example, Herzfeld 1987:21, 40); more importantly, as the anthropologist returns, the actual roles are sometimes inverted, as if the act of writing *up* necessarily presupposed privileged access to the "grammar" of the native world. The novice anthropologist finally becomes the tutor. The journey back to the academic base signifies a rite of passage during which the anthropologist experiences a transformation of his or her role.

The ambivalence of current views of the role of mutualism and dialogue in ethnographic practice is reflected in the image of the native. On the one hand, anthropologists tend to regard the native as not only their chief source of cultural wisdom, on which their writings inevitably depend, but also as an important collaborative or reflexive check on the authenticity of their results. The development of native anthropologists is often seen as a positive sign on the assumption that they are strategically located on the borderland between "us" and "them," providing undiluted access to indigenous realities, a "correct" translation. On the other hand, natives, whether anthropologists or not, are frequently marginalized in anthropological discourse, isolated in their ethnographic bantustans. As Knowlton points out, "It is easier to keep the 'native' safely in our notes or at the end of a journey, rather than among us. Thus we avoid having our caricatures challenged and our categories confused in the messiness of solidary sociality" (1992:78). Such a position grants us the licence and the freedom to associate particular themes with the places we study. In the Icelandic context, such a thematic association is probably best represented by the issue of kinship.[3] Recently, Pinson has argued that the notion of lineage (*ætt*) is "the key to the Icelandic psyche" (1979:189), that the kinship system structures most social relationships, and that "friendship . . . is virtually nonexistent in Iceland" (191). Much evidence indicates, however, that references to kinship relations are opportunistically selected from a large repertoire of Icelandic terms and, moreover, there is ample confirmation of the importance of friendship in modern Iceland. Ironically, Pinson contradicts her own thesis about the absence of friendship in an article which elaborates on the importance of "the institution of friendship" associated with drinking patterns (1985:75). Pinson's thesis about the absence of friendship may have less to do with the realities of Icelandic ethnography than her tacit acceptance of the theoretical hegemony of kinship in anthropological discourse, the analogy to the Bishop's agenda in *Christianity*. Rich remarks that the moment has arrived for the contribution of native scholars to Icelandic kinship studies. Such a contribution, he suggests, at "a moment when the concensus about Icelandic kinship is shifting," might tell us "whether the apparent complexity and latent contrasts in the system are a product of the systematizing gaze of anthropology, a product of Icelandic history and culture, or an apparition" (1989:76–77).

Now, the argument may be developed that the ethnographic notion of "the living discourse" is both anarchist and utopian. Some of the charges levelled against Habermas's notion of "the ideal speech situation" (a "speech situation that is immune to repression and inequality" (1990:85)) may be relevant here as they reflect similar concerns. Benhabib provides a useful summary, drawing attention to the irrelevance of Habermas's discourse ethics in the world of politics:

> Imagine conducting a practical discourse on matters of international relations, state security, maybe even banking and fiscal policy under the constraints of an ideal speech situation! The strategic and instrumental relation of the parties to each other is so fundamentally constitutive of these macroinstitutions of political life that the kind of moralistic utopianism advocated by partisans of discourse ethics, so argues the political realist, would only result in confusion and insecurity. (1990:352)

Critics of Habermas also point out that his approach ignores the fact that dialogues are historically situated and necessarily rooted in power structures.[4] After all, isn't some degree of asymmetry necessary? Isn't the tutor, for example, necessarily on "higher ground" as Vygotsky suggested, emphasizing that "the only 'good learning' is that which is in advance of development" (Vygotsky, cited in Bruner 1986:73)? If we are to believe Aristotle and his followers, young children are simply too irrational to be allowed to participate in sound pedagogical dialogue. Inevitably, perhaps, the contracts that come to prevail in the encounters between ethnographers and their hosts are shaped by established relations of power. There is some truth in Appadurai's remark that "until there are as many persons from Papua New Guinea studying Philadelphia as vice versa, the appearance of dialogue conceals the reality of monologue" (1988:20).

In my view, however, there are good grounds for rethinking the modernist project; indeed, its assumption about the inevitability of monologue are not infallible and self-evident. Many pedagogues have convincingly argued against the one-sidedness implicit in the Aristotelian colonization of the life world of the child, stressing the importance of reciprocity and engagement, humility and mutual trust.[5] The recently developed theory of practice offers a compelling view of apprenticeship and enskilment, including that of ethnographic fieldwork. Not only does such a theory dismiss the dualistic hierarchy of experts and laypersons, it also provides a "pragmatic" view on how people acquire the skills necessary for managing their lives, starting, as Dewey put it, "from knowing as a factor in action and undergoing" (1958[1929]:23). Icelanders sometimes apply a relevant metaphor, the metaphor of "getting one's sea legs" (*sjóast*), to the process of learning and enskilment. For them, enskilment is not only a physical exercise, it is a process involving *both* sociality and bodily dispositions.

Indigenous discourses can be just as monological and responsive to relations of power as the writing of ethnographies. It is quite revealing to compare the ways in which Icelanders have talked about fishing skills and linguistic competence. Some years ago, I argued, largely on the basis of statistical exercises, that differential success in fishing had more to do with the size of boats and how often they went fishing than the personal capabilities of skippers, the so-called "skipper effect." Most Icelanders tended to reject the thesis about negligible individual differences in fishing abilities, to some extent quite rightly (later on, I adopted a revised position), on the grounds that it contradicted everyday experience and "common sense" knowledge.[6] The reactions, however, in both newspapers and informal talks in the communities where I had worked, showed much less heat than in the case of debates on the purity and social basis of everyday speech. Many people in fact found anthropological arguments and analyses relating to the skipper effect a challenging and interesting subject for thought. During my original fieldwork, people would freely discuss differential fishing success and plausible explanatory hypotheses, mixing statistics and serious arguments with humor and personal anecdotes. Frequently scholarly claims were amplified, distorted or simplified mainly for the purpose of amusement. I heard fishermen tell sarcastic stories about the "scientific" evidence against skipperhood: "Skippers are not just equals; they are dispensable!" The dominant discourse on language was far too canonical to tolerate playfulness of this kind. The challenge to the established linguistic notions of the purity and homogeneity of Icelandic was too much to take. Ironically, fishermen seemed more willing to have a good conversation than many academics. Significantly, the discourse on fishing was largely developed from below, in the grass-roots in rural fishing communities, while the one on language was introduced and enforced in the corridors of power and the academy in the capital city. Recently, as we have seen, both patterns have been altered; while to some extent the commoners have been reclaiming language, with the moderation of official language policy and relaxed attitudes with respect to everyday speech (and the publication of a separate "slang-dictionary"), they have been losing ground in the battle about fishing stocks, as fisheries policy becomes subject to state regulations and quotas are being privatized.

During earlier centuries farmers and landowners occupied the central positions of Icelandic society and, consequently, fishing was regarded as merely a supplementary subsistence activity. Those in power presented the growing fishing communities of the nineteenth and early twentieth century as "devoid of culture" (*menningarsnauð*), the source of degeneration, alienation, and deficient language. Finnur Jónsson, an Icelandic ethnologist, once remarked with respect to a fishing village (Garður) near the place of my fieldwork on the south-west coast that while it was always regarded "as one of the best fishing places in the south, . . . its culture was at a rather low stage of development" (cited in Pálsson 1987b:8). With the development of the market economy and the growing importance of fishing, the focus of discussions on economics and production shifted from land to sea, from the landed elite to the grass roots of the fishing communities. Gradually fishermen, particularly skippers, became the key figures of production discourse. In the process, agriculture was redefined as a burden to the national economy. Now, once again, the discursive pendulum has swung in the opposite direction—from sea to land—as a result of strict state management of fishing stocks, the application of a quota system, increased concentration of wealth, and the evolution of property rights in living aquatic resources. Fishing remains a major economic enterprise, but the central economic agents are not fishermen but the land-based owners of quotas and fishing plants and the holders of scientific, textual knowledge.

IMAGINED BOUNDARIES AND REIFIED TEXTS

The problem of where to locate cultural boundaries has always bothered anthropologists. This is the so-called "Galton's problem" often referred to in relation to comparative databases. We can never be sure that the ethnographic cases in our samples are genuinely independent or distinct cases to allow for meaningful "cross-cultural" comparison. How, then, do we elect the members of what Gellner

(1988a) calls the Assembly of Mankind, to which I referred in Chapter three, and on what basis? Do the members vote independently, to speak metaphorically, according to their own judgement, or do they simply reiterate the statements of their neighbors? Recently, such questions have gained a new significance. "In the pulverized space of postmodernity," Gupta and Ferguson suggest, "space has not become irrelevant: it has been *re*territorialized in a way that does not conform to the experience of space that characterized the era of high modernity" (1992:9). While Iceland is located in the middle of the North Atlantic, it is no longer, if it ever was, a cultural island. Nowadays, in the age of satellite television, superconductors, mobile telephones, and exponential growth in international travel and exchange, space has gained a new meaning, for Icelanders as well as many other people.

The manufacture of difference and the celebration of decentredness, endemic in the localization of anthropological voices and the reification of native life in both classical culturalism and recent versions of "culture critique," rests upon concepts which are increasingly subject to reconsideration. The spatial notion of cultural islands and boundaries raises important analytical and conceptual issues. In particular, what are we to make of the cultures of migrants and borderlands? Isn't human life everywhere shaped by a transnational public sphere? As I argued in the second chapter, anthropologists need to reconsider the whole project of cultural translation, the idea of bridging and boundaries. If we do decide to reject or radically revise such key constructs of anthropological discourse, what happens to the comparative culturalist enterprise?

For one thing, a post-Orientalist scholarship, a scholarship that rejects a cultural, essentialist interpretation of the Other and the idea of the cultural mosaic, does not necessarily dismiss differences and comparison. As Pletsch points out, the Other is always defined in terms of its difference from the observer. Only if we can remember this will we have "the epistemological basis for a differentiated understanding of the globe's societies" (1981:590). Although each ethnography is situated in a particular local context, to claim that there are as many kinds of "societies" as there are contexts is to exaggerate. In my view, rather than elaborate on the unique and the idiosyncratic, anthropological analysis should strive to establish both the contrasts and the parallels in the ethnography and to look for explanations for such contrasts and parallels. It is true that an emphasis on ethnicity and uniqueness is very much a fact of the real world. Nationalism, in fact, has not withered away with decolonization and the end of the Cold War. On the contrary. Recently, ethnic conflicts have reappeared on a massive scale in the global ecumene. However, while both nation builders and anthropological theorists have often taken ethnicity for granted, emphasizing its "naturalness" and independence, it is rooted in specific historical circumstances.[7] This is not to say that ethnicity is simply an "ideological" construct or "phantasmic" mystification, but that analyses of its many faces, its appearance in different contexts, ought to be sensitive to the processes which created it, processes closely associated with state organization and social class.

The kind of nation building that is founded on ethnicity tends to adopt one of two approaches with respect to cultural heterogeneity, celebrating differences or dismissing them. In the former case, a dominant group may give the impression of "preserving" the traditions of minority groups while at the same time imposing its own traditions upon them. In Ecuador, as Keesing points out, Spanish-speaking *mestizos* sometimes stage "indigenous" culture (by wearing Indian costumes, playing Indian music, etc.) on specific public occasions where the Indians themselves, the makers of indigenous manners, are not allowed to participate, only to observe. "What greater alienation than watching those who dominate and rule you perform symbolically central elements of your cultural heritage: selling *your* culture?" (Keesing 1989b:31). In such cases, minority identities are merely for marketing and display, "preserved like specimens in jars" (ibid.). To celebrate differences does not, however, necessarily involve alienation and domination. Switzerland, for example, has largely managed to avoid it, despite the coexistence of four major language areas for several centuries.[8] In the other approach, where cultural differences are minimized or denied, existing contrasts tend to be discussed in implicit terms. Twentieth-century Iceland is a case in point.

During the last phase of the "struggle" against Danish colonialism, emerging signs of "modernity"—notably class cleavages—were carefully edited out of the cultural invention of Icelanders, to emphasize harmony and uniqueness. A model of unity and glorious achievements was enforced upon both the present and the past to justify political independence. Later on, in newly independent Iceland, with rapid modernization and the growth of capitalist fishing during the immediate post-war years, everyday life became the euphemistic site of a cultural and economic struggle. The nonstandard speech of lower-class Icelanders was systematically attacked on the grounds that it represented a "pathological" deviation from established standards, a dangerous threat to the "purity" of official Icelandic. Uneducated, lower-class Icelanders were compelled to imitate the language of the learned and the elite, to participate in a "culture" which they did not quite recognize as theirs. For Icelanders language, above all else, assumes the role of the key marker of patriotic ethnicity and sensibility, separating Icelanders from Scandinavians, other Europeans, and the rest of the world's population. In this respect, Iceland follows a well-known European pattern. As Smith has noted, there remains a eurocentric bias "in favour of language as the medium and vessel of ethnicity" (1986:181). Icelanders tend to regard their language not as an extension of their person or a culturally-fashioned tool, but rather as an artifact independent of themselves, analogous to their equally celebrated landscape: in other words, an external condition within which they as a "nation" operate. Icelandic ethnicity, in fact, is erected on the symbolic trinity of "land, language and nation" (*landið, tungan og þjóðin*), frequently referred to in public speeches and political rhetoric.

Icelandic views of language reflect practical local concerns: the "struggle" for independence and the class politics of recent decades. Icelandic ethnolinguistics are characterized by a romantic and nationalistic attitude regarding the "spirit" and "uniqueness" of Icelandic and its place among other languages. The writer Isaac Bashevis Singer is reported to have once said that "being a sociological exception is the essence of being Jewish" and the same may be said about Icelanders, given their emphasis on the quality and uniqueness of their language and culture. In some respects, the idea of Hebrew, the "Holy Language" of another group in possession of ancient scripts (see Rabin 1983), may be the closest ideological parallel to the idea of Icelandic. During the Middle Ages, the attitude of Jews to Hebrew was one of religious awe. Hebrew was considered the language of creation and divine service, a "superior language, primary in eloquence and pedigree" (Halkin 1963:241). In some parts of Portugal, people apply a similar language of purity; a person who speaks badly (*fala mal*) is regarded as impure and the "capacity to avoid 'speaking badly' is used as an index of local stratification" (De Pina-Cabral 1986:101). But in the Portuguese context particular subjects for discussion are regarded as polluting (often they have to do with sex), whereas in Iceland it is primarily the *form* of the utterance which counts. Another national discourse on linguistic form which in many ways is parallel to the Icelandic one is that of Greece. The similarities of their histories at the margins of a larger civilization—in particular, a "struggle" for independence and the possession of a "classic" heritage—have called for comparable kinds of nationalistic and elitist ethnolinguistics.

If the native (the postmodern savage) continues to inhabit a cultural island, as a victim of culture (much like the speaker, according to the followers of Saussure and Derrida, is a victim of language), native culture remains a museum piece for the privileged scrutiny of non-native anthropologists. Some of the acute problems of voice and agency in ethnographic studies of the cultural mosaic are evident as well in some attempts at understanding the past. Thus, in the textual approach to historiography, there is no room for a flesh-and-blood social history of actual persons, let alone the *making* of history, only intertextual echoes and semiotic play. Historical textualism not only reduces the past to a linguistic construction, it virtually amounts to the suppression of time, the dissolution or denial of history. An alternative approach to historiography seeks to locate texts, potentially important avenues to the past, within specific social sites. "Involved in this positioning of the text is an examination of the play of power, human agency, and social experience as historians traditionally understand them" (Spiegel 1990:85). Such a perspective, I suggest, is highly useful to address the issues of authenticity, rhetorics, and the production of texts, including the Icelandic sagas. A number of scholars with varied backgrounds and training are now attempting to make sense of the sagas along those lines, asking a range of questions about the making of texts, medieval society, and similar social formations at other times and other places, questions informed by studies of contemporary societies as well as anthropological, literary, and historical theory.

Why the textual model put its stamp on the imagination of generations of anthropologists working in different countries on a range of issues from production to language, from economic systems to semiotics, remains open to question. Perhaps, as Moerman implies, the textual model was the offspring of the "unhappy marriage" (1988:88) of Saussurean structuralism and American culturalism. Perhaps, too, the method of participant observation is partly to blame: "The particular relationship which binds the anthropologist to his subject, and the neutrality of the 'impartial spectator' conferred by the status of the external observer, made anthropology the prime victim" (Bourdieu 1991:33). In my view, however, there is more to the story. The reasons have more to do with what I have referred to as the political economy of "cultural dyslexia," with Orientalism and othering. Just as the reification of language is more common among students of *foreign* languages than those who study their native language, the perspective of objectivist textualism is more appealing among students of "other" societies than those who work at home. The absence of othering means that one positions oneself *within* the flow of everyday discourse. Othering, however, is not simply a matter of global geopolitics. Some societies within the so-called First World (the academic base of most anthropologists), those that belong to the "Fourth World," continue to be regarded as the subject of anthropologists. The conceptual move which separates science and the civilized from the "everyday" (Lévi-Strauss 1972) effectively distances some other parts of the anthropologist's own society, making the "rest in the west" (women, the lower class, children, etc.) "primitive" and therefore suitable for anthropological analysis.

The idea that anthropology is shaped by the social context in which it is practiced, is not a novel one. Marx, Kuhn and Foucault and many others have pointed out that scientific paradigms and conventional standards of scholarship are inevitably rooted in history. Given the historicity of anthropology and its quest for knowledge, every major transformation in the social world is likely to lead to a reconsideration of the discipline. With decolonization in the 1960s, anthropology was subject to intense criticism. Anthropology, however, did not wither away, contrary to the predictions of some of its critics; rather it was reborn and re-established on new terms, supported by greater institutional backing than ever before and enjoying increasing popularity. Nowadays, anthropologists have good reason to rethink their excessively textualized subject once again.

Anthropology has commonly been thought of as an art of translation, a medium for communicating *between* different worlds, across boundaries, but if the human world is increasingly holistic then, certainly, the anthropological enterprise is bound to be redefined. Rethinking the anthropological project, I think, will involve nothing less than a new ethnographic order, the development of an anthropology which dispenses with, or radically redefines, some of its key concepts—the Other, participant "observation," cultural discontinuities, language, and ethnographic translation—and yet an anthropology that retains its classical concern with fieldwork, social understanding, and the multiple forms of social life. The difference between textualism and being-in-the-world is a crucial one for ethnography. To assume the perspective of the linguistic turn fundamentally impairs our understanding of what happens in the field as well as our attempts to elucidate what it means to be human.

NOTES

[1] The notion of "canonizing" is borrowed from Bakhtin (1981:417, 425). For an example of the application of the concept, and the related notion of *de*-canonizing, to academic discourse, see Brown 1993.

[2] Another example is provided by an account by Gewertz and Errington on the Chambri of Papua New Guinea. Although Chambri lives may be regarded as texts, they argue, "we must not be so preoccupied with textual concerns focusing on representation as to forget that they also have lives, lives affected in important ways by our Western power and interest" (1991:18–19).

[3] Morgan's monumental work on kinship (1871), which briefly mentions Icelanders, sparked a prolonged discussion of the kinship system of Icelanders. It is, no doubt, the source used in Murdock's early work on the *Ethnographic Atlas* in which Icelanders are the only Nordic group represented. Later a series of articles appeared on Icelandic kinship; see, for example, Rich 1976, 1980, 1989, and Pinson 1979, 1985.

[4] For a critical discussion of the position of Habermas, see, for example, Bourdieu 1991 and Love 1989.

[5] See Lave 1988, 1990, Fischer, Rotenberg and Raya 1993, Freire 1972:79–80. Habermas has questioned the assumption of asymmetry in medical work using the example of a person undergoing psychoanalysis (see Young 1990:127). If the treatment is to be effective, he suggests, the conclusions of the analyst must be verified by the patient.

[6] See Pálsson 1987b, Pálsson and Durrenberger 1992, and Pálsson 1994a.

[7] See Comaroff and Comaroff 1992: Chap. 2.

[8] See Bendix 1992. 222

References

Acheson, James M. 1988. *The Lobster Gangs of Maine*, Hanover & London: University Press of New England.
Alexanders saga 1925. Copenhagen: Komissionen for det Arnemagneske laget.
Alþingistíðindi 1945D. Reykjavík.
Amory, Frederic 1991. 'Speech acts and violence in the sagas', *Arkiv för Nordisk Filologi* 106, 57–84.
Anderson, Benedict 1983. *Imagined Communities*. London: Verso.
Appadurai, Arjun 1986. 'Introduction: Commodities and the politics of value', in *The Social Life of Things: Commodities in cultural perspective*, ed. A. Appadurai, Cambridge: Cambridge University Press.
Appadurai, Arjun 1988. 'Introduction: Place and voice in anthropological theory'. *Cultural Anthropology* 3(1), 16–20.
Appadurai, Arjun 1991. 'Global ethnoscapes: Notes and queries for a transnational anthropology', in *Recapturing Anthropology: Working in the present*, ed. Richard G. Fox, New Mexico: School of American Research Press, 191–210.
Ardener, Edwin 1987. '"Remote areas": Some theoretical considerations', in *Anthropology at Home*, ed. A. Jackson, London & New York: Tavistock, 38–54.
Árnason, Kristján and Höskuldur Þráinsson 1984. 'Um reykvísku', *Íslenskt mál* 6, 113–134.
Árnason, Ragnar 1991. 'Efficient management of ocean fisheries'. *European Economic Review* 35, 408–417.
Árnason, Ragnar 1993. 'The Icelandic individual transferable quota system: A descriptive account'. *Marine Resource Economics* 8, 201–218.
Asad, Talal (ed.) 1973. *Anthropology and the Colonial Encounter*, London: Ithaca Press.
Asad, Talal 1986. 'The concept of cultural translation in British social anthropology', in *Writing Culture: The poetics and politics of ethnography*, eds. J. Clifford and G.E. Marcus, Berkeley, CA: University of California Press, 141–164.
Asad, Talal 1987. 'Are there histories of peoples without Europe? A review article', *Comparative Studies in Society and History* 29 (3), 594–607.
Atkinson, Paul 1990. *The Ethnographic Imagination: Textual constructions of reality*, London: Routledge.
Austin, J.L. 1975 [1962]. *How to do Things with Words*, Cambridge, MA: Harvard University Press.
Bakhtin, Mikhail M. 1981. *The Dialogic Imagination: Four essays by M.M. Bakhtin*, ed. M. Holquist, trans. C. Emerson and M. Holquist, Austin, TX: University of Texas Press.
Bakhtin, Mikhail, M. 1986. *Speech Genres and other Late Essays*, transl. V.W. McGee, eds. C. Emerson and M. Holquist, Austin, TX: University of Texas Press.
Barley, Nigel 1983. *The Innocent Anthropologist: Notes from a mud hut*, Middlesex, U.K.: Penguin Books.
Barth, Fredrik 1969. 'Introduction', in *Ethnic Groups and Boundaries: The social organization of cultural difference*, ed. F. Barth, Bergen: Universitets Forlaget, 9–38.
Bauman, Richard 1986. 'Performance and honor in 13th-century Iceland', *Journal of American Folklore* 99, 131–150.
Bauman, Richard 1992. 'Contextualization, tradition, and the dialogue of genres: Icelandic legends of the *kraftaskáld*', in *Rethinking Context: Language as an interactive phenomenon*,

eds A. Duranti and C. Goodwin, Cambridge: Cambridge University Press, 125–145.
Bauman, Richard and Joel Sherzer (eds) 1989 [1974]. *Explorations in the Ethnography of Speaking*, Cambridge: Cambridge University Press. Second edition.
Baxter, Paul T.W. 1972. 'Absence makes the heart grow fonder: Some suggestions why witchcraft accusations are rare among East African pastoralists', in *The Allocation of Responsibility*, ed. Max Gluckman, Manchester: Manchester University Press, 163–191.
Baxler, Paul T.W. 1991. 'From anthropological texts to popular writings', *Bulletin of the John Rylands Library* 73 (3), 105–124.
Beidelman, T.O. 1971. *The Translation of Culture: Essays to E.E. Evans-Pritchard*, London: Tavistock Publications.
Bendix, Regina 1992. 'National sentiment in the enactment and discourse of Swiss political ritual', *American Ethnologist* 19 (4),768–790.
Benediktsson, Einar 1952. *Laust mál: Úrval*, Reykjavík: Ísafoldar-prentsmiðja.
Benediktsson, Hreinn 1959. 'The vowel system of Icelandic: A survey of its history', *Word*, 15 (2), 283–312.
Benediktsson, Hreinn 1961–62. 'Icelandic dialectology: Methods and results', *Lingua Islandica* 3, 72–113.
Benediktsson, Hreinn 1972. *The First Grammatical Treatise*, Reykjavík: Institute of Nordic Linguistics.
Benhabib, Seyla 1990. 'Communicative ethics and current controversies in practical phylosophy', in *The Communicative Ethics Controversy*, eds S. Benhabib and F. Dallmar. Cambridge, Mass., MIT Press, pp. 330–369.
Benhabib, Seyla 1992. *Situating the Self: Gender, community and postmodernism in contemporary ethics*, Cambridge: Polity Press.
Bennett, John W. 1993. *Human Ecology as Human Behavior: Essays in environmental and developmental anthropology*, New Brunswick: Transaction Publishers.
Bessason, Haraldur 1967. 'A few specimens of North American-Icelandic', *Scandinavian Studies*, 39 (2), 115–146.
Bitterli, Urs 1986. *Cultures in Conflict: Encounters between European and non-European cultures 1492–1800*, Stanford, CA: Stanford University Press.
Björnsdóttir, Inga Dóra 1989. 'Public view and private voices', in *The Anthropology of Iceland*, eds E.P. Durrenberger and G. Pálsson, Iowa City: University of Iowa Press, 98–118.
Bloch, Maurice 1991. 'Language, anthropology and cognitive science', *Man* 26 (2), 183–198.
Bloch, Maurice 1992. 'What goes without saying: The conceptualization of Zafimaniry society', in *Conceptualizing Society*, ed. A. Kuper, London: Routledge, 127–146.
Bongie, Chris 1991. *Exotic Memories: Literature, colonialism, and the Fin de Siècle*. Stanford, CA: Stanford University Press.
Boon, James A. 1982. *Other Tribes, Other Scribes: Symbolic anthropology in the comparative study of cultures, histories, religions, and texts*, Cambridge: Cambridge University Press.
Bordo, Susan 1987. *The Flight to Objectivity: Essays on Cartesianism and culture*, New York: State University of New York Press.
Bourdieu, Pierre 1977. *Outline of a Theory of Practice*, trans. R. Nice, Cambridge: Cambridge University Press.
Bourdieu, Pierre 1984. *Distinction: A social critique of the judgement of taste*, trans. R. Nice, Chicago: University of Chicago Press.
Bourdieu, Pierre 1990. *The Logic of Practice*, trans. R. Nice, Cambridge: Polity Press.

Bourdieu, Pierre 1991. *Language and Symbolic Power*, ed. J.B. Thompson, trans. G. Raymond and M. Adamson, London: Polity Press.

Brightman, Robert 1993. *Grateful Prey: Rock Cree human-animal relationships*, Berkeley, CA: University of California Press.

Brown, Vivienne 1993. 'Decanonizing discourses: Textual analysis and the history of economic thought', in *Economics and Language*, eds W. Henderson, T. Dudley-Evans and R. Backhouse, London & New York: Routledge, 64–84.

Bruner, Jerome 1986. *Actual Minds, Possible Worlds*, Cambridge, MA.: Harvard University Press.

Brydon, Anne 1993. 'Review of Kirsten Hastrup's *Island of Anthropology* and *Nature and Policy*'. *Scandinavian Studies* 65 (2), 96–99.

Burch, Ernest S. 1988. 'Modes of exchange in north-west Alaska', in *Hunters and Gatherers 2: Property, power and ideology*, Oxford: Berg Publishers, 95–109.

Byock, Jesse L. 1992. 'History and the sagas: The effect of nationalism', in *From Sagas to Society: Comparative approaches to early Iceland*, ed. G. Pálsson, Middlesex: Hisarlik Press, 43–59.

Carrier, James G. 1992. 'Occidentalism: The world turned upside-down', *American Ethnologist* 19 (2), 195–212.

Carroll, Raymonde 1987. *Cultural Misunderstandings: The French-American experience*, Chicago: University of Chicago Press.

Carucci, Laurence M. 1988. 'Small fish in a big sea: Geographical dispersion and sociopolitical centralization in the Marshall Islands', in *State and Society: The emergence and development of social hierarchy and political centralization*, (eds) J. Gledhill, B. Bender, and M.T. Larsen, London: Unwin Hyman, 33–42.

Chamberlain, Lori 1988. 'Gender and the metaphorics of translation', *Signs* 13 (3), 454–472.

Chomsky, Noam 1980. *Rules and Representations*, Oxford: Basil Blackwell.

Clifford, James 1988. *The Predicament of Culture: Twentieth-century ethnography, literature, and art*, Cambridge, MA: Harvard University Press.

Clifford, James and George E. Marcus (eds) 1986. *Writing Culture: The poetics and politics of ethnography*, Berkeley: University of California Press.

Clover, Carol J. 1988. 'The politics of scarcity: Notes on the sex ratio in early Scandinavia', *Scandinavian Studies* 60, 147–188.

Comaroff, John and Jean Comaroff 1992. *Ethnography and the Historical Imagination*, Boulder: Westview Press.

Coy, M. (ed.) 1989. *Apprenticeship: From theory to method and back again*. New York: SUNY.

Crick, M. 1976. *Explorations in Language and Meaning: Towards a semantic anthropology*, New York: John Wiley.

Cronon, William 1992. 'A place for stories: Nature, history, and narrative,' *Journal of American History* 1347–1376.

Damon, William 1981. 'Exploring children's social cognition on two fronts', in *Social Cognitive Development: Frontiers and possible futures*, eds. J.H. Flavell and L. Ross, Cambridge: Cambridge University Press, 154–175.

De Pina-Cabral, João 1986. *Sons of Adam, Daughters of Eve: The peasant worldview of the Alto Minho*, Oxford: Clarendon Press.

Derrida, Jacques 1985. 'Des tours de Babel', in *Difference in Translation*, ed. J.F. Graham, Ithaca: Cornell University Press, 165–205.

Derrida, Jacques 1992. *Acts of Literature*, (ed.) D. Attridge, New York & London: Routledge.

Dewees, C.M. 1989. 'Assessment of the implementation of individual transferable quotas in New Zealand's inshore fishery', *North American Journal of Fisheries Management* 9, 131–139.

Dewey, John 1958 [1929]. *Experience and Nature*, New York: Dover Publications, Inc.

Dilley, Roy (ed.) 1992. *Contesting Markets: Analyses of ideology, discourse and practice*, Edinburgh: Edinburgh University Press.

Donaldson, Margaret 1978. *Children's Minds*, Glasgow: Fontana.

Donham, Donald L. 1990. *History, Power, Ideology: Central issues in Marxism and anthropology*, Cambridge and Paris: Cambridge University Press and Editions de la Maison des Sciences de l'Homme.

Douglas, Mary 1966. *Purity and Danger: An analysis of concepts of pollution and taboo*, London: Routledge & Kegan Paul.

Douglas, Mary 1991. 'Witchcraft and leprosy: Two strategies of exclusion', *Man* 26, 723–36.

Dreyfus, Hubert L. 1991. *Being-in-the-World: A commentary on Heidegger's* Being and time, *division I*. Cambridge, MAs.: The MIT Press.

Drummond, Lee 1987. 'Are there cultures to communicate across? An appraisal of the 'culture' concept from the perspective of anthropological semiotics', in *Developments in Linguistics and Semiotics: Language teaching and learning communication across cultures*, ed. S.P.X. Battestini, Washington: Georgetown University Press, 215–225.

Dumont, Luis 1972. *Homo Hierarchicus: The caste system and its implications*, London: Paladin.

Dunn, Judy 1988. *The Beginnings of Social Understanding*, Cambridge: Cambridge University Press.

Duranti, Alessandro 1988. 'Ethnography of speaking: Toward a linguistics of praxis', in *Linguistics: The Cambridge survey* (ed.) F.J. Newmeyer, Cambridge: Cambridge University Press, 210–228.

Duranti, A. and Goodwin, C. (eds) 1992. *Rethinking Context: Language as an interactive phenomenon*, Cambridge: Cambridge University Press.

Durrenberger, E. Paul 1975. 'Understanding a misunderstanding: Thai-Lisu relations in northern Thailand', *Anthropological Quarterly* 48, 106–120.

Durrenberger, E. Paul 1982. 'Reciprocity in *Gautrek's saga*: An anthropological analysis', *Northern Studies* 19, 23–37.

Durrenberger, E. Paul 1990. 'Text and tranactions in Commonwealth Iceland', *Ethnos* 55, 74–91.

Durrenberger, E. Paul 1991. 'Sitting Buddha in a Mississippi golf course: Constructing anthropology in exotic and familiar settings', *Anthropology and Humanism Quarterly* 16 (3), 88–94.

Durrenberger, E. Paul 1992. *The Dynamics of Medieval Iceland: Political economy and literature*, Iowa: University of Iowa Press.

Durrenberger, E. Paul and Gísli Pálsson 1986. 'Finding fish: The tactics of Icelandic fishermen'. *American Etnologist* 13, 213–229.

Durrenberger, E. Paul and Gísli Pálsson 1987. 'Ownership at sea: Fishing territories and access to sea resources', *American Ethnologist* 14 (3), 508–522.

Durrenberger, E. Paul and Gísli Pálsson (eds) 1989. *The Anthropology of Iceland*, Iowa: University of Iowa Press.

Eggertsson, Thráinn 1992. 'Analyzing institutional successes and failures: A millennium of common mountain pastures in Iceland', *International Review of Law and Economics* 12, 423–437.

Egil's saga 1960. Translated from the Old Icelandic, with an Introduction and Notes by Gwin Jones. New York: Syracuse University Press.

Egilsson, Ólafur 1969 [1628]. *Reisubok séra Ólafs Egilssonar*, Reykjavík: Almenna bókafélagið.

Einarsson, Níels 1990. 'From the native's point of view: Some comments on the anthropology of Iceland', *Antropologiska Studier* 46–47, 69–77.

Ellen, Roy (ed.) 1984. *Ethnographic Research: A guide to general conduct*, London: Academic Press.

Ellen, Roy 1988. Fetishism, *Man* 23(2), 213–235.

Ellis Davidson, H.R. 1973. 'Hostile magic in the Icelandic sagas', in *The Witch Figure*, ed. V. Newall, London: Routledge & Kegan Paul.

Endicott, K. and K.L. Endicott 1986. 'The question of hunter-gatherer territoriality: The case of the Batek of Malaysia', in *The Past and Future of !Kung Ethnography: Critical reflections and symbolic perspectives. Essays in honour of Lorna Marshall* eds M. Biesele, R. Gordon and R. Lee, Hamburg: Helmut Buske Verlag, 137–162.

England, Paula 1993. 'The separative self: Androcentric bias in neoclassical assumptions'. In *Beyond Economic Man: Feminist theory and economics* (eds.) M.A. Ferber and J.A. Nelson, Chicago & London: The University of Chicago Press, 37–53.

Evans-Pritchard, E.E. 1976. *Witchcraft, Oracles, and Magic Among the Azande*, abridged with an Introduction by E. Gillies, Oxford: Clarendon Press.

Fabian, Johannes 1991. *Time and the Work of Anthropology: Critical essays 1971–1991*, Chur: Harwood Academic Publishers.

Fagan, Brian M. 1984. *Clash of Cultures*, New York: W.H. Freeman.

Featherstone, Mike (ed.) 1990. *Global Culture: Nationalism, globalization and modernity*, London: Sage.

Feleppa, Robert 1988. *Convention, Translation, and Understanding: Philosophical problems in the comparative study of culture*, Albany, NY: State University of New York Press.

Figueira, Dorothy Matilda 1991. *Translating the Orient: The reception of Sakuntala in nineteenth century Europe*, Albany, NY: State University of New York Press.

Finnbogason, Guðmundur 1922. 'Mannkynbætur', *Andvari* 47, 184–204.

Finnbogason, Guðmundur 1943. *Huganir*, Reykjavík: Ísafoldarprentsmiðja.

Finnbogason, Guðmundur 1971. *Íslendingar*, Reykjavík: Almenna bókafélagið.

Fischer, K.W., E.J. Rotenberg, D.H. Bullock, and P. Raya 1993. 'The dynamics of competence: How context contributes directly to skill', in *Development in Context: Acting and thinking in specific environments*, eds R.H. Wozniak and K.W. Fischer. Hillsdale, NJ: Lawrence Erlbaum Associates, 93–117.

Flavell, John H. and Lee Ross 1981. 'Concluding remarks', in *Social Cognitive Development: Frontiers and possible futures*, eds. J.H. Flavell and L. Ross, Cambridge: Cambridge University Press, 306–316.

Frake, Charles O. 1980. *Language and Cultural Description*, essays selected and introduced by A.S. Dil. Stanford: Stanford University Press.

Freire, Paulo 1972. *Pedagogy of the Oppressed*, N.Y.: Herder & Herder.

Fried, Morton H. 1967. *The Evolution of Political Society: An essay in political anthropology*, New York: Random House.

Friedman, Jonathan 1987. 'Beyond otherness or: The spectacularization of anthropology', *Telos* 71, 161–170.

Frye, Northrop 1982. *The Great Code: The Bible and literature*, New York and London: Harcourt Brace Jovanovich, Publishers.

Galt, A.H. 1982. 'The evil eye as synthetic image and its meanings on the island of Pantelleria, Italy', *American Ethnologist* 9 (4), 664–681.

Gaskins, Richard H. 1992. *Burdens of Proof in Modern Discourse*, New Haven: Yale University Press.

Geertz, Clifford 1963. *Agricultural Involution*, Berkeley, CA.: University of California Press.

Geertz, Clifford 1973. *The Interpretation of Cultures*, London: Hutchinson.

Geertz, Clifford 1983. *Local Knowledge: Further essays in interpretive anthropology*, New York: Basic Books.

Geertz, Clifford 1988. *Works and Lives: The anthropologist as author*, Stanford, CA: Stanford University Press.

Gellner, Ernest 1988a. *Plough, Sword and Book: The structure of human history*, Chicago: University of Chicago Press.

Gellner, Ernest 1988b. *State and Society in Soviet Thought*, New York: Basil Blackwell.

Gelsinger, Bruce E. 1981. *Icelandic Enterprise: Commerce and economy in the Middle Ages*, Columbia: University of South Carolina Press.

Gewertz, Deborah and Frederick K. Errington 1991. *Twisted Histories, Altered Contexts: Representing the Chambri in a world system*, Cambridge: Cambridge University Press.

Gledhill, John 1988. 'Introduction: The comparative analysis of social and political transitions', in *State and Society: The emergence and development of social hierarchy and political centralization*, eds. J. Gledhill, B. Bender, and M.T. Larsen, London: Unwin Hyman, 1–29.

Godelier, Maurice 1986. *The Making of Great Men: Male domination and power among the New Guinea Baruya*, Cambridge: Cambridge University Press.

Godelier, Maurice and Marilyn Strathern (eds.) 1991. *Big Men and Great Men: Personifications of power in Melanesia*, Cambridge & Paris: Cambridge University Press & Editions de la Maison des Sciences de l'Homme.

Goldman, L. 1983. *Talk Never Dies: The language of Huli disputes*, London: Tavistock.

Goody, Jack 1987. *The Interface Between the Written and the Oral*, Cambridge: Cambridge University Press.

Goody, Jack 1991. 'The time of telling and the telling of time in written and oral cultures', in *Chronotypes: The construction of time*, eds. J. Bender and D.E. Wellbery, Stanford: Stanford University Press, 77–96.

Grágás, 1852, I. Islendingernes lovbog i fristatens tid, utgivet efter det kongelige Biblioteks Haandskrift. Copenhagen: Brödrene Berlings Bogtrykeri.

Grímsdóttir, Guðrún Ása 1988. 'Um sárafar í Íslendinga sögu Sturlu þórðarsonar', in *Sturlustefna*, eds Guðrún Á. Grímsdóttir and Jónas Kristjánsson, Reykjavík: Stofnun Árna Magnússonar.

Groenke, Ulrich 1966. 'On standard, substandard, and slang in Icelandic', *Scandinavian Studies*, 38, 217–230.

Gudeman, Stephen 1992. 'Markets, models and morality: The power of practices.' In *Contesting Markets: Analyses of ideology, discourse and practice* (ed.) Roy Dilley, Edinburgh: Edinburgh University Press, 279–294.

Gudeman, Stephen and Alberto Rivera 1990. *Conversations in Colombia: The domestic economy in life and text*, Cambridge: Cambridge University Press.

Gudemann, Stephen and Alberto Rivera 1995. 'From car to house.' *American Anthropologist* (In press).
Guðfinnsson, Björn 1946. *Mállýzkur* I, Reykjavík: Ísafoldarprentsmiðja.
Guðfinnsson, Björn 1967. *Íslenzk málfræði*, (sixth edition), Reykjavík: Ríkisútgáfa námsbóka.
Guðmundsson, Helgi 1972. *Pronominal Dual in Icelandic*, Reykjavík: Institute of Nordic Linguistics.
Guðmundsson, Helgi 1977. 'Um ytri aðstæður íslenskrar málþróunar', in *Sjötíu ritgerðir helgaðar Jakobi Benediktssyni*, I, Reykjavík: Stofnun Árna Magnússonar, 315–325.
Gunnarsson, Pétur 1978. *Ég um mig frá mér til mín*, Reykjavík: Iðunn.
Gupta, Akhil and James Ferguson 1992. 'Beyond "culture": Space, identity, and the politics of difference', *Cultural Anthropology* 7 (1), 6–23.
Gurevich, Aaron 1968. 'Wealth and gift bestowal among the ancient Scandinavians', *Scandinavica* 7, 126–138.
Gurevich, Aaron 1977. 'Representations of property during the Middle Ages', *Economy and Society* 6 (1), 1–27
Gurevich, Aaron 1988. *Medieval Popular Culture: Problems of belief and perception*, transl. J.M. Bak and P.A. Hollingsworth, Cambridge: Cambridge University Press.
Gurevich, Aaron 1992. *Historical Anthropology of the Middle Ages*, Cambridge: Polity Press.
Gutt, Ernst-August 1991. *Translation and Relevance: Cognition and context*, Oxford: Basil Blackwell.
Guttormsson, Loftur 1983. *Bernska, ungdómur og uppeldi á einveldisöld: Tilraun til félagslegrar og lýðfræðilegrar greiningar*. Reykjavík: Sagnfræðistofnun Háskóla Íslands.
Guttormsson, Loftur 1989. Læsi, in *Íslensk þjóðmenning VI: Munnmenntir og bókmenning* (ed.) Frosti F. Jóhannsson. Reykjavík: þjóðsaga, 118–144.
Gylfason, þorsteinn 1973. Að hugsa á íslenzku, *Skírnir* 129–58.
Haas, Jonathan (ed.) 1990. *The Anthropology of War*, Cambridge: Cambridge University Press.
Habermas, Jürgen 1989. *The New Conservatism: Cultural criticism and the historians' debate*, ed. and trans. S.W. Nicholsen, Cambridge, MA: The MIT Press.
Habermas, Jürgen 1990. 'Discourse ethics: Notes on a program of philosophical justification', in *The Communicative Ethics Controversy*, eds. S. Benhabib and F. Dallmar, Cambridge, Mass.: MIT Press, 60–110.
Habermas, Jürgen 1992. *Postmetaphysical Thinking: Philosophical essays*, trans. W.M. Hohengarten, London: Polity Press.
Hákonardóttir, Inga Huld 1992. *Fjarri hlýju hjónasængur: Öðruvísi Íslandssaga*. Reykjavík: Mál og menning.
Halkin, Abraham 1963. 'The medieval Jewish attitude toward Hebrew', in *Biblical and Other Studies*, ed. A. Altman, Cambridge, MA.: Harvard University Press, 233–248.
Hallberg, Peter 1974. 'The syncretic saga mind: A discussion of a new approach to the Icelandic sagas', *Medieval Scandinavia* 7, 102–117.
Halldórsson, Halldór (ed.) 1964. *þættir um íslenzkt mál*, Reykjavík: Almenna bókafélagið.
Halldórsson, Halldór 1971a. *Íslenzk málrækt*, Reykjavík: Hlaðbúð.
Halldórsson, Halldór 1971b. 'Allt er mér leyfilegt: þatturinn Daglegt mál', *Morgunblaðið*, November 28th, Reykjavík.
Halldórsson, Halldór 1976. 'Mályrkja Guðmundar Finnbogasonar og framtíð íslenzkrar tungu', *Morgunblaðið*, December 4th, Reykjavík.

Halldórsson, Halldór 1979. 'Icelandic purism and its history', *Word* 30, 76–86.
Halldórsson, Halldór 1983. 'Á móti því að breyta málinu nema þörf sé', *Morgunblaðið*, October 23rd, Reykjavík.
Halldórsson, Helgi J. 1953. 'Nokkur orð um sjómannamál', *Sjómannablaðið Víkingur* 1–2, 3–6. Reykjavík.
Halldórsson, Helgi J. 1975. 'Mál blaða og útvarps', *Skírnir*, Reykjavík, 168–187.
Halldórsson, Helgi J. 1978. 'Málvondun, bókstafstrú og þjóðfélag', *Þjóðviljinn*, May 9th, Reykjavík.
Hanks, W.F. 1989. 'Text and textuality', *Annual Reveiw of Anthropology* 18, 95–127.
Hanna, Susan S. 1990. 'The eighteenth century English commons: A model for ocean management', *Ocean & Shoreline Management* 14, 155–172.
Hannerz, Ulf 1992. *Cultural Complexity*. New York: Columbia University Press.
Hanson, F. Allan 1979. 'Does God have a body? Truth, reality and cultural relativism', *Man* 14, 515–529.
Haralds, Auður 1979. *Hvunndagshetjan*, Reykjavík: Iðunn.
Hardin, G. 1968. 'The tragedy of the commons', *Science* 162, 1243–1248.
Harper, Douglas 1987. *Working Knowledge: Skill and community in a small shop*, Chicago & London: The University of Chicago Press.
Harris, Roy 1980. *The Language-Makers*, London: Duckworth.
Harris, Roy 1988. *Language, Saussure and Wittgenstein: How to play games with words*, London: Routledge.
Harvey, David 1989. *The Condition of Postmodernity*, Oxford: Basil Blackwell.
Haskell, Thomas L. 1985. 'Capitalism and the origin of humanitarian sensibility, part 1', *American Historical Review* 90 (2), 339–361
Hastrup, Kirsten 1985. *Culture and History in Medieval Iceland: An anthropological analysis of structure and change*, Oxford: Oxford University Press.
Hastrup, Kirsten 1987. 'Fieldwork among friends: Ethnographic exchange within the Northern civilization', in *Anthropology at Home*, ed. A. Jackson, London & New York: Tavistock, 94–108.
Hastrup, Kirsten 1990a. *Nature and Policy in Iceland 1400–1800: An anthropological analysis of history and mentality*, Oxford: Clarendon Press.
Hastrup, Kirsten 1990b. *Island of Anthropology: Studies in past and present Iceland*, Odense: Odense University Press.
Hastrup, Kirsten 1990c. 'The anthropological vision: Comments to Niels Einarsson', *Antropologiska Studier* 46–47, 78–84.
Hastrup, Kirsten 1991. 'Eating the past: Some notes on an Icelandic food ritual', *Folk* 33, 229–243.
Hastrup, Kirsten 1992. 'Writing ethnography: State of the art', in *Anthropology and Autobiography*, eds J. Okely and H. Callaway, London & New York: Routledge, 116–133.
Hastrup, Kirsten 1993. 'The native voice—and the anthropological vision', *Social Anthropology* 1, 173–86.
Hatim, Basil and Ian Mason 1990. *Discourse and the Translator*, London: Longman.
Haugen, Einar 1972. *The Ecology of Language*, ed. A.S. Dil, Stanford: Stanford University Press.
Haugen, Einar 1975. 'Pronominal address in Icelandic: From you-two to you-all', *Language in Society* 4, 323–40.
Hauksbók 1892–96. Copenhagen: Det Kongelige Nordiske Oldskrift-selskab.

Helgason. Þorkell and Örn D. Jónsson (eds.) 1990. *Hagsæld í húfi: Greinar um stjórn fiskveiða*. Reykjavík: Sjávarútvegsstofnun.

Herzfeld, Michael 1987. *Anthropology Through the Looking-Glass: Critical ethnography in the margins of Europe*, Cambridge: Cambridge University Press.

Hirschfeld, Lawrence A. 1988. 'On aquiring social categories: Cognitive development and anthropological wisdom', *Man* 23, 611–638.

Hirschman, Albert O. 1982. 'Rival interpretations of market society: Civilizing, destructive, or feeble?', *Journal of Economic Literature* 20, 1463–1484.

Hodgen, Margareth T. 1971. *Early Anthropolgy in the Sixteenth and Seventeenth Centuries*, Philadelphia: University of Pennsylvania Press.

Hong, Keelung 1994. 'Experiences of being a "native"', *Anthropology Today* 10(3), 6–9.

Hvalkof, Sören and Peter Aaby (eds) 1981. *Is God an American? An anthropological perspective on the missionary work of the Summer Institute of Linguistics*, Copenhagen & London: IWGIA & Survival International.

Ingimundarson, Jón Haukur 1992. 'Spinning goods and tales: Market, subsistence and literary productions', in *From Sagas to Society: Comparative approaches to early Iceland*, ed. G. Pálsson, Middlesex: Hisarlik Press, 217–230.

Ingold, Tim 1986. *Evolution and Social Life*, Cambridge: Cambridge University Press.

Ingold, Tim 1987. *The Appropriation of Nature: Essays on human ecology and social relations*, Iowa City: University of Iowa Press.

Ingold, Tim (ed.) 1992. *Language is the Essence of Culture*. Manchester: Group for Debates in Anthropological Theory.

Ingold, Tim 1993a. 'The art of translation in a continuous world', in *Beyond Boundaries: Understanding, translation and anthropological discourse*, ed. G. Pálsson. Oxford: Berg Publishers, 210–231.

Ingold, Tim 1993b. 'Tool use, sociality and intelligence', in *Tools, Language and Cognition in Human Evolution*, eds. K.R. Gibson and T. Ingold. Cambridge: Cambridge University Press, 429–45.

Ingold, Tim 1993c. 'Technology, language, intelligence: A reconsideration of basic concepts', in *Tools, Language and Cognition in Human Evolution*, eds. K.R. Gibson and T. Ingold. Cambridge: Cambridge University Press, 449–472.

Íslendinga sögur og þættir, vols. I-III, 1987. Reykjavík: Svart á hvítu.

Jackson, Michael 1989. 'On ethnographic truth', in *Paths Toward a Clearing*, Indiana: Indiana University Press, 170–217.

James, Henry 1905. *The Question of Our Speech, the Lesson of Balzac: Two lectures*. Boston & New York: Houghton, Mifflin & Company.

Joas, Hans 1993. *Pragmatism and Social Theory*, Chicago & London: The University of Chicago Press.

Jochens, Jenny M. 1980. 'The church and sexuality in medieval Iceland', *Journal of Medieval History* 6, 377–392.

Jochens, Jenny M. 1986. 'The medieval Icelandic heroine: Fact or fiction?', *Viator* 17, 35–64.

Jochens, Jenny M. 1991. 'The illicit love visit: An archaeology of old Norse sexuality', *Journal of the History of Sexuality* 1, 357–92.

Jochens, Jenny M. 1992. 'From libel to lament: Male manifestations of love in Old Norse', in *From Sagas to Society: Comparative approaches to early Iceland*, ed. G. Pálsson, Middlesex, U.K.: Hisarlik Press, 247–264.

Jóhannesson, Jón 1974. *A History of the Old Icelandic Commonwealth: Íslendinga saga*, 2 vols, trans. Haraldur Bessason, Manitoba: University of Manitoba Press.

Johnson, Allen W. and Timothy Earle 1987. *The Evolution of Human Societies: From foraging group to agrarian state*, Stanford: Stanford University Press.

Johnson, Barbara 1985. 'Taking fidelity philosophically', in *Difference in Translation*, ed. J.F. Graham, Ithaca: Cornell University Press, 142–148.

Jones, O.F. 1964. 'Some Icelandic *götumál* expressions', *Scandinavian Studies* 36, 59–64.

Jónsson, Arngrímur 1985 [1609]. *Crymogea: þættir úr sögu Íslands*, Reykjavík: Sögufélag.

Jónsson, Baldur 1978a. *Íslenzk málvöndun*, Reykjavík. (Mimeograph).

Jónsson, Baldur 1978b. 'Íslenska á vorum dögum', *Skíma* 1–2, 3–7.

Jónsson, Finnur 1945. *Þjóðhættir og ævisögur frá 19. öld*, Akureyri: Bókaútg. P.H. Jónssonar.

Jónsson, Hjörleifur R. 1989. 'Haltu hátíð', *Skírnir* 163, 446–458.

Kaplan, Martha 1990. 'Meaning, agency and colonial history: Navosavakadua and the *Tuka* movement in Fiji', *American Ethnologist* 17 (1), 3–22.

Karlsson, Gunnar 1988. 'Upphaf þjóðar á Íslandi', in *Saga og kirkja: Afmælisrit Magnúsar Más Lárussonar fyrrverandi háskólarektors*. Reykjavík: Sögufélag.

Karras, Ruth Mazo 1992. 'Servitude and sexuality in medieval Iceland', in *From Sagas to Society: Comparative approaches to early Iceland*, ed. G. Pálsson, Middlesex, U.K.: Hisarlik Press, 289–304.

Kaysen, Susanna 1990. *Far Afield*. New York: Random House.

Keesing, Roger 1985. 'Conventional metaphors and anthropological metaphysics: The problematic of cultural translation', *Journal of Anthropological Research* 41, 201–217.

Keesing, Roger 1987. 'Models, "folk" and "cultural": Paradigms regained?', in *Cultural Models in Language and Thought*, eds D. Holland and N. Quinn, Cambridge: Cambridge University Press, 369–393.

Keesing, Roger 1989a. 'Exotic readings of cultural texts', *Current Anthropology* 30 (4), 459–479.

Keesing, Roger 1989b. 'Creating the past: Custom and identity in the contemporary Pacific', *The Contemporary Pacific* 1, 19–42.

Kirch, Patrick V. 1984. *The Evolution of Polynesian Chiefdoms*, Cambridge: Cambridge University Press.

Knowlton, D. 1992. 'No one can serve two masters or native anthropologist as oxymoron', *International Journal of Moral and Social Studies* 7 (1), 72–88.

Kress, Helga 1987. 'Bróklindi Falgeirs: Fóstbræðrasaga og hláturmenning miðalda', *Skírnir*, 161, 271–286.

Kress, Helga 1991. 'Staðlausir stafir: Um slúður sem uppsprettu frásagnar í Íslendingasögum'. *Skírnir* 165, 130–156.

Kristjánsdóttir, Bergljót Soffía 1991. ' "... svo mátti höfðingja best farið vera sem honum var...": einige Bemerkungen über das Wort "höfðingi" in den Islandersagas'. (Unpublished paper.)

Kristof, Ladis K.D. 1959. 'The nature of frontiers and boundaries', *Association of American Geographers Annals* 49, 269–282.

Kroeber, A.L. 1945. 'The ancient *Oikoumenê* as an historic culture aggregate', *Journal of the Royal Anthropological Institute* 75, 9–20.

Kroeber, A.L. 1952. 'Culture', in *Papers of the Peabody Museum in American Archaeology and*

Ethnology, eds A.L. Kroeber and C.H. Kluckhohn, Cambridge, MA: Harvard University Press.

Kundera, Milan 1990. *Immortality*, trans. P. Kussi, New York: Harper Collins Publishers.

Kuper, Adam 1988. *The Invention of Primitive Society: Transformations of an illusion*, London: Routledge.

Kvaran, Eiður S. 1934. 'Um mannfræðilegt gildi forníslenskra mannlýsinga', *Skírnir* 108, 83–101.

Labov, William 1970. 'The logic of nonstandard English', *Georgetown University Roundtable on Languages and Linguistics 1969*, Washington: Georgetown University Press.

Larsen, Tord 1987. 'Action, morality, and cultural translation', *Journal of Anthropological Research* 43 (1), 1–28.

Lave, Jean 1988. *Cognition in Practice: Mind, mathematics and culture in everyday life*. Cambridge: Cambridge University Press.

Lave, Jean 1990. 'The culture of acquisition and the practice of understanding', in *Cultural Psychology: Essays on comparative human development*, eds. J.W. Stigler, R.A. Shweder, and G. Herdt. Cambridge: Cambridge University Press, 309–327.

Laxness, Halldór 1942. 'Laxdælumálið: Sex greinar', in *Vettvangur dagsins: Ritgerðir*. Reykjavík: Heimskringla, 324–337.

Laxness, Halldór 1963. 'Fjölskyldulíf í Barcelona', in *Skáldatími*, Reykjavík: Helgafell, 185–198.

Laxness, Halldór 1965 [1962]. 'Persónulegar minnisgreinar um skáldsögur og leikrit', in *Upphaf mannúnaðarstefnu: Ritgerðir*, Reykjavík: Helgafell, 67–79.

Laxness, Halldór 1972 [1968]. *Christianity at Glacier*, trans. M. Magnússon, Reykjavík: Helgafell.

Laxness, Halldór 1986 [1925]. *Af menníngarástandi*, Reykjavík: Vaka-Helgafell.

Le Goff, Jacques 1988. *The Medieval Imagination*, Chicago & London: The University of Chicago Press.

Leach, Edmund R. 1954. *Political Systems of Highland Burma: A study of Kachin social structure*, Boston: Beacon Press.

Leach, Edmund R. 1970. 'The epistemological background to Malinowski's empiricism', in *Man and Culture: An evaluation of the work of Malinowski*, ed. R. Firth, London: Routledge & Kegan Paul, 119–137.

Leach, Edmund R. 1982. *Social Anthropology*, Glasgow: Fontana.

Lederman, Rena 1990. 'Big men, large and small? Towards a comparative perspective', *Ethnology* 29 (1), 3–15.

Lefevere, André and Susan Bassnett 1990. 'Introduction: Proust's grandmother and the Thousand and One Nights: The "cultural" turn in translation studies', in *Translation, History and Culture*, eds. S. Bassnett and A. Lefevere, London: Pinter Publishers, 1–13.

Lepowsky, Maria 1990. 'Big men, big women, and cultural autonomy', *Ethnology* 29 (1), 35–50.

Levack, Brian P. 1987. *The Witch-Hunt in Early Modern Europe*, London: Longman.

Lévi-Strauss, Claude 1963. *Totemism*, Boston: Beacon Press.

Lévi-Strauss, Claude 1972. *The Savage Mind*, London: Weidenfeld & Nicolson.

Lévi-Strauss, Claude 1973 [1955]. *Tristes Tropiques*, Middlesex: Penguin Books.

Lindberg, David C. and Nicholas H. Steneck 1972. 'The sense of vision and the origins of modern science', in *Science, Medicine and Society in the Renaissance: Essays to honor Walter*

Pagel, ed. A.G. Debus. London: Heineman, 29–45.

Linke, Uli 1992. 'The theft of blood, the birth of men: Cultural constructions of gender in medieval Iceland', in *From Sagas to Society: Comparative approaches to early Iceland*, ed. G. Pálsson, Middlesex, U.K.: Hisarlik Press, 265–289.

Long, Norman (ed.) 1989. *Encounters at the Interface: A perspective on social discontinuities in rural development*, Wageningen: Agricultural University Wageningen.

Love, Nancy S. 1989. 'Foucault & Habermas on discourse & democracy', *Polity* 22 (2), 269–293.

Lowenthal, David 1985. *The Past is a Foreign Country*, Cambridge: Cambridge University Press.

Lowie, Robert H. 1924. *Primitive Religion*, New York: Boni & Liveright

Ludwig, D., R. Hilborn, and C. Walters 1993. 'Uncertainty, resource exploitation, and conservation: lessons from history,' *Science* 260, 17& 36.

Löfgren, Orvar 1987. 'Deconstructing Swedishness: Culture and class in modern Sweden', in *Anthropology at Home*, ed. A. Jackson, ASA Monographs 25, London: Tavictock, 74–93.

Lönnroth, Lars 1991. 'Sponsors, writers, and readers of early Norse literature', in *Social Approaches to Viking Studies*, ed. R. Samson, Glasgow: Cruithne Press.

Maine, Henry 1861. *Ancient Law*, London: John Murray.

Malinowski, Bronislaw 1923. 'The problem of meaning in primitive languages', in *The Meaning of Meaning*, eds C.K. Ogden and I.A. Richards, London: Kegan Paul, Trench, Trubner, 451–510.

Malinowski, Bronislaw 1929. *The Sexual Life of Savages in North-Western Melanesia*, New York: Eugenics Publishing Company.

Malinowski, Bronislaw 1937. 'The dilemma of contemporary linguistics', *Nature* 140, 172–173.

Malinowski, Bronislaw 1967. *A Diary in the Strict Sense of the Term*, New York: Harcourt, Brace & World.

Malinowski, Bronislaw 1972 [1922]. *Argonauts of the Western Pacific: An account of native enterprise and adventure in the archipelagoes of Melanesian New Guine*, London: Routledge & Kegan Paul.

Mandelbaum, JoannaLynn K. 1989. *The Missionary as a Cultural Interpreter*, New York: Peter Lang.

Marglin, Stephen A. 1990. 'Losing touch: The cultural conditions of worker accommodation and resistance', in *Dominating Knowledge: Development, culture and resistance*, eds F.A. Marglin and S.A. Marglin, Oxford: Clarendon Press, 217–282.

Marwick, Max (ed.) 1970. *Witchcraft and Sorcery*, Middlesex: Penguin.

Marx, Karl 1961 [1844]. *Economic and Philosophical Manuscripts of 1844*, Moscow: Foreign Language Publishing House.

Marx, Karl 1976 [1867]. *Capital*, vol. 1, Middlesex: Penguin.

Marx, Karl 1979. *The Letters of Karl Marx*, selected and translated with Notes and an Introduction by S.K. Padover, New Jersey: Prentice-Hall, Inc.

Mascia-Lees, Frances E., Patricia Sharpe, and Colleen Ballerino Cohen 1993. 'The postmodernist turn in anthropology: Cautions from a feminist perspective', in *Anthropology and Literature*, ed. Paul Benson, Urbana & Chicago: University of Illinois Press, 225–248.

Mauss, Marcel 1954 [1923–4]. *The Gift: Forms and functions of exchange in archaic societies*, trans. I. Cunnison, London: Cohen & West Ltd.

McCay, Bonnie M. 1984. 'The pirates of piscary: Ethnohistory of illegal fishing in New Jersey', *Ethnohistory* 31 (1), 17–37.

McCay, Bonnie M. 1993. 'Common and private concerns.' (Unpublished paper).

McCay, Bonnie M. and J.M. Acheson (eds) 1987. *The Question of the Commons: The culture and ecology of communal resources*, Tucson: University of Arizona Press.

McCloskey, Donald N. 1985. *The Rhetoric of Economics*, Madison, WI: University of Wisconsin Press

McEvoy, Arthur F. 1986. *The Fisherman's Problem: Ecology and law in the California fisheries, 1850–1980*, Cambridge: Cambridge University Press.

McGovern, Thomas H. 1990. 'The archaeology of the Norse North Atlantic', *Annual Review of Anthropology* 19, 331–351.

McGovern, T. H., G. F. Bigelow, T. Amorosi, and D. Russel 1988. 'Northern Islands, human error, and environmental degradation: A view of social and ecological change in the medieval North Atlantic', *Human Ecology* 16 (3), 225–270.

Melville, Herman 1846. *Typee*, London and Glasgow: Collins Clear-Type Press.

Melville, Herman 1962 [1851]. *Moby Dick*, New York: Macmillan Company.

Merchant, Carolyn 1980. *The Death of Nature: Women, ecology and the scientific revolution*, San Francisco: Harper & Row.

Messick, Brinkley 1993. *The Calligraphic State: Textual domination and history in a Muslim society*, Berkeley: University of California Press.

Meulengracht Sörensen, Preben 1992. 'Some methodological considerations in connection with the study of the sagas', in *From Sagas to Society: Comparative approaches to early Iceland*, ed. G. Pálsson, Middlesex, U.K.: Hisarlik Press, 17–42.

Midgley, Mary 1992. *Science as Salvation: A modern myth and its meaning*, London: Routledge.

Miller, William I. 1986a. 'Gift, sale, payment, raid: Case studies in the negotiation and classification of exchange in Medieval Iceland', *Speculum* 61, 18–50.

Miller, William I. 1986b. 'Dreams, prophecy and sorcery: Blaming the secret offender in Medieval Iceland', *Scandinavian Studies* 58, 101–23.

Miller, William I. 1986c. Review of Kirsten Hastrup's *Culture and History in Medieval Iceland: An anthropological analysis of structure and change*, Scandinavian Studies 58 (2), 183–6.

Miller, William I. 1990. *Bloodtaking and Peacemaking: Feud, law, and society in saga Iceland*, Chicago & London: The University of Chicago Press.

Miller, William I. 1992. 'Emotions and the sagas', in *From Sagas to Society: Comparative approaches to early Iceland*, ed. G. Pálsson, Middlesex, U.K.: Hisarlik Press, 89–109.

Mintz, Sidney W. 1985. *Sweetness and Power: The place of sugar in modern history*, New York: Elisabeth Sifton Books.

Moerman, Michael 1988. *Talking Culture: Ethnography and conversation analysis*. Philadelphia: University of Pennsylvania Press.

Morgan, Henry Lewis 1871. *Systems of Consanguinity and Affinity of the Human Family*, Washington, D.C.: Smithsonian Institute.

Morris, Katherine 1991. *Sorceress or Witch? The image of gender in Medieval Iceland and Northern Europe*, Lanham: University Press of America.

Mudimbe, V.Y. 1988. *The Invention of Africa: Gnosis, philosophy, and the order of knowledge*, Bloomington and Indianapolis: Indiana University Press.

Murdock, G.P. 1967. 'The ethnographic Atlas', *Ethnology* 6.

Nahir, Moshe 1977. 'The five aspects of language planning: A classification', *Language Problems and Language Planning*, 1, 107-123.

Neher, P.A., R. Arnason, and N. Mollett (eds.) 1989. *Rights Based Fishing*, Dordrecht: Kluwer Academic Publishers.

Neild, Elizabeth 1989. 'Translation is a two-way street: A response to Steiner', *Meta* 34 (2), 238-241.

Nelson, Julie A. 1992. 'Gender, metaphor, and the definition of economics,' *Economics and Philosophy* 8: 103-125.

Nelson, Julie A. 1993. 'The study of choice or the study of provisioning?: Gender and the definition of economics,' in *Beyond Economic Man: feminist theory and economics* (eds.) M.A. Ferber and J.A. Nelson, Chicago & London: The University of Chicago Press, 23-36.

Newmeyer, F. J. 1986. *The Politics of Linguistics*, Chicago: University of Chicago Press.

Nordal, Sigurður 1942. *Íslenzk menning*, Reykjavík: Mál og menning.

Nordal, Sigurður (ed.) 1967. *Píslarsaga síra Jóns Magnússonar*, Reykjavík: Almenna bókafélagið.

O'Brien, Jay and William Roseberry (eds.) 1991. *Golden Ages, Dark Ages: Imagining the past in anthropology and history*, Berkeley: University of California Press.

Ochs, Elinor 1988. *Culture and Language Development: Language acquisition and language socialization in a Samoan village*. Cambridge: Cambridge University Press.

Odner, Knut 1974. 'Economic structures in Western Norway in the Early Iron Age', *Norwegian Archaeological Review* 7, 104-112.

Odner, Knut 1992. 'Þorgunna's testament', in *From Sagas to Society: Comparative approaches to early Iceland*, ed. G. Pálsson, Middlesex, U.K.: Hisarlik Press, 125-146.

Okely, Judith 1992. 'Anthropology and autobiography: Participatory experience and embodied knowledge', in *Anthropology and Autobiography*, eds. J. Okely and H. Callaway, London: Routledge, 1-28.

Ólafsson, Jón 1946 [1661]. *Reisubók Jóns Ólafssonar Indíafara*, Vols. 1 & 2, Reykjavík: Bókfellsútgáfan.

Ólason, Vésteinn 1971. 'Nokkrar athugasemdir um Eyrbyggja sögu', *Skírnir* 145, 5-25.

Ólason, Vésteinn 1989. 'Bóksögur', in *Íslensk þjóðmenning VI: Munnmenntir og bókmenning* (ed.) Frosti F. Jóhannsson. Reykjavík: þjóðsaga, 159-227.

Ong, Walter J. 1982. *Orality and Literacy: The technologizing of the word*. London & New York: Routledge.

Ortner, Sherry B. 1984. 'Theory in anthropology since the sixties', *Comparative Studies in Society and History* 26, 126-166.

Ortner, Sherry B. 1991. 'Reading America: Preliminary notes on class and culture', in *Recapturing Anthropology: Working in the present*, ed. R.G. Fox, Santa Fe: School of American Researh Press, 163-189.

Ostrom, Elinor 1990. *Governing the Commons: The evolution of institutions for collective action*, Cambridge: Cambridge University Press.

Pálsson, Einar 1991. *Alþingi hið forna*. Reykjavík: Mímir.

Pálsson, Gísli 1979. 'Vont mál og vond málfræði', *Skírnir* 153, 175-201, Reykjavík.

Pálsson, Gísli 1987a. 'Tungan, bakarinn og þjóðarkakan: Er málfarsleg stéttaskipting á Íslandi?', *þjóðlíf*, October, Reykjavík.

Pálsson, Gísli 1987b. *Sambúð manns og sjávar*, Reykjavík: Svart á hvítu.

Pálsson, Gísli 1989. 'Language and society: The ethnolinguistics of Icelanders', in *The*

Anthropology of Iceland, eds. E.P. Durrenberger and G. Pálsson, Iowa City: University of Iowa Press, 121–139.

Pálsson, Gísli 1991. *Coastal Economies, Cultural Accounts: Human ecology and Icelandic discourse*, Manchester & New York: Manchester University Press.

Pálsson, Gísli (ed.) 1992. *From Sagas to Society: Comparative approaches to early Iceland*, Middlesex: Hisarlik Press.

Pálsson, Gísli (ed.) 1993. *Beyond Boundaries: Understanding, translation and anthropological discourse*, Oxford: Berg Publishers.

Pálsson, Gísli 1994a. 'Enskilment at sea', *Man* 29(4).

Pálsson, Gísli 1994b. 'The name of the witch: Sagas, sorcery, and social context', in *A River of Blessings: Essays in Honor of Paul Baxter*, (ed.) D. Brokensha, Syracuse, New York: Maxwell School of Citizenship and Public Affairs (African Series of Foreign and Comparative Program). 287–305.

Pálsson, Gísli and E. Paul Durrenberger 1983. 'Icelandic foremen and skippers: The structure and evolution of a folk model', *American Ethnologist* 10 (3), 511–528.

Pálsson Gísli and E. Paul Durrenberger 1992. 'Icelandic dialogues: Individual differences in indigenous discourse', *Journal of Anthropological Research* 48 (4), 301–316.

Pálsson, Gísli and E. Paul Durrenberger 1995. *Images of Iceland.* Iowa City: University of Iowa Press.

Pálsson, Gísli and Agnar Helgason 1994. 'Figuring fish and measuring men: The quota system in the Icelandic cod fishery'. Paper submitted to the Annual Science Conference of the International Council for the Exploration of the Sea, St. John's, Newfoundland, 22–30 September.

Pálsson, Hermann 1984. *Uppruni Njálu og hugmyndir*. Reykjavík: Menningarsjóður.

Panofsky, Erwin 1991 [1927]. *Perspective as Symbolic Form*, trans. C.S. Wood. Cambridge, Mass.: Zone Books.

Parkin, David 1980. 'The creativity of abuse', *Man* 15, 45–64.

Parry, Jonathan 1985. 'The Brahmanical tradition and the technology of the intellect', in *Reason and Morality*, ed. J. Overing, London & New York: Tavistock Publications.

Partner, Nancy F. 1986. 'Making up lost time: Writing on the writing of history', *Speculum* 61, 90–117.

Patterson, Lee 1987. *Negotiating the Past: The historical understanding of medieval literature*, Madison: University of Wisconsin Press.

Phillpotts, Bertha Surtees 1913. *Kindred and Clan in the Middle Ages and After: A study in the sociology of the Teutonic races*, Cambridge: Cambridge University Press.

Pinson, Ann 1979. 'Kinship and economy in modern Iceland: A study in social continuity', *Ethnology* 18, 183–197.

Pinson, Ann 1985. 'The institution of friendship and drinking patterns in Iceland', *Anthropological Quarterly* 58 (2), 75–82.

Pirsig, Robert M. 1974. *Zen and the Art of Motorcycle Maintenance: An inquiry into values*. New York: William Marrow & Company, Inc.

Pletsch, Carl E. 1981. 'The three worlds, or the division of social scientific labor, circa 1950–1975', *Comparative Studies in Society and History* 23 (4), 565–590.

Polanyi, Michael 1958. *Personal Knowledge: Towards a post-critical philosophy*, Chicago: University of Chicago Press.

Postmodernism, 1988. Special issue of *Theory, Culture and Society* 5 (2–3).

Prakash, Gyan 1990. 'Writing post-Orientalist histories of the third world: Perspectives from Indian historiography', *Comparative Studies in Society and History* 32 (2), 383–408

Quine, W. 1960. *Word and Object*, Cambridge, MA.: MIT Press

Rabin, Chaim 1983. 'The sociology of normativism in Israeli Hebrew', *International Journal of the Sociology of Language* 41, 41–56.

Rabinow, Paul 1989. *French Modern: Norms and forms of the social environment*. Cambridge, Mass.: MIT Press.

Reed, Edward S. 1993. 'The intention to use a specific affordance: A conceptual framework for psychology', in *Development in Context: Acting and thinking in specific environments* (eds.) R.H. Wozniak & K.W. Fischer. Hillsdale, NJ: Lawrence Erlbaum Associates, 45–76.

Rich, George W. 1976. 'Changing Icelandic kinship', *Ethnology* 15, 1–20.

Rich, George W. 1980. 'Kinship and friendship in Iceland', Ethnology 19, 475–493.

Rich, George W. 1989. 'Problems and prospects in the study of Icelandic kinship', in *The Anthropology of Iceland*, ed. E.P. Durrenberger and G. Pálsson, Iowa City: University of Iowa Press, 53–79.

Ricoeur, Paul 1965. 'Universal civilization and national cultures', in *History and Truth*, Evanston, IL: Northwestern University Press, 271–284.

Robinson, Douglas 1991. *The Translator's Turn*, Baltimore, MD: Johns Hopkins University Press.

Rodman, Margaret C. 1992. 'Empowering place: Multilocality and multivocality', *American Anthropologist* 94 (3), 640–656.

Rosaldo, Renato 1980. *Ilongot Headhunting 1883–1974: A study in society and history*, Stanford: Stanford University Press.

Rosaldo, Renato 1987. 'Where objectivity lies: The rhetoric of anthropology', in *The Rhetorics of the Human Sciences*, eds. J.S. Nelson, A. Megill, and D.N. McCloskey, Madison, Wisc.: The University of Wisconsin Press, 87–110

Rosaldo, Renato 1989. *Culture and Truth: The remaking of social analysis*, Boston: Beacon Press.

Rose, Carol M. 1985. 'Possession as the origin of property', *The University of Chicago Law Review* 52, 73–88.

Rose, Carol M. 1986. 'The comedy of the commons: Custom, commerce, and inherently public property', *The University of Chicago Law Review* 53 (3), 711–781.

Rose, Dan 1980. 'Malinowski's influence on Wittgenstein on the matter of *use* in language', *Journal of the History of the Behavioral Sciences*, 16, 145–49.

Roseberry, William 1991. 'Potatoes, sacks, and enclosures in early modern England', in *Golden Ages, Dark Ages: Imagining the past in anthropology and history*, Berkeley: University of California Press.

Ruthven, Malise 1990. *A Satanic Affair: Salman Rushdie and the rage of Islam*. London: Chatto & Windus.

Rögnvaldsson, Eiríkur 1983. 'þágufallssýkin og fallakerfi íslensku', *Skíma* 16, 3–6.

Sabean, David Warren 1984. *Power in the Blood: Popular culture and village discourse in early modern Germany*, Cambridge: Cambridge University Press.

Sahlins, Marshall 1963. 'Poor man, rich man, big man, chief', *Comparative Studies in Society and History* 5, 283–303.

Sahlins, Marshall 1976. *Culture and Practical Reason*, Chicago: The University of Chicago Press.

Said, Edward 1978. *Orientalism*, New York: Vintage Books.

Said, Edward 1989. 'Representing the colonized: Anthropologys interlocutors', *Critical Inquiry* 15, 205-225.
Samson, Ross (ed.) 1991. *Social Approaches to Viking Studies*, Glasgow: Cruithne Press.
Samuel, Geoffrey 1990. *Mind, Body and Culture: Anthropology and the biological interface*, Cambridge: Cambridge Univesrity Press.
Sangren, P. Steven 1988. 'Rhetoric and the authority of ethnography: "Postmodernism" and the social reproduction of texts', *Current Anthropology* 29 (3), 405-424.
Sanjek, Roger (ed.) 1990. *Fieldnotes: The makings of anthropology*, Ithaca & London: Cornell University Press.
Sartre, Jean-Paul 1959 [1938]. *Nausea*, trans. L. Alexander, Norfolk: New Direction Books.
Saussure, Ferdinand de 1959 [1916]. *Course in General Linguistics*, New York: McGraw-Hill.
Schieffelin, Edward L. and Robert Crittenden (eds.) 1991. *Like People You See in a Dream: First contact in six Papuan societies*. Stanford: Stanford University Press.
Schlauch, Margaret 1934. *Romance in Iceland*, New York: Russel & Russel.
Scott, Anthony D. 1989. 'Conceptual origins of rights based fishing', in *Rights Based Fishing*, eds. P.A. Neher, R. Arnason and N. Mollett, Dordrecht: Kluwer Academic Publishers, 11-38.
Scott, James C. 1990. *Domination and the Arts of Resistance: Hidden transcripts*, New Haven & London: Yale University Press.
Sharabi, Hisham (ed.) 1990. *Theory, Politics and the Arab World*, New York: Routledge.
Sharp, Henry S. 1988. 'Dry meat and gender: The absence of Chipewyan ritual for the regulation of hunting and animal numbers', in *Hunters and Gatherers 2: Property, power and ideology*, eds. Tim Ingold, David Riches and James Woodburn, Oxford: Berg Publishers, 183-191.
Smith, Anthony D. 1986. *The Ethnic Origins of Nations*, Oxford: Basil Blackwell.
Spiegel, Gabrielle M. 1990. 'History, historicism, and the social logic of the text in the Middle Ages', *Speculum* 65, 59-86.
Spiro, Melford 1990. 'On the strange and the familiar in recent anthropological thought', in *Cultural Psychology: Essays on comparative human development*, eds J.W. Stigler, R.A. Schweder and G. Herdt, Cambridge: Cambridge University Press, 47-61.
Spiro, Melford 1991. *Anthropological Other or Burmese Brother? Studies in Cultural Analysis*. New Brunswick, N.J.: Transaction Publishers.
Starr, June 1989. 'The "invention" of early legal ideas: Sir Henry Maine and the perpetual tutelage of women', in *History and Power in the Study of Law: New directions in legal anthropology*, eds J. Starr and J.F. Collier, Ithaca & London: Cornell University Press, 345-368.
Stearn, G.E. 1967. *McLuhan: Hot and cool*, New York: The Dial Press.
Stefánsson, Halldór 1992. Review of Kirsten Hastrup's *Island of Anthropology*. *Ethnos* 3-4, 278-280.
Stefánsson, Halldór 1993. 'Foreign myths and sagas in Japan: The academics and the cartoonists', in *Beyond Boundaries: Understanding, translation and anthropological discourse*, ed. G. Pálsson, Oxford: Berg, 75-99.
Steiner, George 1976. *After Babel*, London: Oxford University Press.
Stocking, G.W. (ed.) 1983. *Observers Observed: Essays on ethnographic fieldwork*, Madison, WI: University of Wisconsin Press.
Strathern, Andrew 1979. 'Introduction', in *Ongka: A self-account by a New Guinea big-man*,

transl. A. Strathern, New York: St. Martin's Press, xii–xxii.
Strathern, Marilyn (ed.) 1987. *Dealing with Inequality: Analysing gender relations in Melanesia and beyond*, Cambridge: Cambridge University Press.
Strathern, Marilyn 1988. *The Gender and the Gift: Problems with women and problems with society in Melanesia*, Berkeley, CA: University of California Press.
Strathern, Marilyn 1991. 'One man and many men', in *Big Men and Great Men: Personifications of power in Melanesia*, eds. M. Godelier and M. Strathern, Cambridge & Paris: Cambridge University Press & Editions de la Maison des Sciences de l'Homme, 197–214.
Street, Brian (ed.) 1993. *Cross-Cultural Approaches to Literacy*. Cambridge: Cambridge University Press.
Sturlunga saga, I–III, 1988. Reykjavík: Svart á hvítu.
Svavarsdóttir, Ásta 1982. '"þágufallssýki": Breytingar á fallnotkun í frumlagssæti ópersónulegra setninga', *Íslenskt mál* 4, 19–62.
Svavarsdóttir, Ásta, Gísli Pálsson, and Þórólfur Þorlindsson 1984. 'Fall er fararheill: Um fallnotkun með ópersónulegum sögnum', *Íslenskt mál* 6, 33–55, Reykjavík.
Sveinsson, Einar Ó. 1959. *Handritamálið*, Reykjavík: Hið íslenska bókmenntafélag.
Sæmundsson, Matthías Viðar 1992. *Galdrar á Íslandi: Íslensk galdrabók*, Reykjavík: Almenna bókafélagið.
Tambiah, Stanley J. 1968. 'The magical power of words', *Man* (n.s.) 3, 175–208.
Tambiah, Stanley J. 1990. *Magic, Science, Religion, and the Scope of Rationality*, Cambridge: Cambridge University Press.
Tannen, Deborah 1989. *Talking Voices: Repitition, dialogue, and imagery in conversational discourse*, Studies in Interactional Sociolinguistics, Cambridge: Cambridge University Press.
Tannen, Deborah 1990. *You Just Don't Understand: Women and men in conversation*, New York: Ballantine Books.
Tapper, Richard L. 1988. 'Animality, humanity, morality and society', in *What is an Animal?*, ed. T. Ingold, London: Unwin Hyman, 47–62.
Taussig, Michael T. 1980. *The Devil and Commodity Fetishism in South America*, Chapel Hill: The University of North Carolina Press.
Tedlock, Barbara 1991. 'From participant observation to the observation of participation: The emergence of narrative ethnography', *Journal of Anthropological Research* 47 (1), 69–94.
The Hávamál: With selections from other poems of the Edda, illustrating the wisdom of the North in heathen times 1923, ed. and trans. by D.E. Martin Clarke, Cambridge: Cambridge University Press.
Thomas, George 1991. *Linguistic Purism*, London & New York: Longman.
Thomas, Nicholas 1991. *Entangled Objects: Exchange, material culture, and colonialism in the Pacific*. Cambridge, Mass.: Harvard University Press.
Thoroddsen, Þorvaldur 1892. *Landfræðisaga Íslands, vol. 2*, Copenhagen: Hið íslenzka bókmenntafélag.
Todorov, Tzvetan 1984. *The Conquest of America*, New York: Harper & Row.
Todorov, Tzvetan 1988. 'Knowledge in social anthropology', *Anthropology Today* 4 (2), 4–7.
Todorov, Tzvetan 1990. *Genres in Discourse*. Cambridge: Cambridge University Press.
Todorov, Tzvetan 1993. *On Human Diversity: Nationalism, racism, and exoticism in French thought*, trans. C. Porter, Cambridge, Mass.: Harvard University Press.

Tomasson, Richard F. 1980. *Iceland: The first new society*. Minneapolis: University of Minnesota Press.
Torgovnick, Marianna 1990. *Gone Primitive: Savage intellects, modern lives*, Chicago & London: The University of Chicago Press.
Turner, V.W. 1971. 'An anthropological approach to the Icelandic saga', in *The Translation of Culture: Essays to E.E. Evans-Pritchard*, ed. T.O. Beidelman, London: Tavistock, 349-374.
Tyler, S.A. 1986. 'Post-modern Ethnography: From document of the occult to occult document', in *Writing Culture*, eds. J. Clifford and G.E. Marcus, Berkeley, CA: University of California Press, 122-140.
Ulin, Robert C. 1991. 'Critical anthropology twenty years later: Modernism and postmodernism in anthropology', *Critique of Anthropology* 11 (1), 63-89.
Upham, Steadman 1990. 'Decoupling the processes of political evolution', in *The Evolution of Political Systems*, ed. S. Upham, Cambridge: Cambridge University Press, 1-17.
Veblen, Thorstein 1925. 'Introduction', in *The Laxdæla Saga*, trans. T. Veblen, New York: B.W. Huebsch, v-xv.
Veblen, Thorstein 1964 [1914]. *The Instinct of Workmanship and the State of the Industrial Arts*, with an Introduction by J. Dorfman, New York: Sentry Press.
Volosinov, V.N. 1973 [1929]. *Marxism and the Philosophy of Language*, trans. L. Matejka and I.R. Titunik, Cambridge, MA.: Harvard University Press.
Warner, Michael 1990. *The Letters of the Republic: Publication and the public sphere in eighteenth-century America*. Cambridge, Mass.: Harvard University Press.
Watson, Graham 1984. 'The social construction of boundaries between social and cultural anthropology in Britain and North America', *Journal of Anthropological Research* 40 (3), 351-366
Wax, R.H. 1969. *Magic, Fate and History: The changing ethos of the Vikings*, Lawrence, Kansas: Coronado Press.
Wengle, John L. 1988. *Ethnographers in the Field: The psychology of research*, Tuscaloosa & London: The University of Alabama Press.
Wenzel, George 1991. *Animal Rights, Human Rights: Ecology, economy and ideology in the Canadian Arctic*. London: Belhaven Press.
Whitehouse, Harvey 1992. 'Leaders and logics, persons and polities', *History and Anthropology* 6 (1), 103-124.
Williams, Raymond 1976. *Keywords: A vocabulary of culture and society*, Glasgow: Fontana.
Willis, Paul 1978. *Learning to Labour: How working class kids get working class jobs*, New York: Columbia University Press.
Willis, Roy G. 1990. 'Introduction', in *Signifying Animals: Human meaning in the natural world*, ed. R.G. Willis, London: Unwin Hyman, 1-24.
Wilson, J.A., J.M. Acheson, M Metcalfe and P. Kleban 1994. 'Chaos, complexity and community management of fisheries', *Marine Policy* 18 (4), 291-305.
Wolf, Eric R. 1982. *Europe and the People Without History*, Berkeley, CA: University of California Press.
Wolf, Margery 1990. 'Chinanotes: Engendering anthropology', in *Fieldnotes: The makings of anthropology*, Ithaca & London: Cornell University Press, 343-355.
Worster, Donald (ed.) 1988. *The Ends of the Earth: Perspectives on modern environmental history*, Cambridge: Cambridge University Press.

Wright, Sue 1992. 'Method in our critique of anthropology: A further comment', *Man* 27 (3), 642–644.

Young, Oran R. 1986. 'International regimes: Toward a new theory of institutions', *World Politics* 39 (1), 105–122.

Young, Robert E. 1990. *A Critical Theory of Education: Habermas and our children's future*, New York & London: Teachers College Press.

Þórólfsson, Björn K. 1925. *Um íslenskar orðmyndir á 14. og 15. öld og breytingar þeirra úr fornmálinu*, Reykjavík: Félagsprentsmiðjan.

Index

aboriginality, 12, 20
agency, 87, 148, 177
    see also pragmatist approach
Alaska, 48
Alþing, 12, 88, 98n.7, 131, 133
Amory, Frederic, 98n.11, 120n.4
Anderson, Benedict, 24n.6
Annales school, 75
anthropocracy, 4
anthropology at home, *see* native
Appadurai, Arjun, 62, 96, 142n.2, 173
Arabs, 1, 46n.3, 56, 58, 118
archaeologists, 78, 82
Ardener, Edwin, 68
Aristotelian philosophy, 3, 4, 172–3
Árnason, Ragnar, 153
Asad, Talal, 28–9, 41
Atkinson, Paul, 72n.7
Austin, J.L., 99, 120n.4
Azande, 105

Babel, tower of, 41, 59
Bacon, Francis, 4–5, 24n.3, 165
Bakhtin, Mikhail M., 5, 8, 49–51, 71, 103, 140–1, 179n.1
barbarí, concept of, 118
Barley, Nigel, 56
Barth, Fredrik, 32
Baruya, 91–2, 94
Bassnett, Susan, 34–5, 39
Batek, 48
Bauman, Richard, 18, 76, 98n.11, 120n.3, 125
Baxter, Paul T.W., 75, 120n.1
Beidelman, T.O., 28
being-in-the-world, 47, 60, 179
Benediktsson, Einar, 128–9

Benediktsson, Hreinn, 12, 24n.8
Benhabib, Seyla, 5, 172
Bennett, John W., 145
Bessason, Haraldur, 142n.4
Biblical scholarship, 33, 82
big men, 91–5
    see also chiefs
Bitterli, Urs, 41
Björnsdóttir, Inga Dóra, 133
Black Report, 155, 162
Bloch, Maurice, 5, 65
Boas, Franz, 27, 82, 148
Bobb, Franz, 124
Bongie, Chris, 24n.1
book prose theory, 83, 85
Boon, James A., 3
Bordo, Susan, 24n.3
boundaries, cultural, *see* cultural; translation
Bourdieu, Pierre, 21, 130, 135, 169–71, 178, 179n.4
bridging, 32
    see also translation
Brightman, Robert, 46n.4
Brown, Vivienne, 72n.7, 179n.1
Bruner, Jerome, 172
Brydon, Anne, 72n.11
Burch, Ernest S., 48
Byock, Jesse L., 14

Canada, 142n.4, 160
Canadian Icelanders, 142n.4
canonizing, notion of, 170, 179n.1
capital, *v* labor, 157
Carneiro, R.L., 91
Carrier, James G., 2, 68, 71n.1
Carroll, Raymonde, 41
Carucci, Laurence M., 85

Catholicism, 51
Chamberlain, Lori, 34, 36
Chambri, 179n.2
chaotic aspects, of fisheries, 163
chiefs, 83-5, 88, 92-6, 109-111, 114, 115
child development, 43, 44, 172, 173
China, 46
Chomsky, Noam, 5, 125
Christianity, 13, 17, 83, 84, 97n.1, 100, 112-13, 117-20, 164
Christianity at Glacier, 22, 47, 50-62, 64, 70, 75, 164, 169, 172
Clifford, James, 7, 56, 72n.7
Clover, Carol J., 98n.11
cod equivalents, 167n.9
Cod Wars, 150, 155, 156
Cohen, Colleen B., 6
Cold War, 16, 30-1, 33, 37, 45-6, 175
Colombia, 170
colonialism, 1, 2, 12, 13, 35, 85, 87, 118, 119
Comaroff, Jean, 71n.5, 179n.7
Comaroff, John, 71n.5, 179n.7
Commonwealth, 12-13, 17-18, 22, 81-100, 105-120, 133, 135
  collapse of, 12, 13, 114
  concept of, 88
competence, cultural, 125, 126
conversation, 22, 45, 68, 70, 171
creation myths, 94
creative writings, 47, 49, 50, 56, 59, 75, 84, 124, 178
  see also life; sagas
Cree, 46n.4, 149
Crick, M., 27, 105
Crittenden, Robert, 46n.5, 48
Cronon, William, 24n.4
cultural
  boundaries, 7, 21, 31, 37, 41, 43, 46, 67, 170, 174, 179
  continuity, 31, 32, 44
  critics, 8, 47, 56, 60, 82, 175
  dyslexia, see dyslexia
  invention, 2, 12-17
  relativism, 35, 42
  theory, 41
  translation, see translation
  turn, 39
culture
  concept of, 41, 68, 82, 140
  v nature, see nature
  shock, 11
  as text, 1, 6, 21, 37

dative disease (*þágufallssýki*), 131, 137, 138, 139, 142n.11
da Vinci, Leonardo, 4
De Pina-Cabral, João, 177
decolonization, 14, 29, 44, 178
deconstruction, 97
Denmark, 12-14, 62, 119, 127, 151
  colonialism of, 13, 19, 117, 127, 176
Derrida, Jacques, 2, 35, 97, 177
Descartes, 4
Dewey, John, 165, 167n.11, 175
dialogue, see conversation
Dilley, Roy, 167n.7
displacement, and language, 58
divination, 102, 106, 113
domestic discipline (*húsagi*), 19
domesticated, *v* wild, 62, 63
  see also inside
Donaldson, Margaret, 135
Donham, Donald L., 146
Douglas, Mary, 116, 120n.1, 133
Dreyfus, Hubert L., 141
Drummond, Lee, 41-2
Dumont, Luis, 136
Dunn, Judy, 43
Duranti, Alessandro, 143n.14, 143n.16
Durkheim, Emile, 42, 125
Durrenberger, E. Paul, 40, 67, 80-1, 90, 98n.2, 112, 115, 179n.6
dwelling, perspective of, 141, 165
dyslexia, 27, 37-G9, 42, 44, 178
dönsk tunga (Danish language), 127

Earle, Timothy, 90
economics, 59, 149, 155, 156, 159, 160, 165
  provisioning definition of, 156-7
ecumene, 31, 175

Eggertsson, Þráinn, 98n.3, 150
Egilsson, Ólafur, 118
Einarsson, Níels, 63–8, 72n.9
Ellen, Roy, 72n.7, 142n.1
Ellis Davidson, H.R., 120n.2
Embi, 51–8, 61, 64, 70, 169
emotion, 86–7
Endicott, K., 48
Endicott, K.L., 48
England, Paula, 36, 167n.7
English language, position of, 17
Enlightenment, 5, 19, 40
enskilment, 43
  see also learning
environmental
  discourse, 21, 24n.4, 145
  Orientalism, 145–6, 152, 163
Eskimos, 31
essentialism, of language, 141
  see also textualism
ethnic markers, 142n.4
ethnicity, 32, 35, 175–6
ethnographic
  authenticity, 6, 22, 64
  authority, 62, 64, 69, 84
  dialogue, *see* living discourse
  disagreement, 22, 62–9
  fieldwork, *see* fieldwork
  present, 84, 113
  production, modes of, 33–7, 169–73
  see also conversation
ethnography of speaking, 125–6, 139–40
ethnolinguistics, 127–8, 136, 177
ethnologists, 15–16, 57
ethnoscience, 29, 140
eugenics, 128
Europe, 2–3, 14, 16, 19–20, 30, 45, 49, 51, 78, 80, 119, 164
Evans-Pritchard, E.E., 28, 75, 100, 105
exotic, 1–3, 8, 16, 39, 53, 67, 86
exoticism, 33, 56
Eyrbyggja saga, 99, 106–12, 114

Fabian, Johannes, 6
fact, *v* fiction, 56–9, 83–5
  see also creative writings

Fagan, Brian M., 41
family sagas, 76, 81–3, 94, 97n.1, 99–100, 109–14, 117
fast fish, 147–8
feasts, 114
Feleppa, Robert, 27
Ferguson, James, 175
fetish, concept of, 123, 142n.1
  see also language
feudalism, in fishing, 157–61
feuds, 90, 110–12
fiction, *see* fact
fieldwork, 1, 8–11, 47, 51, 55, 63–5, 67, 69, 85, 138, 179
  as apprenticeship, 171, 173
Figueira, Dorothy Matilda, 1
Finnbogadóttir, Vigdís, 133
Finnbogason, Guðmundur, 13, 128–9, 142n.8
first contact, 41, 46n.5
First Grammatical Treatise, 12, 17, 127
Fischer, K.W., 179n.5
fishing, 23, 63–4, 145–66, 173–4
  history, 152, 157
  limits, 151–2
  management of, 145, 152–3, 156, 160, 164
  success, 9, 23, 173
Flavell, John H., 46n.6
folk linguistics, *see* ethnolinguistics
Foucault, Michel, 48, 178
Frake, Charles O., 125, 140
free prose theory, 83
Free State, 88
Freeman, D., 39, 69
Freire, Paulo, 179n.5
Freud, S., 6
Fried, Morton H., 91, 115
Friedman, Jonathan, 7
friendship, 76, 96, 172
Frye, Northrop, 33, 146

galdrabækur (magic sheets), 115
  see also witchcraft
galdur (magic), concept of, 103
  see also witchcraft

Galt, A.H., 120n.1
Galton's problem, 174
Gaskins, Richard H, 72n.7
Geertz, Clifford, 37, 72n.7, 82
Gellner, Ernest, 37-8, 48, 174
gender, 34, 40, 63-5, 84, 92, 103, 107, 124, 133, 138
generosity, 91, 114
geometry, 4
Germany, 34, 118-19, 129, 151, 154-5
"getting one's sea legs", 8, 10, 55, 70, 173
Gewertz, Deborah, 179n.2
gifts, 18, 76, 96, 97n.2, 114
Gledhill, John, 91
global context, 39, 41, 45, 175
globalization, 33, 45
goðaveldi (reign of *goðar*), 84
goði (chief), concept of, 88, 94, 99
  see also chiefs
Godelier, Maurice, 89, 91-2, 94, 98n.12
goðorð (chieftaincy), 88-9, 95, 115
  confiscation of, 95
  notion of, 88
Goffman, Ervin, 11
Goldman, L., 18
Goodwin, C., 143n.14
Goody, Jack, 86, 126
gossip, 101, 102-3, 150
Grágás, 83, 97n.1, 99, 102-3, 106, 113, 150
great men, 92-4
Greece, 12, 20, 24n.11, 31, 33, 77, 136, 177
Greenland, 78, 113
  see also Inuit
Greenpeace International, 154
Grímsdóttir, Guðrún Ása, 83
Groenke, Ulrich, 130
Gudeman, Stephen, 8, 167n.7, 170-1
Guðfinnsson, Björn, 131, 137
Guðmundsson, Helgi, 135
Guðmundsson, Sigurður, 21, 164
Gunnarsson, Pétur, 138
Gupta, Akhil, 175

Gurevich, Aaron, 75, 83, 86, 96, 97n.2, 103, 164
Gutt, Ernst-August, 35
Guttormsson, Loftur, 24n.9, 24n.10
Gylfason, Þorsteinn, 132
götumál (street language), 130

Haas, Jonathan, 120n.5
Habermas, Jürgen, 7-8, 44, 172, 179n.4, 179n.5
habitus, 21, 164
Hagen, 94-5
Hákonardóttir, Inga Huld, 120n.11
Halkin, Abraham, 177
Hallberg, Peter, 86
Halldórsson, Halldór, 131-2, 135, 137, 139
Halldórsson, Helgi J., 131, 143n.13
Hanna, Susan S., 164, 166n.5
Hannerz, Ulf., 46n.2
Hanson, F. Allan, 71n.5
Haralds, Auður, 138
Hardin, G., 146, 149, 166
Harper, Douglas, 163-4
Harris, Roy, 5, 41, 125
Harvey, David, 72n.6
Haskell, Thomas L., 40
Hastrup, Kirsten, 12, 15-16, 22, 47, 62-9, 72n.9, 80-1, 98n.2, 117, 120n.5, 142n.5, 170
Hatim, Basil, 34
Haugen, Einar, 125, 129-30, 135, 142n.4
Hávamál, 76, 96, 102
Hebrew, 33, 99, 177
Heidegger, M., 32, 43, 47, 141
Helgason, Agnar, 159, 167n.9
Herder, J.G. von, 34, 133
hermeneutics, 36, 148
Herzfeld, Michael, 4, 12, 20, 35, 136, 171
hidden people (*huldufólk*), 64
hidden transcripts, 81, 138
Hilborn, R., 164
Hirschfeld, Lawrence A., 71n.1
Hirschman, Albert O., 40
historical anthropology, 75
  see also history

history, 22–3, 65, 75–6, 83–4, 87, 177–8
historiography, 4, 83, 87, 177
Hodgen, Margareth T., 78
Hong, Keelung, 70
honorifics, 129–30, 135, 142n.9
Huli, 18
Human Rights, declaration of, 48
hunches, in fishing, 162
   see also practitioner's knowledge
hunter-gatherer-fishermen, 36, 58, 147
Hymes, Dell, 125–6
höfðingi (chief), 89, 95
   see also chiefs

Iceland, 2, 8–24, 47, 50–2, 54, 62–70, 75–8, 80–120, 127–143, 145, 147, 150–64, 170, 172–77, 179n.3
Icelandic language
   history of, 12
   pollution of, *see* purism
   properties of, 129, 177
   "resurrection" of, 127
   unification of, 16, 127
   variability of, 124, 130, 136–8
Icelandic school, 14, 19, 77, 85
ideal speech situation, 44, 172
Ilongot, 90
India, 46n.3, 77, 118
indigenous critique, of language, 136–9
individual, concept of, 125, 164
inequality
   in fishing, 159–61, 165, 174
   linguistic, 124–33, 135, 136–8
   euphemistic theory of, 124, 131–3, 135–6
Ingimundarson, Jón Haukur, 98n.3
Ingold, Tim, 7, 42, 44, 126, 143n.17
inside, *v* outside, 9, 43, 59–60, 62–64, 66, 69, 87
interface, 31–2
Inuit, 48, 51, 149
Iron Curtain, 37
irony, metaphor of, 146, 161

Jackson, Michael, 11, 72n.7
Jakobson, R., 28

James, Henry, 142
Japan, 80
Joas, Hans, 143n.15, 167n.11
Jochens, Jenny M., 98n.4, 120n.3
Jóhannesson, Jón, 98n.10
Johnson, Allen W., 90
Johnson, Barbara, 32, 35
Jolly, M., 98n.12
Jones, O.F., 130
Jónsson, Arngrímur, 13, 127, 142n.6
Jónsson, Baldur, 128, 132, 135
Jónsson, Finnur, 174
Jónsson, Hjörleifur R., 15–16

Kachin, 32, 84
Kaplan, Martha, 87
Karlsson, Gunnar, 142n.5
Karras, Ruth Mazo, 81, 98n.4
Kaysen, Susanna, 56
Keesing, Roger, 29–30, 38–9, 126, 140, 176
kinship, 95, 172, 179n.3
   v friendship, 172
Kirch, Patrick V., 89
Knowlton, D., 171
Koran, the, 34
kraftaskáld (power poet), 101
Kress, Helga, 98n.4, 102–3
Kristjánsdóttir, Bergljót S., 98n.9
Kristof, Ladis K.D., 31
Kroeber, A.L., 28, 31
Kuhn, Thomas, 178
Kundera, Milan, 57–8
Kuper, Adam, 29, 45
Kvaran, Eiður S., 129

labor, *v* capital, *see* capital
Labov, William, 6, 120n.4, 125
language
   as fetish, 5, 20, 123–4
   game, 5, 141, 143n.15, 148
   and gender, 124
   as instrument, 128
   policy, 16, 20, 23, 124, 128, 132–3, 135, 174

and social context, 124–5, 136–9, 141, 173–4
  see also Icelandic language; text; textualism
langue, v parole, 5, 125, 139, 141
Larsen, Tord, 29
Lave, Jean, 179n.5
Laxness, Halldór, 22, 47, 50–2, 56–60, 62, 64, 70, 75, 84, 127, 142n.7, 164
Le Goff, Jacques, 3
Leach, Edmund R., 32, 41, 48, 69, 84
learning
  as bodily involvement, 10, 24n.5
  decentering of, 162–3
Lederman, Rena, 91
Lefevere, André, 34–5, 39
Lepowsky, Maria, 92
Levack, Brian P., 118
Lévi-Strauss, Claude, 28, 56, 68, 132, 178
Lewis, I, 39, 69
libel, 101, 105, 107
life, *v* text, 2, 8, 21–2, 43–4, 47, 50, 59, 61, 64, 76
Lindberg, David C., 3
linguistic
  inequality, *see* inequality,
  model, 27
    see also textualism
  turn, 1, 5–7, 39, 179
Linke, Uli 1992, 81, 94
Lisu, 40–1
literacy, 17–20, 82
  individual *v* group, 18, 20
living discourse, 23, 44, 60, 166, 169–71
Locke, John, 147
Long, Norman, 32
Love, Nancy S., 179n.4
Lowenthal, David, 87
Ludwig, D., 164
lying sagas, 77, 84
Löfgren, Orvar, 136
Lönnroth, Lars, 24n.9

Maghreb world, 118
magic, *see galdur*
Magnússon, Árni, 13
Magnússon, Jón, 116
Maine, Henry, 38
Malaysia, 48
maleficium, 117
Malinowski, Bronislaw, 1–2, 8, 18, 27–8, 35, 57, 69, 141, 143n.15
  diaries of, 6, 56
Mandelbaum, JoannaLynn K., 71n.5
manuscripts, 13–14
  "homecoming" of, 14–15
  see also sagas
Marcus, George E., 56, 72n.7
marine biology, 145–6, 160–2
Marshall Islands, 85
Marwick, Max, 120n.1
Marx, Karl, 20, 41, 59, 92, 123, 129, 165–6, 178
Mascia-Lees, Frances E., 6
Mason, Ian, 34
Mauss, Marcel, 76, 97n.2, 142n.2
McCay, Bonnie M., 146, 166, 166n.5
McCloskey, Donald N., 66, 72n.7, 167n.7
McEvoy, Arthur F., 40, 149, 166n.1
McGovern, Thomas H., 78
McLuhan, M., 126
Mead, Margaret, 39, 69
Melanesia, 27, 89, 91–2, 94–6
Melville, Herman, 49–50, 147
mentality, 68, 81
merchants, 95
Messick, Brinkley, 21
Meulengracht Sörensen, Preben, 82
Middle Ages, 2, 29, 49, 55, 164–5
Middle East, 45
Midgley, Mary, 5
Miller, William I., 63, 80, 86, 90, 98n.2, 120n.7
Mintz, Sidney W., 57, 71n.3
missionaries, 71n.5
misunderstanding, 33, 39–41
modernism, 4, 66, 69, 84, 145, 159, 163, 165–6
Moerman, Michael, 178
Montesquieu, 40
Morgan, Henry Lewis, 179n.3

Morris, Katherine, 117
"Mountain", 21
"Mountain Woman", the, (*Fjallkonan*), 133-4
Mudimbe, V.Y., 71n.5
Murdock, G.P., 179n.3
mutedness
  in fishing, 156, 161
  and gender, 64-6

nation building, 129, 145, 176
nationalist movement, 13-16, 85, 127, 135, 177
native
  concept of, 171
  anthropologists, 67, 171
  see also inside
nature, 5
  v society, 3-4, 36, 67, 133, 146, 149, 164-6
Nazi regime, 129
Neher, P.A., 166n.4
Neild, Elizabeth, 34, 36
Nelson, Julie A., 156, 167n.7
neo-Orientalism, 62, 69-70
  see also Orientalism
new ethnography, *see* ethnoscience
Newmeyer, F. J., 129, 142n.3, 143n.12
nið (libel), *see* libel
non-state society, 91
Nordal, Sigurður, 13-14, 116
Nordic neighbors, 12, 16
North America, 14
Norway, 12-14, 17, 78, 89, 98n.2, 150, 160

O'Brien, Jay, 87
observer's paradox, 6
Occidentalism, 1
Ochs, Elinor, 141
Ólafsson, Jón, 118
Ólason, Vésteinn, 24n.9, 114, 120n.7
Old Testament, the, 33
Ong, Walter J., 2
Orientalism, 1, 2, 22, 33, 35, 38, 47, 49, 56, 70, 77, 84, 145-6, 169-70, 170

Ortner, Sherry B., 37
othering, 1, 2, 5, 49, 70, 85-6, 118, 165, 175, 178

Pálsson, Einar, 98n.7
Pálsson, Gísli, 24n.5, 59, 64, 98n.2, 125, 136-8, 166n.2, 167n.9, 167n.10, 174, 179n.6
Panofsky, Erwin, 4-5
paper, 19
Papua New Guinea, 18, 46n.5, 49, 91, 94, 141, 173, 179n.2
Paredes, Americo, 69
Parkin, David, 130
Parry, Jonathan, 14n.6
participant observation, 6, 85, 179
Partner, Nancy F., 4-5
Patterson, Lee, 75, 87
perception, 3
  see also visual sensibilities
Perspectiva, laws of, 3
Phillpotts, Bertha Surtees, 76
philologism, 123
philosophy, 61
Pinson, Ann, 172, 179n.3
Pirsig, Robert M., 167n.11
Píslarsaga, 116
Plato, 47
Pletsch, Carl E., 30-1, 175
Plus X, 60, 64-5, 83
Polanyi, Michael, 167n.11
political organization, 90-1, 113-14
pollution, *see* language
Polynesia, 91
Portugal, 177
positivists, 4, 7-8, 37, 60, 66
post-Orientalism, 23, 36, 44, 171, 175
postmodernism, 5, 24n.4, 36, 59, 66, 71n.6, 165, 175
practice theory, 68, 82, 142, 162
practitioner's knowledge, 145-6, 161-4, 171
pragmatist approach, 62, 141, 143n.15, 167n.11, 173
Prakash, Gyan, 46n.3
predator - prey, metaphor of, *see* translation

print capitalism, 17, 19
printing, 19
privatization, of resources, 145, 149, 174
private language, 40
problem of voice, 62, 65, 177
profiteering (*brask*), 157-9
   see also quotas
pronominal dual (*þerun*), 129-30, 135
property regimes, 147, 149, 164
purism, 127-33, 135, 174-5
   see also pollution
Pygmies, 31

Quine, W., 37
Quota base, 158, 167n.9
quota-kings (*kvótakóngar*), 158
quotas, in fishing, 23, 150, 152-3, 155-61, 163, 165, 174
   catch, *v* effort, 157, 167n.8

Rabelais, F., 103
Rabin, Chaim, 177
Rabinow, Paul, 24n.2
"racial pollution" (*kynspell*), 128-9
Rask, R., 19, 127, 129
Raya, P., 179n.5
Redfield, R., 39, 69
reflexive approach, 38
Reformation, 19, 21, 115-17, 119
Renaissance, 3-5, 58-9, 146, 164
representation, 6, 47, 51, 56-61, 179n.2
resource-tax, 156
rhetorics, 6
Rich, George W., 172, 179n.3
Ricoeur, Paul, 42
Rivera, Alberto, 8, 170-1
Robinson, Douglas, 36, 39, 43, 98n.6
Roman alphabet, 17
romance, metaphor of, 146, 166
Rorty, Richard, 167n.11
Rosaldo, Renato, 41, 69, 90, 120n.5
Rose, Carol M., 147-8, 166n.1
Rose, Dan, 143n.15
Roseberry, William, 87, 164
Ross, Lee, 46n.6
Rotenberg, E.J., 179n.5

rowing time, 153
runes, 17, 101, 115
Rushdie, Salman, 56
Russia, 37-8, 77
Ruthven, Malise, 56, 71n.4
Rögnvaldsson, Eiríkur, 139

Saami, 100
Sabean, David Warren, 118-19
sagas, 12, 18, 19, 51, 62-3, 75-115, 127, 133
   and comparative studies, 22-3, 62, 76, 87-96, 100, 109
   as fieldnotes, 76, 80
   genres of, 76, 98n.1
   scholarship on, 19, 77, 81, 83-4, 89-90, 97
   translation of, 80
   see also manuscripts
Sahlins, Marshal, 91-2, 94, 114
Said, Edward, 1, 22, 43, 49, 51
Samoans, 39, 69, 141
Samson, Ross, 98n.2
Samuel, Geoffrey, 46n.7
Sanjek, Roger, 72n.7
Sapir, E., 27
Sartre, Jean-Paul, 70
Saussure, Ferdinand de, 5, 20, 42, 82, 125, 139, 141, 177-8
Schieffelin, Edward L., 46n.5, 48, 141
Scott, Anthony D., 149
Scott, James C., 81, 138
scribal culture, 17
scriptism, 20
Searle, J.R., 120n.4
sexual
   exploitation, 81
   idiom, 5
   see also gender
shamans, 100
Sharabi, Hisham, 46n.3
Sharp, Henry S., 6
Sherzer, Joel, 125
Simmel, Georg, 40
Singer, I.B., 177
skipper

effect, 157, 173
   in fishing, 63, 152-3, 157, 161-3, 173
skrælingi (barbarian), 78
slang, 135
   dictionary, 174
   see also purism
slaves, 114
Smith, Anthony D., 75, 176
social
   historians, 176
   understanding, 39-46
   see also misunderstanding; translation
sociolinguistic rules, 102, 139
sound mistake (hljóðvilla), 131-2
source, v target, see translation
speech acts, 7, 18, 99, 120n.4, 140, 148
Spiegel, Gabrielle M., 177
Spiro, Melford, 38
Sprachethik, 22, 68
   see also conversation
Starr, June, 65
Stearn, G.E., 126
Steblin-Kamenskij, S., 86
Stefánsson, Halldór, 64, 68, 72n.10, 72n.11, 80
Stefánsson, V., 51
Steinør, George, 34-5
Steneck, Nicholas H., 3
Stocking, G.W., 72n.7
Stone Age, 48-9
storyteller (sagnamaður), 51
storytelling, 17-18
strangers, 40, 48, 67
Strathern, Andrew, 94
Strathern, Marilyn, 89, 92, 96, 98n.12
street language, see götumál
Street, Brian, 24n.9
Sturlunga saga, 76, 81, 94, 97n.1, 99-100, 111-15
Svavarsdóttir, Ásta, 131, 137
Sveinsson, Einar Ó., 14, 98n.5, 114, 127
Switzerland, 176
symbolic capital, 23, 123, 135
Sæmundsson, Matthías Viðar, 120n.10

TAC (total allowable catch), 155

Tambiah, Stanley J., 29, 105
Tannen, Deborah, 40
target, v source, see translation
Taussig, Michael T., 117-18, 120n.1, 123
taxes, 88
tenancy, in fishing, see feudalism
Tepoztlan, 39
text
   etymology of, 1, 8
   as metaphor, 1, 27, 42, 146, 148
   see also translation; written
textualism, 1, 7, 8, 17, 36, 41, 60, 86, 119, 126, 141, 145, 170, 178-9
Thai, 40-1
"them" and "us", 48-9, 171
theology, 61
Thomas, George, 128
Thomas, Nicholas, 1
Thoroddsen, Þorvaldur, 13
Thorsson, Örnólfur, 120n.8
three world scheme, 29-31, 178
Tithe Law, 114
Todorov, Tzvetan, 7, 24n.1, 68-9, 76
Tomasson, Richard F., 20
Torgovnick, Marianna, 24n.1
totemism, 105, 131-2
tournaments of value, 96
tragedy of the commons, 146, 149, 155, 163-4, 166
translation
   cultural, 21, 27-9, 33, 42, 44, 175, 179
   empathic, 36
   faithfulness, 39
   literary, 33
   metaphor of, 45, 169, 178
   as predator-prey relationship, 34, 36-7
   source, 33
   studies, 38-9
   target, 33
translationese, 38
translinguistics, 5, 139-41
travel novel, 50
   see also creative writings
trawling rally, 161-2
Trobrianders, 6, 18, 28, 69
Turner, V.W., 80, 90, 94, 97n.2, 112-13

typological schemes, 90
Ulin, Robert C., 7
United States, 16, 40, 51, 148, 154, 160, 163
Upham, Steadman, 90

Veblen, Thorstein, 76, 167n.11
Vietnam war, 15, 36
Vikings, 12, 15, 77–8, 80, 89, 102, 128
violence, rhetoric of, 66, 170
visual sensibilities, 3, 4, 21, 116
Volosinov, V.N., 43, 123, 141, 143n.15, 148
Vygotsky, L., 172

Walters, C., 164
warfare, "primitive", 120n.5
Warner, Michael, 24n.7
Watson, Graham, 37
Wax, R.H., 97n.2
Weberian ideal types, 35
Wenzel, George, 166n.3
whaling, 147, 154
White, Hayden, 146
Whitehouse, Harvey, 92
Whorf, Benjamin, 27
wild, *v* domesticated, *see* domesticated
Williams, Raymond, 164
Willis, Paul, 135
Wilson, James A., 163

witch-acts, 107
witch-hunts, 115–19
witchcraft, 19, 23, 98n.11, 99–120
  context of, 101–5
  decline of, 100, 111–15
  frequency of, 19, 106, 111–12
  and gender, 107–8, 111, 117–19
  manuscripts, 115
  morality of, 108, 117
  semantics of, 105–7, 111, 116, 120n.8
  upsurge in, 115–19
Wittgenstein, L., 5, 40–1, 141, 143n.15
Wolf, Eric R., 45, 87
Worsley, Peter, 29
Wright, Sue, 70, 72n.12
written, *v* oral, 7, 81, 99, 108, 118–19, 126

Young, Robert E., 179n.5

þingmaður (follower of goði), 88–9, 95–6
þjóðveldi, 88
  see also Commonwealth
Þorláksson, Guðbrandur, 129
Þórlindsson, Þórólfur, 137
þorrablót, 15–16, 67
  etymology of, 15

Örlygsstaðir, battle at, 114

For Product Safety Concerns and Information please contact our EU representative GPSR@taylorandfrancis.com
Taylor & Francis Verlag GmbH, Kaufingerstraße 24, 80331 München, Germany

www.ingramcontent.com/pod-product-compliance
Lightning Source LLC
Chambersburg PA
CBHW080335170426
43194CB00014B/2577